MODERN
AMERICAN
HISTORY ★ A
Garland
Series

Edited by
FRANK FREIDEL
Harvard University

A HISTORY OF THE
INTERCULTURAL EDUCATIONAL MOVEMENT
1924–1941

Nicholas V. Montalto

Garland Publishing, Inc.
New York & London ★ 1982

Library of Congress Cataloging in Publication Data

Montalto, Nicholas V.
   A history of the intercultural educational movement,
1924–1941.

   (Modern American history ; [34])
   Originally presented as the author's thesis:
University of Minnesota, 1978.
   Bibliography: p.
   Includes index.
   1. Intercultural education—United States—History—
20th century.   I. Title.   II. Series.
LC1099.M64   1982   370.19'6'0973   80-8479
ISBN 0-8240-4863-6   AACR2

All volumes in this series are printed on acid-free,
250-year-life paper.
Printed in the United States of America

"...let me plead with you to appreciate your own background, and never be ashamed of it....If your parents speak Italian or Polish, or any other foreign language, don't answer them in English; learn to speak the language yourself...just as your parents are learning English. Learn what it stands for and what the people from that country have brought to America...."

(What a teacher might say to her students--from "A Sample Homeroom Discussion" [1934-1935], Rachel Davis DuBois papers)

TABLE OF CONTENTS

Preface.. iii

PART I: THE UNRESOLVED PROBLEMS OF MASS IMMIGRATION

Chapter
I.   Historians and the Aftermath of Restriction......... 1

II.   The Second Generation: Perilous Presence or
        Hope of America................................ 22

PART II: HISTORY OF THE SERVICE BUREAU FOR INTERCULTURAL EDUCATION

III.   Rachel Davis DuBois: From Pacifist to Ethnic
        Studies Advocate............................... 77

IV .   The Service Bureau: "Specialized Work for the
        Second Generation"............................. 109

V.   Joining the Vanguard for Educational Reform· The
        Progressive Education Association, 1936-1938...... 124

VI.   The Bureau Broadcasts to the Nation: Americans
        All--Immigrants All, 1938-1939.................. 149

VII.   Intercultural Education and the Jewish Search For
        Self-Definition in American Society.............. 171

VIII.   Upheaval in the Service Bureau, 1939-1941........ 218

IX.   Signposts to the Present........................ 268

Conclusion. 280

A Note on Manuscript and Interview Sources. 288

Select Bibliography. 294

Index. 312

PREFACE

In 1945, the Commissioner of Investigations of the City of
New York, Louis E. Yavner, issued a comprehensive report on a
dispute that had erupted over the operation of intercultural education programs in the New York City public schools. In the report,
he remarked that "intercultural and intergroup education activities
have in recent years assumed the character of a social movement."[1]
He also noted that a consensus had not been reached over the
principles and practices of an intergroup education program. The
variety of pursuits that by 1945 had become "big business" in the
United States--the business of controlling cultural dynamics and
engineering group relations--had been growing and gaining momentum
over the previous two decades, stirring the consciences of thousands
of individuals, altering, one would presume, the self-conceptions
of minority children,[2] and laying a foundation for the post-World

---

[1]Louis E. Yavner, "Administration of Human Relations
programs in New York City Schools," Report to Mayor Fiorello
LaGuardia, Dec. 20, 1945, p. 12.

[2]Throughout this study, I use the term "minority" to refer
to both racial groups and ethno-linguistic groups of recent
immigrant origin.

War II surge of interest in "human relations." Yavner's investigation had been prompted by a rash of well-publicized resignations from the City's Advisory Commission on Human Relations. These resignations had been marked by an acrimonious exchange of charges between members of the dissident faction, led by Frank Karelsen, and members of the rump committee and the Board of Education. The resultant din may well have been unprecedented in the history of the intercultural education movement, but similar conflicts had taken place previously, the news of which had never reached the outside world. No one will ever know how many times such battles had broken out, how many times organizations devoted to spreading "good will" had been torn apart because they could not reach a consensus on methodology or could not solve their own internal intergroup problems. This dissertation will tell the story of one such organization, the first and the most ambitious endeavor in the field of intergroup education: the Service Bureau for Intercultural Education, founded in New York City in 1934.

The Service Bureau was always a shaky operation, forever struggling to stay afloat financially, constantly trying to assert its independence from financial backers, constantly searching for a program that could weather the changing tides in the social sciences. Although the Bureau struggled against serious handicaps, although its resources were severely limited, and its staff inadequate to the tasks it faced, the Bureau had an impact on American society far out of proportion to its small size. In part, this was due to its adroit use of publicity and its constant concern with the development and dissemination of curriculum materials. In part, this was also due to the galaxy of notables who at one time or another lent their names, talents or prestige to the advancement of the Bureau's cause. Among these individuals were leading progressive educators such as Harold Rugg, Frederick L. Redefer, William H. Kilpatrick and H. Harry Giles; social scientists such as Ruth Benedict, Franz Boas, Margaret Mead, Otto Klineberg and Bruno Lasker; intergroup education specialists such as Everett Clinchy, Rachel Davis DuBois, and Stewart G. Cole. Also hovering about the Bureau were leading dissenters of the Depression Decade: Louis Adamic, who raised his voice so eloquently on behalf of the trouble-ridden second generation, i.e. the sons and daughters of the immigrants; Eduard C. Lindeman, who decried the narrow specialization and de-humanization of the social work profession; Milton Steinberg, who called attention to what he considered the cultural suicidal tendencies of American Jewry; and W.E.B. DuBois, who mounted an attack upon the Old Guard, assimilationist leadership of the NAACP. These were not individuals who reserved their criticisms for the conservative upholders of the old order; they also attacked

the "liberal" and "progressive" elements who--in their pursuit

of a sometimes self-serving vision of society--trampled on the

rights of others.

Since the stream of the Service Bureau's history is fed

from many different sources and breaks into many different

channels, this study will limit its scope to the ten-year period

prior to the formation of the Bureau (1924 to 1934) and the first

seven years of the organization's twenty-year lifetime (1934 to

1941). The year of American entrance into World War II is no

arbitrary point of termination. From 1938 to 1941--a period of

time during which the Bureau attained national prominence--the

organization underwent an agonizing and protracted internal

crisis that eventually left it a shell of its former self, under

caretaker direction until the bombshell of America's racial problem

exploded in 1943 and gave the organization a new direction, a

new mission and a new name.[3] I have considered the year 1924

as an approximate point of origin for the intercultural education

movement. The passage of the Quota Law in that year marked the

temporary resolution of the first controversy over immigration to

_____

[3]In 1943, the word "service" was dropped. The organization
became known as the "Bureau for Intercultural Education."

America: how to cut off the limitless flow of aliens entering American society; it also marked the onset of a second controversy: how to assimilate the progeny of the immigrants. The "second generation problem," as it was called, was a preoccupation of many of those who advocated intercultural education during the inter-war years.

The story of the Service Bureau needs to be placed in historical perspective and context. The excesses of the World War I Americanization movement, the witch-hunts, the deportations, the Klan rallies, and the vogue of racism, were haunting memories for liberal-minded Americans--memories which served to crystalize an alternative to coercive assimilation. Cultural diversity came to be seen as an inescapable though transitory condition of American life and--for some--a potential source of national enrichment. Assimilation, in this view, would have to be voluntary and it would have to win the support of ethnic group leaders. Organizations such as the Foreign Language Information Service, the International Institutes and other immigrant service agencies gave expression to this enlightened impulse and laid a groundwork of ideas and concerns upon which the Service Bureau could build. Developments in the social sciences, such as the popularization of Freudian psychology and the influence of the Boasian school of Anthropology, lent intellectual credibility to the Service Bureau's program.

During the 1930's great events on the domestic and international scenes altered the course of the Bureau's history. The
Great Depression, as William Stott points out,[4] was a period of
intense social analysis, of probing into the hidden corners of
American life. One of the discoveries made at this time was that
America was still a fragmented society, that the alchemy of the
Melting Pot had not worked. The rise of Nazism in Europe spurred
many Americans into vigorous action to contain the disease of race
hatred and keep it from spreading to America. Leaders of American
Jewry worked to quell the outbreaks of anti-Semitism that--with
encouragement from abroad--threatened to engulf them. By the end
of the decade, as war clouds drifted closer on the horizon, so
many of the concerns of the decade appeared as dangerous flirtations
clearly subordinate to the need to ensure national unity in the
approaching titanic struggle.

The story of the Service Bureau and of the larger movement
of which it was part is also biographical. It is the story of a woman
who--through the power of her convictions and the force of her
personality--carried a message to an entire generation of Americans.
Rachel Davis DuBois was the driving force behind a new concept of

---

[4]William Stott, Documentary Expression and Thirties America
(New York, 1974).

education. Recognized as a pioneer by both her friends and adversaries, she experienced both the glory and the grief of all pioneers, arousing passionate devotion among her followers and deep antagonism among those who did not share her convictions. DuBois' accomplishments were many - as were her failures. The organization she struggled to create and with which she identified so completely, the Service Bureau for Intercultural Education, came to spurn her and the philosophy she represented. The ethnic studies curriculum materials, which she may have been the first American educator to produce, were eventually cast aside and forgotten. This dissertation will take a close look at this extra-ordinary woman, whose vision seldom failed to captivate but whose single-mindedness and inflexibility, in the eyes of her critics, were both perplexing and confounding.

It is my hope that a study of this type may provide an historical perspective on current trends in American education. Proponents of the "New Pluralism" often assume that American education has been generally unresponsive to the special needs of minority children. This dissertation will try to demonstrate that this had not been the case. Far from being scornful of, or oblivious to, the ethnic background of school children, a number of innova-tive educators during the inter-war years attempted to introduce ethnic studies into the school curriculum both for the purpose of self-esteem of minority children and overcoming erroneous group stereotypes. While they encountered strong resistance to their efforts to revamp the curriculum, they did alter the conventional wisdom with regard to the "melting pot". As Eduard Lindeman remarked in 1945, the melting pot is "in disrepute." This was not an uncommon observation.[5] What happened to this brief honeymoon with "pluralism" in American education? How were the values and expectations of these early reformers different from those of today? How and why did the movement fade away?

I began this study with a strong conviction that there was an important and an exciting story to be told. I only hope that my recounting of these events conveys some sense of the drama and passions which I have seen revealed in the sources and that my analysis of the forces underlying these events provides a helpful

---

[5]Eduard C. Lindeman, "Foreword" to Rachel Davis DuBois, Build Together Americans: Adventures in Intercultural Education for the Secondary School (New York, 1945), p. VII. For remarks similar to Lindeman's, see: "The Council Against Intolerance in America: What and Why?" American Unity, I (November, 1942), 22; Dan W. Dodson, "Constructive and Destructive Factors and Trends in Intergroup Understanding: A General Survey," (Speech before the Common Council for American Unity, April 3, 1946) in ff. American Common - Discussion Series on Intergroup Understanding, 1946, Records of the American Council for Nationalities Service, Immigration History Research Center, University of Minnesota (hereinafter referred to as ACNS Mss.); Clyde V. Kiser, "Cultural Pluralism," Annals of the American Academy of Political and Social Science, CCLXII (March, 1949),128.

framework for understanding the period. The author admits to certain biases which may have shaped his perceptions of the period and influenced his conclusions. I believe that ethnicity is a vital and inevitable expression of human individuality. I believe that the disorders of our society, the spiritual unrest, the materialism that provides the only confirmation of self-worth, the loss of creativity and freedom, are consequences of an out-moded social system, which attempted to suppress those centers of valuation and opinion in conflict with the "core culture." In its uncorrupted form, the revival of ethnic consciousness is but one aspect of a larger movement for social change, a movement to protect the environment, to adapt technology to human needs, to find satisfaction in work, to regain power over our lives, to eliminate racism, and to reorder relations among the nations.

I would like to express my gratitude to those who have guided me and sustained me in carrying this project through to completion. Professor Rudolph J. Vecoli, of the University of Minnesota, has been a gentle task-master and a steadfast friend. It was he who sparked my interest in the intercultural education movement and who first established contact with Rachel Davis DuBois. Other scholars have given generously of their time and their insights. These include: Clarke A. Chambers, Henry A. Christian, Walter Feinberg, Ronald K. Goodenow, Patricia Albjerg Graham, Michael

Karni, Paul W. McBride, Michael Rapp and Frank Renkiewicz.

In tracking down manuscript sources, I have relied upon the assistance of a number of outstanding archivists and librarians. These include: Ruth Rauch, director of the AJC Archives, and Harry J. Alderman, former director of the AJC Library; Philip F. Mooney and Catherine Stover of the Balch Institute; Sara L. Engelhardt, Secretary of the Carnegie Corporation; Sandra Keith, Halyna Myroniuk, and Lynn Schweitzer of the Immigration History Research Center, University of Minnesota; Carmen Delle Donne of the National Archives, Washington D.C.; Elizabeth Norris, of the National Board of the Young Women's Christian Association; the late Dr. Bernhard E. Olson, National Director of Interreligious Affairs, National Conference of Christians and Jews; Dr. Irene Jones, of the National Council of Churches; Larry Allen of the New York Foundation; and Dr. J. William Hess and Warren Hovious of the Rockefeller Archives Center.

I have been particularly fortunate in making the acquaintance of so many "veterans" of the thirties, men and women who have not only graced my life but also--by sharing their recollections and observations with me--have deepened my understanding of the events described in this dissertation. I am especially grateful to Rachel Davis DuBois, who gave me access to all her personal papers and was ever ready to answer questions about her career and concerns. Her undimmed vision and undaunted spirit helped me to recapture the mood of an earlier generation of reformers. A full list of those who granted me interviews appears in the final "Note on Manuscript and Interview Sources." To all of these individuals, I express my sincere appreciation.

In concluding these words of recognition, I wish to pay tribute to my family, both extended and immediate. I wish to thank my mother and father, Carmen and Frank, for the example they set and the inspiration they gave. I wish to thank my father-in-law and mother-in-law, Andrew and Clare Struzzieri, for their countless acts of generosity. To my children, Franco and Chiara, who bore up well under the strain of a part-time father, I owe a degree of comic relief and the silent joy of their presence. Finally, I wish to express my gratitude to my wife Gloria for her support, infinite patience and fortitude. Although she would never agree, she held us all together, and that is the highest achievement of all.

PART I

THE UNRESOLVED PROBLEMS OF MASS IMMIGRATION

CHAPTER I

HISTORIANS AND THE AFTERMATH OF RESTRICTION

Very little has been written about the kaleidoscope of events
and interplay of forces which will be discussed in this dissertation.
We do not intend this observation to be an indictment of the
historical profession. The period is still too recent and the sources
too fragmentary to rush to a judgment of this sort. Yet, the paucity
of research has created certain misimpressions about the post-World
War I era that persist to the present time. One recent writer, for
example, refers to the 1930 to 1950 period as a time when there
was a "dissipation" of pluralist thought in America;[1] another suggests
that preoccupation with economic problems during the Great Depression and the challenge of totalitarianism during World War II "muted
any reference to ethnic divisions" during the period;[2] another writer,

---

[1]Seymour W.Itzkoff, Cultural Pluralism and American Education
(Scranton, Pa., 1969), p.121

[2]Richard Kolm, "Ethnicity and Society: A Theoretical Analysis
and its Implications for the United States", unpublished paper, Center
for Studies of Metropolitan Problems, National Institute of Mental
Health, Rockville, Md., October, 1971, p.52

1

looking back over a half century of educators' dealings with

minority children, saw "no evidence of any effort to employ the

immigrants' language and culture as educational vehicles."[3] How

and why has the ethnic disunity of the depression era, so alarm-

ing and perplexing to contemporaries, escaped the attention of

historians? How and why have we erased the memory of a

determined group of reformers who, although they disagreed among

themselves, were united in their condemnation of the Melting Pot?

In a curious way, it may be the vivid impressions of the

World War I period which obscure our vision of the post-war

period. The year 1924 ended an epoch in the history of the United

States. For three centuries the country had been the destination

of millions of the persecuted and poverty-stricken peoples of the

world. With the passage of the Johnson-Reed Act of 1924, which

drastically reduced the number of immigrants permitted annual

entry, the era of mass immigration came to an abrupt end. Like

the framers of the new law, who believed that they had ended once

and for all the threat to Anglo-Saxon cultural and political domina-

tion, historians have similarly viewed the story of the domestic

pressures leading up to the new law as the final chapter in the

[3]David K. Cohen, "Immigrants and the Schools," Review of
Educational Research, XL (1970), 25-26

history of immigration to America. With the supply of fresh recruits from abroad cut off, with assimilation expected to sap the strength of foreign communities in the years ahead, 1924 has been viewed as a major watershed in American history. The new law sealed the fate of minority communities in America. Whatever potential for discord and disunity that had existed prior to 1924 disappeared later. Even if class and political conflicts remained, the cultural consensus would be restored either through ethnic adjustments to Anglo-Saxon modes of behavior or through mutual accommodations of majority and minority groups leading to the emergence of a "cosmopolitan nationality." The post-restriction period as it relates to the immigrant and his descendents constitutes one of the last remaining beachheads of the Consensus School of American Historiography. Until recently, few have dared to challenge the assumption of unity triumphant.

Some of the most widely-read syntheses of the history of American immigration reinforce this view of the larger finality of the restriction movement. John Higham's Strangers in the Land, a masterful analysis of nativist movements in American history, drew to a close in 1924, leaving the impression that no new national crisis, such as the Depression or World War II, could ever fan the flames of nativist hysteria. With the triumph of the restrictionist movement, wrote Higham, "The country would never be the same again . . . [A] new equation between national loyalty and a large measure of political and social conformity would long outlive the generation that

established it."[4] In a more recent essay, Higham reiterated this

view, observing that a "great leap forward in assimilation" took

place after the enactment of the immigration law.[5] A similar

conclusion was reached by Maldwyn Allen Jones, who argues that

the dwindling number of "reinforcements" from overseas in the years

after 1924 "accelerated the Americanization" of recent immigrant

groups.[6] The consequences, according to Jones, were total and

irreversible: the "disintegration of ethnic ghettos," the "dissolving"

of ethnic identity, and the cultural "estrangement" of the second

generation from their immigrant parents.[7] Although Philip Taylor

acknowledged that "the processes of ethnic history in America are

not yet at an end," he also asserted that "when reinforcements from

the old country ceased . . . assimilation [was] likely to accelerate

markedly."[8] The nativist argument that restriction would ensure the

---

[4]John Higham, Strangers in the Land: Patterns of American Nativism, 1860-1925 (2nd ed.; New York, 1963), p. 330.

[5]John Higham, Send These to Me: Jews and Other Immigrants in Urban America (New York, 1975), p. 211.

[6]Maldwyn Allen Jones, American Immigration (Chicago, 1960), p. 297.

[7]Ibid., pp. 297-299.

[8]Philip Taylor, The Distant Magnet; European Emigration to the U.S.A. (New York, 1971), pp. 278, 258.

survival of American institutions and ideals has been accepted by historians.

The theoretical assumptions made by historians in analyzing the process of ethnic adjustment to American society have also clouded our understanding of the post-restriction period. In his poignant study of the immigrant experience, The Uprooted, Oscar Handlin saw restriction as an affront to immigrant peoples that temporarily incited a defensive nationalism during the Depression era, a reaction that quickly and "ingloriously" flickered out as assimilation moved relentlessly forward.[9] Handlin's interpretation of the ethnic experience was in part due to the sociological framework in which he viewed his subject. Handlin accentuated the break between the all-encompassing and restraining ties of traditional communities in Europe and the expansive, individualistic society of America. He argued that the very act of migration, pulling up primordial roots and striking out into a strange land, was an assertion of human freedom whose consequences were in most cases irreversible. Immigration, for Handlin, was the acquisition of something new, not the perpetuation of something old. America was the land of separated

---

[9]Oscar Handlin, The Uprooted: The Epic Story of Great Migrations that Made the American People (New York, 1951), pp.294-300

men and in that shared fate would be the ultimate "resolution of the immigrants' problem."[10] Handlin's view of the transformative nature of the American environment, according to Rudolph Vecoli, is typical of many older American historians who--having absorbed the environmentalism of Frederick Jackson Turner or Robert Park--saw no need to turn their attention to the dying or vestigial force of ethnicity in American society.[11] Both men had exalted the regenerative and purgative qualities of the American environment, its capacity to allow men to transcend the human condition, whether in the vast expanse of the frontier, as Turner argued, or in the hustle and excitement of the modern city, as Park suggested. Dampened with the heady dew of freedom, America enticed its newcomers to put aside their old ways and take on the new.

It seems paradoxical that those writers, such as Handlin, who have seen community disintegration and cultural decline as norms for the post-restriction period are mindful of the rise of ethnic nationalism during the inter-war years. To accord with their model

---

[10]Ibid., p. 299. Handlin's sociological perspective is analyzed in Rudolph Vecoli, "Contadini in Chicago: A Critique of The Uprooted," Journal of American History, LI (December, 1964), 404-417.

[11]Rudolph J. Vecoli, "Ethnicity: A neglected Dimension in American History," in Herbert J. Bass, ed., The State of American History (Chicago, 1970), 70-88.

of inevitable assimilation, this phenomenon must be depicted as
a temporary aberration resulting from the insecurities of the
Depression decade or the residue of social rejection remaining as
an aftermath of the restrictionist controversy. Handlin speaks of
the "defiant nationalism" of ethnic groups during the thirties, but
considers their mood a kind of reverse racism: "These sentiments . . .
were rather the equivalents of the narrow feelings that swayed the
members of the Klan."[12] Jones sees the ethnic divisions that
surfaced so visibly during the Depression as temporary formations
soon to be "swept away" in the patriotic frenzy of World War II.[13]
Louis Gerson depicts ethnic-Americans as mindless pawns lured
from their loyalty to America by foreign agents eager to stir up
internal dissension or party hacks willing to appeal to tribal feelings in order to win votes.[14]

What appears as a post-script in the standard accounts of

---

[12] Handlin, The Uprooted, p. 296. Handlin later modified his position, devoting much attention to the vitality and "fluidity" of group life in America. See, for example, his The American People in the Twentieth Century (Cambridge, 1954). However, he came to view the resilience of ethnic communities as the outcome of structural requirements in American society, not cultural persistence.

[13] Jones, American Immigration, p. 302.

[14] Louis L. Gerson, The Hyphenate in Recent American Politics and Deplimacy (Lawrence, Kansas, 1964), pp. 109-31.

immigration to America takes on added significance when one

reviews the important developments of the inter-war years. It

was a time when American social science made great advances in

understanding the dynamics of ethnic interaction. It was a time

when the children of the immigrants, entering adolescence and

young adulthood, pondered their place and future in American

society. It was a time when American Jews, acutely conscious of

the crisis of their co-religionists in Germany, searched for ways to

check the contagion of hate from abroad. It was a time when

"enlightened educators" struggled to "build dykes to hold back the

flood of dangerous chauvinism" that threatened to inundate the

schools.[15] It was a time when, as James Henry Powell noted,

"cultural pluralism" as an instrumental strategy for the achievement

of assimilation had its greatest vogue.[16] While some professional

educators were uncompromising guardians of unity, others became

so absorbed by method that "pluralism" was transformed into an end

---

[15]Miriam R. Ephraim, "Service for Education in Human Relations,"
in Selected Writings of Miriam R. Ephraim (New York: National
Jewish Welfare Board, 1966), p. 17.

[16]James Henry Powell, "The Concept of Cultural Pluralism
in American Social Thought" (Unpublished Ph.D.Dissertation,
University of Notre Dame, 1971), pp. 75-115.

in itself.

Institutional policy and educational strategy toward ethnic communities in the inter-war years were not implemented without reference to the great debate over restriction that had taken place a decade earlier, and out of which various strategies for dealing with diversity had been devised. For leading social thinkers of the thirties, Americanization had a pejorative character, an ignorant and bungling policy that only served to exacerbate the problem it tried to solve. Though they were as concerned about the slow acquisition of "democratic ideals" and national loyalties by recent immigrant peoples, though their policies were perhaps as repressive in intent as those of the nativists, they carefully disassociated themselves from the jawboning element that had attempted to mold and transform the immigrant. The most important intellectual context for the educational controversies of the thirties was the crosscurrents of ideas that had appeared during the Americanization controversy.

Just as historians have tended to close the book on immigration in 1924 so also have they rushed to pronounce Americanization dead around the same time. Their haste can be attributed to some embarrassment over the naked racism and "un-American" aspects of the movement which abated somewhat after 1924. The two major studies of the Americanization movement have tried to de-emphasize the virulent ideas that flourished at the time, the first by denying

10

that they were characteristic of the movement, the second by
implying that they were episodic. Edward Hartmann argues that
the leadership of the Americanization movement, as opposed to the
crank racists who sometimes stole the headlines, were interested
in "a positive program of education and guidance...," that the
true significance of the movement was the clear evidence it gave
of a self-confident American nationalism that refused to discount
the ability of the nation to absorb the recent arrivals.[17] Higham
does not dismiss the currency of racist ideas so easily, but he
offers us a psychological explanation why this departure from "the
nation's traditional values" of openness and hospitality toward the
immigrant took place, and at the end of his study, we are left with
a movement in disarray and retreat.[18] Both books fail to explore in
any great depth the liberal alternative that outlived the flood of
xenophobia and had a greater and more permanent impact on public
policy and the national consciousness. Hartmann is correct in
suggesting that the liberal alternative held greater sway over policy-
makers, but he errs by misconstruing its benign quality. Higham--by
concentrating so heavily on the extreme and glaringly racist elements
of the movement--creates the impression that the ideological and

---

[17]Edward George Hartmann, The Movement to Americanize the
Immigrant (New York, 1948), pp. 7-8

[18]Higham, Strangers, pp. 300-30, passim. (The quoted phrase is
on p. 329).

institutional assault on the immigrant was broken after 1924.

Problems arising from immigration as well as policies for coping

with those problems were a continuing concern of the years ahead.

The tendency in recent scholarship has been to make sweep-

ing generalizations about the liberal Americanization movement

that--although valid to a limited degree--have operated to cloud

the deep and sometimes bitter disagreements that erupted during

the inter-war years. Higham traced the tension in American history

between faith in the absorptive capacity of American society and

fear that the nation would be over-run and subverted by alien forces.

He convincingly argued that xenophobic movements rise and crest

during periods of national crises, and that as the crisis subsides,

the abiding tradition of tolerance and hospitality regains the

ascendency. By concentrating so heavily on this one particular

polarity in American history, Higham paradoxically supports a

consensus view of the past. The liberal tradition survives its cyclic

challenges as a pure and uniform stream of ideas that has suffered

no pollution and no inner agitation, as the constant and humane

counterpoise to the outbreaks of intolerance that have periodically

afflicted American society. In highlighting this dichotomy, Higham

overlooks evidence that would indicate conflict within the center of

the liberal tradition, and latent repressive functions of liberal

ideology. A major reassessment of liberalism is now underway, and

Higham's admiration of the liberals is being replaced by a more objective approach somewhat laced with suspicion.

In an important recent study,[19] Daniel Weinberg examined an organization that typified the liberal approach to the immigrant: the Foreign Language Information Service (FLIS). Founded in 1917 as a wartime agency, the Service tried to bridge the linquistic barriers that separated ethnic communities from the larger society. It prepared news dispatches in foreign languages for the ethnic press and championed the cause of the immigrant in appeals to the general American public. Weinberg argues that FLIS exemplified another side of the Americanization movement, one that does not conform to the "coercive, shrill and intolerant" stereotype of the movement popularized by historians like Higham. Midway between the poles of anglo-Conformity and cultural pluralism, between the racist rhetoric of Madison Grant and the thorough-going pluralism of Horace Kallen, Weinberg discerned a point of view that tried to reconcile the need for social unity with the realization that ethnic groups would resist attempts at forced assimilation. To actively intervene in the slow process of cultural assimilation, these leaders realized, would invite a self-defensive reaction on the part of these groups--counter-productive to the goal of eventual assimilation. Weinberg also saw

---

[19]Daniel Erwin Weinberg, "The Foreign Language Information Service and the Foreign Born, 1918-1939: A Case Study of Cultural Assimilation viewed as a Problem in Social Technology" (Unpublished Ph.D. Dissertation, University of Minnesota, 1973).

FLIS leaders as specialists in the flow of information, individuals who believed that misunderstandings and differences could be eradicated through educational means. FLIS leaders, according to Weinberg, differed from the nativists in tactics, not in goal. Despite their call for restraint in dealing with immigrant communities, despite their openness to immigrant cultural "contributions", they still bent all of their efforts to achieving the goal of the nativists: social and cultural unity. The liberal tradition, seen as adversary of Americanization in Higham's work, appears as silent and powerful partner in Weinberg's study.

Whereas Weinberg examines the technical approach of professionals in the immigrant service field, another recent writer, Michael Passi, analyzes the ideological underpinnings of that approach. Passi argues that Anglo-Saxon racism was anathema to most intellectuals and social scientists, that the superiority of American culture was rarely seen in racial terms, but in economic terms.[20] Nevertheless, few of these individuals endorsed pluralism because, in their view, urban industrial civilization broke down traditional, peasant cultures even if temporary ethnic formations, as Robert Park and W.I. Thomas argued, appeared to ease the transition.

---

[20]Michael Passi, "Mandarins and Immigrants: The Irony of Ethnic Studies in America since Turner" (Unpublished Ph.D. Dissertation, University of Minnesota, 1971).

Passi argues that the idea of assimilation formed "an essential part of a formidable ideological defense of twentieth century capitalism . . . ."[21] Few challenged this assumption because few challenged the system that spawned this assumption.

The liberal tradition appears in a darker and more malevolent light in a recent study by Paul McBride.[22] Although his study ends with American entrance into World War I, it is nonetheless relevant to an analysis of post-war Americanization since it critically examines aspects of the liberal posture that spanned both periods. McBride argues that despite the rhetoric of tolerance, receptivity toward cultural "gifts", and efforts to disassociate the liberal position from the strident nativism that surfaced during World War I, both liberals as well as nativists feared "cultural mongrelization" and "insisted that the ethnic minorities purge themselves of old world cultures and conform to the new".[23] Both groups were beset by similar fears, both envisioned similar goals; while the nativists pursued their goals openly, the liberals waged a clandestine "cultural cold War" against ethnic minorities. McBride viewed the

---

[21] Ibid., p. 13

[22] Paul Wilbert McBride, "The Cultural Cold War: Immigrants and the Quest for Cultural Monism, 1890-1917" (Unpublished Ph.D. Dissertation, University of Georgia, 1972).

[23] Ibid., p. 111

settlement workers, the most renowned of which was Jane
Addams--heretofore considered the most humane and tolerant of
the liberal elements in the pre-war period--as close cousins of
the openly-condescending charity workers. Had the settlement
workers practiced what they preached about cultural preservation,
they would have supported self-help efforts of immigrants to maintain their cultures through the instrumentality of the schools and
political machines. Instead they presumed to be arbiters of the
immigrant's fate and opposed any initiatives that went beyond the
narrow limits of their professed tolerance.

The posture of social workers is treated in a much more
detached and less conspiratorial fashion in a study by John F.
McClymer, who nonetheless sees ulterior motives for their efforts
to "defend" the immigrant. McClymer notes that social workers,
in particular settlement workers, have received very favorable
comment in the writings of historians.[24] Their respectable image,
he points out, rests in part on their condemnation of racism and
their opposition to the restrictionist movement. McClymer argues
that the basic reason for their well-publicized dissent was their

[24]John Francis McClymer, "The Emergence of Social
Engineering in America, 1890-1925: An Essay in the History of the
'New' Middle Class" (Unpublished Ph.D. Dissertation, State
University of New York at Stony Brook, 1974), p. 152.

realization that racist solutions to the immigrant problem would preclude the exercise of their special expertise. If immigrant "races" were considered inferior to the Anglo-Saxon race, it was futile to advocate, as they did, the uplift and absorption of immigrant peoples through a massive program of education.[25] McClymer sees the social workers as the vanguard of a "new middle class," a class of "experts" who realized that opportunities for advancement within the American industrial system were waiting for those who possessed a specialized body of knowledge. Social workers were the custodians of the knowledge of how to deal with the "immigrant problem." Despite the boldness of their vision and the surfeit of compassion for misfortunate members of society, they were, as McClymer points out, largely ineffectual in altering the course of events and easily controlled by the "eastern philanthropic establishment."

The revisionists have cleared away the air of sanctity surrounding early twentieth century "reformers." They have broken through the rhetoric of immigrant "gifts"; they have unmasked the true intentions of the immigrant's "friends", and they have related the reform impulse to occupational needs. But the newer studies, with their broad generalizations and their stinging criticisms

---

[25]Ibid., pp. 143-44

(however deserved in some cases), have left us unprepared for unravelling the events and understanding the controversies that took place after 1924. These studies have obscured internal contradictions within the liberal ideology that became apparent as that ideology was applied in specific situations. These conflicts were--because of the positions of influences held by these individuals--perhaps of larger significance and greater moment than the intellectual gulf that separated the liberal Americanization school and the more coercive school of Americanization, which traditionally has received the bulk of scholarly attention. There were various interpretations that could be given to the concept of immigrant "gifts". There were different expectations concerning the time required for total assimilation. There were those who sought to conserve American values and institutions and those who sought to transform them. Among those who endeavored to educate the immigrant child, there were different priorities that dictated different approaches to curriculum development.

This dissertation will attempt to show that anxiety over the consequences of mass immigration did not subside after 1924, that if anything, this anxiety intensified as new conditions such as the collapse of the world economy and the rise of Fascism touched the raw nerve of social disunity in the United States. Much of the concern over disaffected and half-assimilated minorities, as will be pointed out in Chapter Two, was directed at the children of the immigrants, who became the subject of much interest and much

controversy during the inter-war years. As a result of the perceived

cracks in the melting pot, efforts to restore social order and wipe

out unacceptable cultural differences were continued after 1924.

As Weinberg has shown, these efforts were made in a much more

sophisticated and low-key fashion and with a rhetoric that seemed

hardly at all hostile to the people it sought to transform. Because

this ostensibly benign approach rested on the findings of social

scientists during the inter-war years, I have labelled it "Scientific

Americanization." An important motivation for this non-inflamatory

and optimistic approach, as will be discussed in Chapters Five

and Six, was that it was as much directed toward the Anglo

majority, which had to be calmed and reassured (if nativism was

to be held in check), as it was toward the immigrants and their

children. The rhetoric of immigrant gifts served this purpose well

as did the reminder that--in the words of the title of a national

radio series (discussed in Chapter Six)--we are "Americans All -

Immigrants All."

For many liberals,[26] however, there was an important gap

between what was said and what was intended, especially with

regard to the delicate question of cultural maintenance. No such

------

26The word "liberal," as used in this study, refers to Native-
American social reformers who believed that meaningful change was
possible within the existing institutional structure of American
Society.

gap existed in the thoughts and deeds of others. During the 1930's, a more vocal and self assured generation of ethnic leadership began to succeed the older generation of immigrant leaders. Reared in America and articulate in the English language, these leaders were proponents of a position which we have called "cultural integrationism"--a logical extension of liberal ideology but one which, in its practical application, proved to be unacceptable to many liberals. The call for cultural integration was endorsed by a group of female reformers, militant defenders of the immigrant, many of whom were products of the training in leadership and social consciousness provided by the Young Women's Christian Association. The combined efforts of these individuals could be seen in the many "Festivals of Nations" that took on such lavish proportions during the inter-war years and in the many programs to instill in the second generation a pride in ancestry and an appreciation for ethnic culture.

There were some "ethnics", however, who were indifferent or hostile to the programs of the "cultural integrationists." In Chapter Seven, we examine the response of the American Jewish community to the intercultural education movement. The experience and the problems of American Jewry were, of course, atypical in many respects. There had been a long-standing difference of opinion within the Jewish community over the relative weight of religion or ethnicity on the scale of Jewish identity. In the period before the foundation of the state of Israel, the bond of common ancestry did not have the same appeal as it has today. Jews in the thirties also had to defend themselves against a world-wide campaign of villification conducted by the Nazis. The task of ensuring the survival of the Jewish community in a hostile world relegated all other concerns to secondary importance. Nevertheless, the fact that many Jewish leaders sought shelter in the "triple melting pot" does raise certain questions with regard to the solidity of ethnic support for cultural pluralism.

It is difficult to set down a definition for "intercultural education" that would subsume the varied meanings that were given to the term. During the inter-war years, scientific American-izers, cultural integrationists, and leaders of endangered minorities all endorsed the call for "improved intergroup relations," but the motivation for pursuing that goal and the strategies employed to achieve it were not the same. In this study, I use the term in the manner in which it was used by those who first employed it: the cultural integrationists. As they saw it, intercultural education was the study of the history and cultural contributions of ethnic groups to American society. Such a study was intended to achieve three basic objectives: raising minority self-esteem, building attitudes of mutual appreciation among groups and promoting inter-group harmony, and stimulating a "renaissance" of American culture.

The inability of the cultural integrationists who controlled the

Service Bureau for Intercultural Education for five years to convince both scientific Americanizers and leaders of American Jewry of the wisdom of their "separate approach" is the central theme of this dissertation. As we narrate the history of the Bureau, we will attempt to understand the several strands of thought that existed on the subject of socio-cultural diversity and the reasons for the ultimate rejection of the "separate approach."

CHAPTER II

THE SECOND GENERATION: PERILOUS

PRESENCE OR HOPE OF AMERICA

"Footloose, prowling and predacious adolescents," is

what one sociologist called them; "noisy painted girls [and] . . .

sneering hats-over-the-eye' smart alecs,'" is how one social

worker described them.[1] Who were these--depending on your

point of view--contemptible or pathethic creatures? They were

what Louis Adamic called in 1934 those "Thirty Million New

Americans," the sons and daughters of the millions of immigrants

who landed on American shores during the early decades of the

twentieth century. Their morale and fate, Adamic argued, would

have a profound impact on the future course of American society.[2]

---

[1]Robert Park, "Preface" to The Gang by Frederick M. Thrasher
(Chicago, 1936), p. ix; Evelyn W. Hersey, "The Emotional Conflicts
of the Second Generation: A Discussion of American-born children
of Immigrant Parents," Interpreter Release Clip Sheet (Informational
Bulletin of the Foreign Language Information Service), XI (July 10,
1934), 85.

[2]Louis Adamic, "Thirty Million New Americans," Harper's
Magazine, CLXIX (November, 1934), 648-93.

Many agreed with Adamic as evidenced by the heated debate that took place on "the second generation problem" during the inter-war years. The very appearance of the second generation on the American scene as a distinct social group with a special set of problems was unexpected, for immigrant apologists had predicted the disappearance of the "immigrant problem" with the growth to maturity of an American-born generation. But there they were to confound Americans with their strident behavior and lingering Old World attachments. Was the separation of the second generation in the public mind and the sense of alienation that they felt the avoidable consequence of barriers that had been erected against their full and equal participation in American life? Was their marginal status, as some social scientists argued, a natural transitional stage, the prelude to complete assimilation in the third generation? Were they the torchbearers of ethnic culture to future generations of Americans, signalling the collapse of the melting pot ideal and the transformation of American civilization? How these questions were answered influenced the policies that were adopted by social workers, politicians and educators in deal-ing with the second generation. Ultimately, those who labored in the schools would wrestle with the policy implications of these questions.

Pre-World War I Comments on the
Second Generation Problem

The special syndrome of behavior that became so well-known

in the years after World War I was not unknown in the pre-war

years. Jane Addams, who shaped the conscience of a generation

on the subject of immigration, had expressed concern over the break-

down of family cohesiveness and tendency toward criminality

displayed by the children of the immigrants, and had blamed these

problems on the "premature fling" of the second generation into

city life with a too rapid abandonment of ancestral traditions.

Like other social analysts of the time, she prescribed a regimen

of greater "reverence of the past" and through the settlement she

worked to acquaint the children with the cultural contributions of

immigrant cultures. Her ultimate objective, however, was not

the establishment of pluralism in American society, but that the

contributions of diverse cultures be released from "the restraining

bond of one country into the land of the universal."[3] Settlement

workers who lived in close proximity to immigrant peoples soon

realized that a special set of problems grew out of the marginal

status of the second generation. Many seemed to be haunted by

the nightmare of a lawless and anti-social generation of alienated

---

[3]Jane Addams, Twenty Years At Hull House (New York, 1910),
pp. 172, 81, 268, 169-85, passim.

25

youth preying upon society.

Mary McDowell, alumna of Hull House and later Head Resident of the University of Chicago Settlement, worried that the rapid acculturation of the children would undermine the authority of the parent and leave no "new restraints" to take the place of the old. She was alarmed by the spectre of "lawlessness" in the second generation, and urged efforts to publicize "all that is admirable" in the immigrant past through the medium of the school curriculum in order to reinforce the authority of the parents.[4] The link between law and order and ethnic pride was an early discovery of American liberals. Another former resident of Hull House, Grace Abbott, who later became director of the Immigrant Protective League was also disturbed by the "family tensions and youthful alienation" in the second generation and blamed these manifestations on their "too rapid assimilation."[5] Randolph Bourne, never one to mince words, did not equate rootlessness with assimilation; the second generation, he wrote, were "cultural half-breeds" who substituted for their ancestral culture the tinsel culture of

[4]Mary E. McDowell, "The Struggle in the Family Life," Charities (December 3, 1904), 196-97 [reprinted in Stanley Feldstein & Lawrence Costello, eds., The Ordeal of Assimilation (Garden City, New York, 1974), pp. 361-63].

[5]Grace Abbott, The Immigrant and the Community (New York, 1917), p. 225.

"the cheap newspaper, the 'movies,' the popular song, the ubiquitous automobile . . . the unthinking who survey this class call them assimilated."[6]

These pre-war comments on the adjustment problems of the second generation appear to have been rather peripheral to the major concerns of the period and overshadowed by the controversies surrounding the restriction movement. Although the Immigration Commission undertook an exhaustive study of the children of immigrants in the schools, seeking to determine drop-out and "retardation" rates of immigrant children from various groups, there was no effort to relate the poor performance of these children to cultural maladjustment.[7] Other major studies of the school experiences of immigrant children failed to mention cultural conflict between the home and school environment.[8] Liberal-minded Americans found it hard to abandon their faith in the absorptive quality of the American environment, an argument they had used so often in their combat against the racist assumptions of the nativists.

----

[6]Carl Resek, ed., War and the Intellectuals: Essays by Randolph S. Bourne, 1915-1919 (New York, 1964), p. 113.

[7]U.S., Congress, Reports of the Immigration Commission, Vols. 29-33, "The Children of Immigrants in School" (Washington, 1911).

[8]Herbert A. Miller, The School and the Immigrant (Cleveland, 1916); Frank V. Thompson, Schooling of the Immigrant (New York, 1920).

The Dawning of the Second Generation Problem

As time passed, a number of developments combined to place the plight of the second generation into clearer public focus. These included: demographic changes, the impact of World War I, and the effect of immigration restriction on social service agencies.

The millions of immigrants who had arrived on American shores prior to World War I continued to bear children--adding to the pool of potential criminals, deviants and drop-outs. More and more of these children were entering the critical stage of adolescence, emerging from the cloistered confines of the home and making their presence known to the rest of society. They came from cultural backgrounds more at variance with the core American culture than previous waves of immigrants, and unlike earlier immigrants they settled in the crowded tenaments and congested streets of urban America. Some turned to lives of crime, lured by the illicit opportunities opened up by the Prohibition experiment. Many paraded their shallow Americanism in the conspicuous consumption of the popular culture of dance hall and movie idol. With the onset of the Great Depression, millions were compelled to stay in school longer where they tried the tolerance of their teachers. The second generation had become a very visible and very disturbing social element.[9]

World War I had also exposed a sensitive nerve in the body politic. The United States had moved beyond its preoccupation with internal expansion and development and had assumed a position of world leadership with interests that extended to every corner of

---

[9]The literature on the criminality and anti-social behavior of the second generation is extensive. Some examples are: Louis Wirth, "Culture Conflict and Misconduct," Social Forces, IX (June, 1931), 484-92; John Levy, "Conflicts of Culture and Children's Maladjustment," Mental Hygiene, XVII (January, 1933), 41-50; Lawrence Guy Brown, Immigration, Cultural Conflicts and Social Adjustment (New York, 1933); Frederick Thrasher, The Gang (Chicago, 1936); Eleanor T. Glueck, "Culture Conflict and Delinquency," Journal of Mental Hygiene, XXI (January, 1937), 46-66; Eleanor T. Glueck, "Newer Ways of Crime Control," Harvard Educational Review, IX (March, 1937), 184-203. The above studies employed the culture conflict hypothesis in explaining second generation crime, i.e. that the conflicting standards and values to which the second generation was exposed contributed to the high incidence of criminal behavior. That interpretation was challenged by a group of experts who argued that the environmental factor, i.e. the concentration of second generation individuals in low income areas, was the most important single cause of second generation criminality. See, for example, Floyd H. Allport, "Culture Conflict vs. the individual as Factors in Delinquency," Social Forces, IX (June, 1931), 493-97; and Thorstein Sellin, "Crime and the Second Generation of Immigrant Stock," in Foreign Language Information Service, Report of Principal Speeches Delivered at the Conference on the Alien in America (Mineographed), Washington, D.C., May 2, 1936, pp. 38-44. For further discussion of the environmentalist position, see below pp.

the world. Suddenly the sentiments of its polyglot population
took on a new importance; continued identification with countries
of origin would either support or impede the objectives of U.S.
foreign policy. During World War I, Americans awoke to the
realization that even the second and third generations of an older
immigrant group like the Germans were still sufficiently nationality-
conscious to exert pressure against American intervention. The
illusion of unity had been shattered and the measures of repression
which followed were consequences of this traumatic experience.
Although the hysterical reaction against hyphenism subsided somewhat after 1924, an undercurrent of anxiety and suspicion remained
that would surface again as a new international threat appeared
during the thirties. In that later context, the second generation
could no longer be counted upon to support and defend the interests
of American foreign policy. Constant vigilance and an active
program to win the allegiance of the second generation would be
necessary. Intercultural education came to be seen as one way
of building morale and instilling loyalty in the children of the
immigrants.[10]

---

[10]For expressions of concern by educators over the uncertain
loyalties of the second generation see: Rachel Davis DuBois, "Danger
or Promise?" Speech delivered at San Francisco State College, 1936,
ff. Speeches and Radio Talks, 1934-1945, Rachel Davis DuBois
Papers, Immigration History Research Center, University of
Minnesota (hereinafter cited as DuBois Mss.); James Marshall, "How
the Schools can Help to Solve the Second Generation Problem,"

A third factor of importance in bringing the plight of the second generation into clearer public focus was the attention given to the problem by professionals in the immigrant service field. The pre-World War I flood-tide of immigration had brought into being a number of public and private agencies that tried to facilitate the adjustment and assimilation of immigrants. Settlement houses, municipal and state Americanization committees, adult education centers, employment bureaus etc.--each tried to meet the varied needs of foreigners in a new society: learning English, finding employment, dealing with government bureaucrats, and adapting to a new way of life. Some of these organizations, by their political connections and national scope, were much more influential than others, and their leaders became recognized experts in the field. The International Institutes of the YWCA, an organizational endeavor begun in 1911 by Edith Terry Bremer, experienced accelerated growth during World War I and became by 1920 a national network of immigrant service centers in more than fifty industrial cities of the

Interpreter Releases, XII (May 13, 1935), 194-96; Joseph Roucek, "Editorial," Journal of Educational Sociology, XII (April, 1939), 449; Francis J. Brown, "New Tensions and Cultural Minorities," (Address delivered at the joint luncheon of the Adult Education Division of the National Education Association and the National Council on Naturalization and Citizenship, St. Louis, Missouri, Feb. 28, 1940), ff. E-G, Records of the International Institute of Boston, Immigration History Research Center, University of Minnesota (Hereinafter cited as Boston Mss.).

United States. The Foreign Language Information Service (FLIS)

was an outgrowth of efforts undertaken by the government during

World War I to spread pro-war propaganda. By 1923, the Service

was an independent, private agency under the direction of Read

Lewis, which specialized in the translation and dissemination of

government reports to the foreign language press. Other localized

agencies proliferated throughout the country. Although the skills

required for immigrant social service were varied and sometimes

eluded exact definition, the field had become a recognized sub-

division of the social work profession with the organization of

"Division X" of the National Conference of Social Work in 1919,

which came to be known as "The Immigrant." The interests of

professionals in organizations such as these were seriously

jeopardized by the end of open immigration. Restriction cut off

the constant flow of new clients from abroad and threatened the

very existence of the organizations which these professionals

staffed. The drift of events became apparent in the twenties as

public support for these organizations eroded, financial sources

dried up and budgets were trimmed.[11] The professionals who

---

[11]The appearance of the second generation on the stage of
concerns felt by International Institute workers coincided with a
period of budgetary retrenchment at the National Board of the
YWCA. The national department's name change in 1924 (From
"National Department for Work with Foreign Born Women" to
"Department of Immigration and Foreign Communities") was symbolic
of the new emphasis in Institute programming (See minutes, Department for Work with Foreign Born Women, Young Women's Christian

suddenly faced an uncertain future did not resign themselves to

slow obsolescence, but instead searched for ways to enlarge their

constituencies and branch out in new directions. The second

generation was a means of salvation for them, a vast and ever-

expanding population group that, in the eyes of social workers,

cried out for professional assistance. The creation of the

"Commission on the Study of the Second Generation Girl" by the

Conference of International Institutes held in Niagara Falls and the

setting up of the "Division of Foreign Language Organizations"

by FLIS in 1928 were events that marked the advent of the new

orientation. While many liberals--spurred on by sociologists and

Association, 1924 [especially Feb. 13, 1924], Records of the
National Board of the YWCA, New York City [Hereinafter referred
to as YWCA Mss.]). The Foreign Language Information Service's
request for financial support from the Carnegie Corporation in 1928
to establish the Division of Foreign Language Organization, a
project designed to reach the second generation through the vast
network of foreign language organizations, occurred at a time
of shrinking foundation outlays for the Service See Read Lewis
to Frederick P. Keppel, Nov. 7, 1928, ff. Common Council
for American Unity [formerly FLIS] , 1930, Records of the Carnegie
Corporation of New York, Archives of the Carnegie Corporation
of New York [Hereinafter cited as Carnegie Mss.]).. FLIS drew
Louis Adamic--the foremost interpreter and popularizer of the
second generation problem during the inter-war years--into its
orbit of influence at the nadir of its financial fortunes in the
year 1933.

by internal pressures within their organizations--were now prepared
to view assimilation as a protracted, multi-generational process,
there were those who continued to insist that environmental
influences would triumph over familial and traditional forces, and
that the cure for the ills of the second generation was an effort
to educate public opinion to the evils of discrimination. These
stalwart environmentalists were an obstacle to those who were
calling for a broadening of professional concern for they refused
to accept important assumptions upon which the new orientation
was based, that the second generation faced a conflict of identity
and needed the guidance of sympathetic professionals.

Environmentalism

The environmentalist position was one of many that crystal-
ized on the second generation problem during the post-World
War I period. While environmentalists tended to simplify the
steps that needed to be taken to solve the second generation
problem, and to reject completely the cultural interpretation of the
problem, they too--unlike their pre-war forebearers--were forced
to turn their attention to the criminal tendencies, lingering Old
World attachments and problems of social and scholastic maladjustment that plagued the second generation. Environmentalists
believed in the irresistible pull of the American environment, that
unprecedented physical, mental and emotional changes had taken

place in the space of one generation. For them, the problems

of the second generation were external in causation, largely

avoidable if Americans had not raised barriers against the full

and equal participation of minority groups in American life.

Misunderstood by teachers and segregated in school life, the

children of immigrants became discipline problems: denied access

to better-paying jobs, they turned to lives of crime; denied accep-

tance as first-class Americans, they continued to identify with

their ancestral homelands. The problem of reconciling two

ways of life, of living in two worlds, was an artificial problem

concocted by well-meaning liberals, who confused forced retreat

into the ethnic enclave with a deliberate choice of life style.

For environmentalists, efforts to enlighten the majority

of Americans, rather than direct work with the second generation,

was the most promising type of approach. Old stock Americans

would have to be educated to the presence of new Americans in

their midst, who--although they differed superficially perhaps

in skin color, facial features or vocal intonation--were culturally

indistinguishable from themselves. Emphasis would have to be

laid on the importance of fair play and brotherhood, the material

contributions of ethnic groups to American life, the adverse affects

of discrimination, and the speed of assimilation. An important

representative of this approach was Harold Rugg of Teachers College,

Columbia University, who with the cooperation of staff members at

the Lincoln School of Columbia University, developed a set of
curriculum materials for secondary schools on the subject of
American immigration history. Although these materials, widely
used in progressive schools during the inter-war years, inserted
immigrant peoples into the mainstream of American history and
stressed the important material and social contributions made
by these people to American development, they also emphasized
the rapid strides that all groups had made toward complete
assimilation.[12]

Insistence on the Americanism of the second generation was
a position that received support from some members of the second
generation, who realized that outward signs of conformity to
American ways provided a ticket for mobility in American society.[13]
This tactic did not appeal to more than a small segment of the
second generation. Environmentalism no longer had the same appeal

---

[12]See Harold Rugg, America and her Immigrants (New York, 1926),
pp. 7-14. Rugg's book was designed as a textbook for secondary
school students. Classroom units on special topics were prepared
by students at Teachers College. See, for example, Gertrude
Van Hise, Ancestral History of a Class (New York, 1931), a pamphlet
in the Teachers' Lesson Unit Series.

[13]See for example, Young Women's Christian Association, What
it Means to be a Second-Generation Girl: Talks Given at the Second-
Generation Youth Dinner of the National Board of the YWCA (New
York: The Woman's Press, 1935), and the first person accounts
published in The Record, XLIII (January, 1935), the journal of the
Girls' Friendly Society of the United States.

to ethnic leaders in the post-restriction period for it no longer functioned as an ideological expedient to gain the admission of more of their countrymen.

Although education of the general public was the preferred way of dealing with the second generation problem, some environmentalists did advocate a limited program of direct work with the second generation, a kind of mopping-up operation to remove the last traces of foreignism. At the 1927 annual conference of International Institutes, some delegates argued that the best way to help the second generation was to encourage them to drop all hint of foreign accent, conform in dress and style as closely as possible to the American pattern, and move out of the ethnic neighborhood as quickly as possible. It was partly at the insistence of one of these delegates, Ruth Crawford Mitchell, who believed that emphasis should be placed on the Americanism of the second generation, that the name of the standing commission examining the problem was changed in 1928 from "Commission on the Study of the Second Generation Girl" to "Commission on First Generation Americans."[14]

---

[14]Ninth Annual National Conference of International Institutes of the Young Women's Christian Association, Report of Proceedings (Des Moines, Iowa, 1927), pp. 66-73; Tenth Annual National Conference of International Institutes of the Young Women's Christian Association, Report of Proceedings (Pocano Manor, Penn., 1928) Section IX, pp. 4-5. (Proceedings for 1927 and 1928 are found in Section 6, Microfilm Reel 100, YWCA Mss.)

Although it became harder in the years ahead to tout the Americanism of the second generation, the environmentalist position never completely disappeared. It was difficult to disprove the environmentalist contention that the chief roadblock to assimilation was the benighted attitudes of other Americans. The persuasiveness of the environmentalist argument with regard to the cultural evolution of the second generation was another matter, however. As time went by, and as new evidence began to mount from the investigations of social scientists, it became harder to argue that the American environment of school, neighborhood, peer group and work place had successfully weaned the second generation away from the ethnic culture. If many members of the second generation still clung to the values, life style and communal patterns of the past, then consideration would have to be given to the function of the ethnic group in the transition to Americanism.

The Second Generation and American Social Science

Environmentalist assumptions concerning the speed of the assimilation process could not stand up against the weight of evidence gathered by social scientists during the twenties and thirties. Sociologists, anthropologists and psychologists--all from different vantage points--tended to agree that culture was a much more persistent psychic and social reality than previously thought, that cultural change was a gradual process subject to certain regularities and taking a number of generations to accom-

plish. For most social scientists, the disappearance of minority

cultures within American industrial society was both inevitable

and desirable; their counsel of forbearance to policy-makers,

their belief in non-intervention in the internal life of minority

groups was not intended to perpetuate ethnic cultures and collectiv-

ities, but to put no obstacles in the way of assimilation. In the

view of American social scientists, the second generation, rather

than being the first Americanized generation, was the transitional

generation, the generation that straddled two worlds.

After World War I, Freudianism enjoyed a great vogue in

the United States; Freud's works were translated and popularized,

and New York City joined Vienna in becoming a major center of

the psychoanalytic school.[15] Freud taught that the shadow of

the individual's past could not easily be shaken; early childhood

experiences left a deep and lasting impression on the individual,

which the weight of later experience could not easily erase.

Although Freud concerned himself primarily with the etiology of

individual abnormality and the universal aspects of psychological

conditioning, it was easy to deduce from his theories that culture,

to the extent that it influenced child-rearing practices, was an

---

[15]William E. Leuchtenburg, The Perils of Prosperity, 1914-
1932 (Chicago, 1958), pp. 163-177.

important variable in personality development, and as resistant
to later modification as purely idiosyncratic behavior. Such
influences could not possibly be swept away in the space of one
generation. The concept of the inferiority complex as developed
by Alfred Adler,[16] also put into theoretical perspective the
demoralization and anti-social behavior that seemed to occur
so often in the second generation. Since an individual's self-
esteem was dependent upon the status of the group to which he
belonged, rejection of the immigrant way of life by the larger
society led to self-rejection by the children of immigrants. The
lessons of psychology were well-learned by a number of social
workers who came to appreciate the resilience of immigrant
cultures and who began to argue that the way to solve the second
generation problem was to raise the status of the immigrant group
through some form of public recognition or selective praise of
immigrant cultures.[17]

---

[16]Alfred Adler, The Science of Living (New York, 1929).

[17]Florence Cassidy, "Report of the Commission on First
Generation Americans," (Presented to the Eleventh Annual National
Conference of International Institutes meeting in Detroit, April 22-25,
1930), pp. 22, 25, ff. YWCA, International Institutes, Bulletins on
Immigration and Case Work with Foreign-Born, 1924-1937, Shipment
3, Box 1, ACNS Mss; Thomas L. Cotton, "Folk Festival Council of
New York: Report of Activities, Jan. 1 to June 1, 1933," ff. ACNS-
Folk Festival Council, Shipment 3, Box 1, ACNS Mss.

Anthropology did not lead Americans to change their
expectations with regard to the longevity of ethnic cultures within
American society, but instead created a climate of tolerance for
those cultures, when they did persist longer than expected.
Franz Boas and his students at Columbia University had toppled
the elaborate edifice of evolutionism, that had characterized
nineteenth century anthropology, premised on a humanistic conception of culture as a singular phenomenon, which various
peoples possessed or lacked to a degree commensurate with their
progress on the scale of evolution.[18] Now instead of people having culture, they had a culture, which fitted the historical
development, psychic dispositions, and material preconditions
of their society. The efforts of Boas and other anthropologists
to show parallels in valuation and cultural form between "primitive"
and modern societies raised the status of primitive peoples in
western eyes. Anthropologists were also fond of pointing out the
shortcomings of American civilization as seen from the vantage
point of other cultures, and thus helped to create a greater

---

[18]George W. Stocking, Jr., "Franz Boas and the Culture
Concept in Historical Perspective," in George W. Stocking, Jr.,
Race, Culture and Evolution: Essays in the History of Anthro-
pology (New York, 1968), pp. 195-233.

receptivity to alien cultural influence.[19] Moreover, by showing

how all great civilizations had arisen at the point of convergence

of different peoples and cultures, anthropology supported those

who advocated a blending of cultural patterns in American society.[20]

Probably more than any other discipline, sociology colored

the perceptions that people had of ethnic group dynamics within

American society. The vital center for the dissemination of

sociological theory in the United States during the inter-war

years was the Sociology Department of the University of Chicago,

under the leadership of Robert Ezra Park. Some of the most

important commentators on the second generation problem during

this period were trained by Park or deeply influenced by him:

Louis Wirth, Frederick Thrasher, Harvey Zorbaugh, Everett Stone-

quist, Pauline Young, E. Franklin Frazier and William C. Smith.

Park constructed a framework of conceptualization that was filled

---

[19]See, for example, Franz Boas, Anthropology and Modern Life (New York, 1928), especially ch. 9; Margaret Mead, Coming of Age in Samoa (New York, 1928); and Ruth Benedict, Patterns of Culture (Cambridge, Mass., 1934), especially Ch. 8.

[20]A book that epitomized this anthropoligcal insight was Alain Locke and Bernhard J. Stern , eds. When Peoples Meet: A Study in Race and Culture Contacts (New York, 1942). The editors set the tone for the readings contained in the collection when they wrote: " . . . from the new scientific evidences of culture contacts, between all varieties and levels of culture, and from every quarter of the globe, comes convincing testimony of the universality and constructive role of cultural interchange " (p.38).

in by his students. His global and historical view of cultural

change form the backdrop for his consideration of the immigrant

problem in American society. Park saw traditional cultures

as the outgrowths of human separation. During the long millenia

of mankind's "Great Dispersion," when transportation and

commerce were relatively undeveloped and most men lived off

the land in rural isolation, a great variety of cultures took root,

each localized in a particular corner of the earth. "Centripetal

forces" partially counteracted these localizing tendencies. As

groups of men came into contact with each other, especially in

the cities of the ancient world, new cultures arose that replaced

the older cultures of separated men. These new cultures incorpo-

rated the best features of the older cultures but discarded the out-

worn and outmoded customs of the past.[21]

The progress that had occurred during the long youth of

mankind was minimal in comparison with the quantum leap foward

that humanity had taken in the new, industrial age. The modern

world had spawned a whole new moral order, a new way of organiz-

ing productive activity along universal, rationalistic lines, a new

liberated man freed from the social constraints of the past, a new

---

[21]Robert Park, Race and Culture (Chicago, 1950), pp. 85, 24.

society which Park called "civilization" to distinguish it from

the cultures of old.[22] Although Park admitted that traditional

cultures operated to restrain anti-social impulses and internalize

patterns of group cooperation, he also saw traditional cultures

as forms of bondage that stifled creativity and restricted the

expression of human individuality.[23] In the new cities of the

industrial world, which Park called "the natural environment of

free men," the precedents of the past were no longer relevant

or binding. "Profound differences in individual opinion, senti-

ments, and beliefs" appear in the city which contrast sharply

with the "monotonous sameness" of attitude in traditional

cultures.[24] Men are free to follow their natural talents and

inclinations. The occupational group, rather than the cultural

group, becomes the prime agent of socialization and the locus

of individual identification. The city becomes an interconnected

web of "natural areas," each reflecting the occupational profile

of its inhabitants.[25]

---

[22]Ibid., pp. 16, 29.

[23]Robert Park, Society: Collective Behavior, News and Opinion, Sociology and Modern Society (Glencoe, Ill., 1955) p. 337.

[24]Robert Park & Ernest W. Burgess, The City (Chicago, 1967), p. 12; Robert E. Park, On Social Control and Collective Behavior (Chicago, 1967), pp. 115-16.

[25]Park & Burgess, The City, pp. 13-14.

44

Park's major contribution to the ongoing debate over
immigration was to interpret the disappearance of ethnic cultures
as an advance, rather than a setback, for human freedom. His
theories masked the intra-national cultural imperialism practiced
by professional elites during this period. Park felt that assimilation was inevitable, but warned that it would take a considerable
length of time, and that attempts to speed the process through
coercive-style Americanization could boomerang. He argued that
the vigorous institutional life of ethnic communities did not
contravene his prediction of eventual cultural assimilation and
community breakdown; rather the immigrant press, fraternal and
mutual aid societies, etc. were a confirmation of his prophecy, an
indication of self-help efforts on the part of the immigrant to "find
his place and make his way in America."[26] For those who
suspected that such organizations served as vehicles for cultural
maintenance, Park made the reassuring argument that they
represented a collective surge of ethnic communities toward
assimilation. There were probably those who were not convinced
of such benign intent, especially as efforts were made to recruit
the second generation into these organizations. Park himself
later wondered why many people preferred to "hug their chains"

[26]Park, Society, p. 164.

instead of adopting the cosmopolitan and emancipated life-style

of the cities.[27] How account for this servility to the past?

The concept of marginality was a refinement of Park's

thought that tried to explain the disorientation and traditionalism

of rural peoples transplanted to urban America. As early as 1925,

Park had taken note of the second generation problem. At this

point, he viewed the signs of social disorganization that appeared

in the second generation as evidence of a kind of cultural void

into which the children of the immigrants had fallen. They had

lost the old culture but were not yet in full possession of the new;

they had refused to submit to the social controls of the immigrant

community, but had not yet found a new code of behavior. In

1928, in a seminal article in the American Journal of Sociology,

Park coined the phrase "marginal man." In the original formulation

of the concept, Park had in mind the cultural conflicts experienced

by the first generation of immigrants, although later extrapolators

of Park's thought, and Park himself, would shift the locus of the

problem to the second generation.[28] Park saw marginality less

---

[27]Ibid., p. 337.

[28]Park's 1925 essay, "Culture and Cultural Trends," is
reprinted in Race and Culture, pp. 24-35 (see especially pp. 26-27);
Robert Park, "Human Migration and the Marginal Man," American
Journal of Sociology, XXXIII (May, 1928), 881-93. For an example of
how Park used the concept of marginality to apply to the second
generation, see: Park, Race and Culture, p. 317.

as a transitional state and more as a condition of modern life.
All men who step outside the geographical bounds of their ancestral
culture obtain a new vision of themselves and their society;
"Things at home look different to the man who has enjoyed a
sojourn abroad."[29] Through such broadening experiences, an
individual is challenged to reconcile the new with the old, to
reevaluate old values and old ways. Park tended to romanticize
the marginal man as the representative of a new "personality type"
composed of certain distinctive attributes; the marginal man,
wrote Park, has "the wider horizon, the keener intelligence, the
more detached and rational viewpoint . . . [he is] the more
civilized human being." He saw the marginal man as the progen-
itor of a new culture that would spread throughout the world. "It
is in the mind of the marginal man--where the changes and fusions
of culture are going on--that we can best study the processes of
civilization and progress." This was a paean to the immigrant,
but at the same time a warning that his life was lived in "permanent
crisis," and that retreat into the ghetto was one way of shirking
the responsibilities of freedom.[30]

The theory of marginality was developed further by Park's

---

[29]Park, Society, p. 255.

[30]Park, Race and Culture, pp. 373-76; Park, "Human Migration," p. 893.

students and others. These later commentators shifted the problem to the second generation. The immigrant's upbringing in the Old Country, his habituation to the old ways, his segregation into ethnic neighborhoods, they thought, had strengthened his resolve to resist assimilation. Wrote Everett Stonequist, in a major treatise on the subject of marginality in 1937, the immigrant community "insulate[d] him [the immigrant] from the higher temperatures of the melting pot, and so [made] him less of a marginal man."[31] Stonequist and others challenged the notion that the American environment had completely stripped the second generation person of his ancestral culture. Heretofore, the problems of social maladjustment that were visible in the second generation had been blamed upon de-culturalization: loss of the old culture without gain of the new; now these problems were considered the outcome of culture conflict, being influenced at one and the same time by the values and standards of the Old World and those of the new. In 1939, William Smith, another of Park's disciples, called the second generation person "the marginal man par excellence."[32] A certain sophistication was

[31]Everett V. Stonequist, The Marginal Man (New York, 1937), p. 95.

[32]William Carlson Smith, Americans in the Making: The Natural History of the Assimilation of Immigrants (New York, 1939), p. 246.

achieved by these later writers in categorizing the varied responses

of the second generation to the problem of marginality.

Pauline Young was impressed by the tenacity with which many

second generation youths held on to the old ways, and cautioned

outside observers to take into consideration the problems of

social masks and the age factor before rushing to make rash judg-

ments about Americanization. Many second generation people,

she argued, behaved differently in their private than in their

public lives, and many returned to the ethnic fold after periods

of youthful rebellion.[33] William Smith, in his study of the second

generation Oriental, isolated eleven different response patterns,

ranging from "the conformist type" to "the emancipated type."[34]

Irwin Child, in his study of second generation Italian youths, found

a similar variation of response and urged social workers to take

into consideration the problem of "individual differences" in

_____

[33]Pauline V. Young, "Social Problems in the Education of
the Immigrant Child," American Sociological Review, I (June, 1936),
419-29. Young was an astute observer of the American ethnic
scene. Her earlier book, The Pilgrims of Russian Town (Chicago,
1932) was a perceptive analysis of a Russian Molokan community in
southern California. The book drew attention to the disorientation of
the second generation.

[34]William Carlson Smith, Americans in Process: A Study of
our Citizens of Oriental Ancestry (Ann Arbor, Mich., 1937), pp. 251-
63.

patterns of adaptation to American society, instead of assuming a single, normative response.[35]

The applicability of this new understanding of the cultural dynamics involved in ethnic adjustment to American society to the realm of policy was unclear. Would it be desirable to slow down the process of assimilation, encourage programs of cultural maintenance in the second generation, prop up the authority of the immigrant community over its wayward youth? Or was non-interference with the relentless advance of assimilation the desirable alternative? In part, the answer one gave depended on one's attitude toward immigrant cultures. In positing such a sharp contrast between traditional cultures and modern civilization, Park lent support to those who viewed immigrant cultures with disdain and modern urban culture with approval. However, in his analysis of cumulative cultural development, where societies advance and new cultures arise forged out of the best elements of the past, and in his exposition of the creative role of the marginal man in building world civilization, Park lent support to those who worked for the incorporation of immigrant "gifts" in a dynamic and changing national culture. This ambiguity in Park's thought was translated into two conflicting positions on the crisis of the

---

[35]Irvin L. Child, Italian or American? The Second Generation in Conflict (New Haven, 1943), p. 200.

ɔn.

Scientific Americanization

The first position, which could be called scientific
Americanization, was a strategy designed to hasten assimilation
through careful attention to the social and psychological
processes through which immigrant peoples passed in adjusting
to a new society. Advocates of this position were reluctant to
describe themselves as "Americanizers," since they carefully
disassociated themselves from the brow-beating element that
had resorted to coercive practices to effect conformity to
American ways. They realized that " . . . the process of adjustment . . . is a natural and slow one, and cannot be forced or
artifically hastened without disastrous result."[36] The tactics
of the nativists, they feared, could easily backfire, stiffening the
will of immigrants and their children to hold on to old world ways
and slowing the onward march of Americanization. "Scientific
Americanizers" also disavowed the label of Americanizer for another
reason: many cf them believed that assimilation in America was
not to an ethnic type which could be called American but to a

---

[36]Samuel Koenig, "Second- and Third- Generation Americans,"
in Francis J. Brown and Joseph Slabey Roucek, Eds., One America;
the History, Contributions, and Present Problems of Our Racial and
National Minorities (New York, 1945), p. 522.

universal type that had supranational legitimacy. The adjustment problems of immigrants and their children, they believed, were but one manifestation of a world-wide phenomenon, the adjustment of peasant populations to urban, industrial civilization.[37] Through this modern variant of manifest destiny, scientific Americanizers disguised their ethnocentrism behind a denial of the ethnic character of American civilization.

Although scientific Americanizers – thinking that the way of life of American technological society exerted an irresistible pull upon immigrant peoples – refused to force-feed Americanism, they believed that they could render valuable services to immigrant peoples. One way was to surmount the linguistic barrier that separated immigrant peoples from the mainstream of American society. Such an impulse must have motivated the many thousands of idealistic young university students who went out to teach English to immigrants in factories and plants as volunteers for the YMCA.[38]

---

[37]Michael Passi made this point in "Mandarins," pp. 13, 143-54. For expressions of this point of view, see the following: Seventh Annual National Conference of International Institutes of the Young Women's Christian Association, Report of Proceedings (Niagara Falls, 1925), p. 54 (Section 6, Microfilm Reel 100, YWCA Mss.); Eighth Annual National Conference of International Institutes, Report of Proceedings (Milwaukee, 1926), pp. 5-6 (Section 6, Microfilm Reel 100, YWCA Mss.).

[38]The Industrial Service Movement, as it was called, captured the imagination and appealed to the idealism of a generation of college students. The movement is documented in the Microfilm Records of the Young Men's Christian Association, ff. 5,6,28,29, Immigration History Research Center, University of Minnesota.

It also motivated the free translation services for the foreign

language press provided by the Foreign Language Information

Service, the motto of which was "to interpret the Immigrant to

America and America to the Immigrant." Scientific Americanizers

worked to speed the two-way flow of information to and from

ethnic communities, hoping in this manner to suffuse the highest

ideals and best traditions of American society to these communities

and to educate old stock Americans to the ordeal of immigrant

communities.[39] Scientific Americanizers believed that compassion

and high-mindedness were valuable assets for dealing success-

fully with immigrant peoples. Writing of the sons of immigrants,

Fred Rindge, senior secretary of the YWCA specializing in American-

ization work, cautioned that "what they most need is not a

forcible feeding of our language and citizenship, but justice, sympathy,

understanding. opportunity, brotherhood, Christian service."[40]

Scientific Americanizers were not disturbed by the elaborate

---

[39]Speaking at the 1926 Annual Conference of International
Institutes, Ernest W. Burgess urged the assembled Institute workers
to perform the role of "social interpreters." It was necessary, he
said, "to interpret immigrant groups to each other and to the
American public, to interpret parents to children and children to
parents, and finally to interpret the changes taking place in our social
life . . . ." (Proceedings [1925] p. 31, YWCA Mss.). The efforts
of the scientific Americanizers to improve communication are emphasized in Daniel Weinberg's study of the Foreign Language Information
Service. See Weinberg, "The Foreign Language Information Service,"
pp. 180-246.

[40]Fred Rindge, "Foreign Boys in America," Service, V (June,
1929), 1.

network of organizations within immigrant communities nor by

the presence of the second generation within their membership.

Organizations such as fraternal groups, mutual benefit societies,

arts clubs, and sports groups were predominantly American in

character, they felt, growing up out of the American tradition

of self-help and voluntarism: they were not transplantations of

alien institutions. They worked to cushion the shock of cultural

change by advancing entire communities to assimilation in a

collective fashion. Such organizations should be helped and

encouraged, not condemned.[41] Comprehending the burden of

marginality for the second generation, scientific Americanizers

were willing to support a restricted program of ethnic cultural

education (mostly in the form of folk arts performances and handi-

craft displays) sufficient to raise the status of immigrant parents

in the eyes of their children and reestablish the social control

function of the immigrant family. Their intention was to instill

an identity without substance, a sentimental attachment to the

superficial aspects of culture, a submission without conformity--not

---

[41]The Foreign Language Information Service called for the induction of the second generation into these organizations as "the surest way to make these organizations thoroughly American in spirit and purpose, and to bring the older generation within the full influence of American Life" (Foreign Language Information Service, "Work with Foreign Language Organizations: An Opportunity," Nov. 7, 1928 [document inserted in bound volume entitled "Division of Foreign Language Organizations"], ACNS Mss.).

a perpetuation of immigrant cultures per se. The almost hypo-

critical nature of all this was well-expressed by Clara Hardin and

Herbert A. Miller: "Paradoxical as it may seem, the most valuable

aid in the transition stage is the promotion of the exactly opposite

program from that desired by ardent patriots, namely, the

stimulation of interest and enthusiasm for Old World cultural

traditions."[42]

Notwithstanding their pragmatic support for multi-cultural

education in the field of the arts, scientific Americanizers did

not value very highly the cultural achievements of the immigrants.

Marian Schibsby, former director of the Immigrants Protective

League of Chicago,who became editor of the FLIS organ The

Interpreter in 1923, disagreed with both the super-patriotic nativists

and their adversaries,whom she derisively called the "friends of the

immigrant." Both groups, she felt, operated from the same flawed

assumption: that the immigrants possessed a culture worthy of

the name, which the former wanted to destroy and the latter wanted

to preserve. "It is the rare native," she wrote, "who appreciates

the fact that, as far as the mass of immigrants goes there is

[42]Clara A. Hardin and Herbert A. Miller, "The Second
Generation," in Francis J. Brown and Joseph S. Roucek, Eds.,
Our Racial and National Minorities (New York, 1937), pp. 720-
21.

precious little either to forget or prize."[43] Schibsby saw the

arriving immigrants as "raw and unkempt," who as members of

the peasant and laboring classes, were excluded from participa-

tion in the national cultures of their countries of origin. Ludmilla

Foxlee, chief YWCA social worker at Ellis Island during the

twenties, echoed similar views. At the 1925 conference of

International Institutes, she contended that immigrants came

from exhausted and impoverished lands, that they had little

of value in a cultural sense to pass on to their children, and

that--rather than trying to foster the transmission of barren

traditions as some misguided Institute workers were suggesting--

Institute staff members should take second generation girls by

the hand and lead them gradually into the light of American civiliza-

tion. The second generation girl, she asserted, "is plastic--

wonderful material in our hands--and what are we going to do to

make her see a lovely vision and try to realize that vision in her

home life."[44] Few YWCA workers were as self-consciously manipu-

lative as Mrs. Foxlee, but that there were ulterior motives to the

"friendly" approach of some social workers seems apparent.

---

[43]Marian Schibsby, "When the Immigrant Goes to School,"
The Interpreter, V (December, 1926), 4-6.

[44]YWCA, Report of Proceedings (1925), p. 57.

served in 1934 that there was a "predisposition

social workers] to an unbalanced alliance with

younger against the older generation" of an immigrant group.[45]

Cultural Integrationism

The faith in the future, the uncritical acceptance of

industrialism, the rejection of immigrant cultures that character-

ized the scientific Americanizers were not shared by a group of

reformers whom we shall call the "cultural integrationists." Less

ethnocentric than the Americanizers, they doubted whether the

world was entering the new age of freedom and resurgent

individualism under American leadership. Integrationists sometimes

had regrets over the passing of a simpler age, were less enraptured

with the technological imperative, were more alienated from their

own society, and tended to be further to the left politically. They

were restless witnesses of the "monotony of industry, the dry

dreariness of grim-tinted streets, the physical exhausion of over-

work." They tended to see American culture as "still in the making,"

as unformed, incomplete and lacking in refinement. At the same

time, integrationists found much to admire, and sometimes

---

[45]Grace Marcus, "The Emotional Conflicts of the Second
Generation," Interpreter Release Clip sheet, XI (July 10, 1934),
p. 91.

romanticized, the cultural heritages of immigrants. They were

missionaries for the "enrichment" and "vitalization" of American

culture to be accomplished through the "conservation" of the

cultural resources of immigrant peoples.

Integrationists sought to make the intermingling of peoples in

America a process of mutual adjustment, a give and take between old

stock and new stock American. As one of them explained: "We were

continually seeking a method which would bring about the integration

of the foreign group with the American group so that there might be

an interpenetration of ideas with the resultant mutual adjustment of

groups and individuals."[46] Like the scientific Americanizers,

integrationists were aware of the predicament of marginality facing

the second generation, but whereas the Americanizers adopted an

attitude of patience coupled with cautious efforts to restore the

social control function of the ethnic community, integrationists--

considering the rapid loss of ethnic culture by the second genera-

tion a diminution of the powers of the individual and a tragic loss

to the nation--recommended strenuous efforts to re-awaken pride in

cultural heritage. Multi-cultural education, if advocated at all,

was an expedient for scientific Americanizers, but an imperative

[46]Thomas L. Cotton, "The Group Approach," Proceedings of the National Conference of Social Work (Chicago, 1925), p. 364.

for cultural integrationists. Many integrationists were second generation Americans themselves concerned to legitimate their own sense of cultural difference within an ideological climate that was predominantly Parkian in nature. The integrationist approach permitted them to promote cultural maintenance in the guise of bringing about a richer and more unified American culture.

The Flowering of Integrationism

During the inter-war years, the integrationist outlook gained great currency, especially within influential immigrant service agencies and among the ethnic groups. The dilemma of the second generation became the context for the discussion of integrationism as an alternative to Americanization. This is not to say that integrationism did not encounter any opposition. There were always those, as previously pointed out, who looked askance at a program that set out to preserve peasant cultural elements, but many were willing to suspend judgment until such time as it became clear whether the social benefits of such a program, in the form of greater social cohesion and tighter social control, warranted running a necessary risk. The various programs that were proposed and carried out by cultural integrationists were among the most daring and innovative ever attempted by American social reformers, and led directly to a new role for the schools in the creation of a new American culture.

Integrationism was an especially strong ideology within the International Institute network. One reason for the appeal of integrationism to Institute personnel may have been the presence within the Institute movement of a large number of second generation staff members. Edith Terry Bremer, the founder and for half a century the guiding light of the movement, had insisted upon the importance of reaching out to immigrant communities with workers familiar with their languages and cultures.[47] To implement this policy, each Institute recruited "nationality secretaries" for the major ethnic communities within its jurisdiction, individuals who could function as intermediaries between those communities and the larger society. Second Generation eastern and southern Europeans came to fill most of these positions; they had the necessary facility in English and at least one immigrant language; they could comprehend the "thought language" of the immigrants; and there were a sufficient number of such individuals with university training. The YWCA thus became one of the first American social service agencies to exploit the talents and skills possessed by indigenous community personnel. These individuals had a hand in shaping the policies of the Institutes both locally and nationally.

---

[47] Young Women's Christian Association, Report of Miss Edith Baldwin Terry to the Association Extension Commission for the year 1911, p. 2, and Edith Terry Baldwin, "Foreign Born Women and Girls" (1920), p. 21, in bound volume of documents entitled, "Immigration and Foreign Community, Reports 1910-1921," YWCA Mss.

As one Institute officer said: "At an International Institute Conference or a YWCA convention we are conscious that to a large extent we are talking about ourselves when we are talking about the second generation."[48] The concerns of these individuals were shared by a remarkable group of female social reformers from old stock backgrounds, who served as officers of the YWCA Department of Immigration and Foreign Communities. Individuals such as Mrs. Bremer, Dorothy Gladys Spicer, Ethel Bird, Mable Brown Ellis and Florence Cassidy were strong proponents of cultural integration and pioneers in developing new programs to attain this objective. Although the strictly utilitarian rationale for multi-cultural education adopted by the scientific American-izers was sometimes borrowed by the cultural integrationists (just as the rhetoric of the cultural integrationists was sometimes borrowed by the scientific Americanizers), there can be little doubt that cultural integration was a deeply-held commitment on the part of the majority of these individuals.

Cultural integrationists were as opposed to laissez-faire in the area of cultural change as they were opposed to laissez-faire in the realm of economics; indeed, there was a strong parallel between their call for concerted efforts to reverse the cultural impoverishment of the second generation and halt the "wasting of

---

[48]Florence Cassidy, "Report," p. 19, ACNS Mss.

cultural resources" and the growing liberal demand to break up

the monopoly of class privilege, prevent economic chaos, and

conserve natural resources. The Commission on First Generation

Americans, which had been charged by the 1925 Annual Conference

of International Institutes to make an in-depth study of the second

generation problem, issued its final report in 1930. Written by

Florence Cassidy, the report contained an excellent summary of

the state of thinking on the subject and was a call to action for

dealing with the problem. The Report recommended the formation

of clubs along nationality lines for second generation young

people "wherever there is lack of security, manifested either by

intense nationality concern in the first generation or by blatant,

extreme and noisy disregard for nationality in the second

generation . . . ."[49] This was a controversial recommendation

given the strong feeling among some members of the Association

that age, occupation or school experience should be the sole

criteria for organizing such clubs. The Commission also emphasized

the importance of conferring upon the second generation a "'sense

of continuity,' that is a sense of having a place in society, of

really belonging to a group which is continuing a dignified and

esteemed cultural tradition." In order to instill such a sense,

the Commission recommended the staging of plays based on Old

---

[49] Ibid., p. 29.

World themes, the setting up of folk dance groups, organizing
city-wide folk festivals, and programs of instruction in immigrant
languages, either offered exclusively by the Institute or in
conjunction with interested private or public schools.[50] The
Report censured the schools for helping to create the second
generation problem; it urged teachers to render a less biased
account of American historical development, place greater emphasis
on the geography of eastern and southern Europe, and teach
immigrant languages. It also suggested that teachers in training
should dilligently study nationality backgrounds.[51] Probably no
other American agency went as far as the YWCA in recognizing
the value and legitimacy of immigrant cultures.

Among the more spectacular techniques for building intergroup cultural awareness and appreciation was the city-wide
international folk festival, which was a major innovation of the
inter-war years. Performances of immigrant music and dance and
handicraft exhibitions had pre-dated the war, but they usually had
a limited audience, participation by only a few ethnic groups, and
the sponsorship of a single agency. Their purpose was to bring
joy and fellowship into the leisure time activities of the immigrants
and inform the general public of the "gifts" of the immigrants. Two

---

[50]Ibid., pp. 32-33.

[51]Ibid., p. 34.

elements appear to be unique to the post-war period: the development of large-scale, city-wide festivals attracting great numbers
of people, and the more conscious use of the festival to solve the
second generation problem. A quickening of the festival impulse
took place during the post-war Americanization period. In New
York State, Allen H. Eaton, a field secretary for the American
Federation of Arts, began organizing large-scale exhibitions in
Buffalo, Albany and Rochester. More than 40,000 people attended
the Buffalo exhibition during its two week showing at the Albright
Art Gallery in 1919.[52] Eaton also lent a hand in planning the well-
publicized "America's Making Exposition" in New York City in
November of 1921, which brought together more than thirty ethnic
groups in a two week program of song, dance, and exhibition at
the 71st Regiment Armory. The actual exposition was preceded by
more than one thousand local performances in schools, parks and
playgrounds.[53] Eaton became somewhat of an elder statesman of
the festival movement, joined the staff of the Russell Sage Foundation,
and continued his advocacy of the cause of immigrant cultural
conservation. Another life-long exponent of the festival approach

---

[52]Allen H. Eaton, Immigrant Gifts to American Life (New York,
1932), pp. 10, 63.

[53]See article entitled "Bearing Gifts," The Survey, XLVII
(Nov. 5, 1921), p. 203, and souvenir journal entitled: "The Book of
America's Making Exposition" (Held at the 71st Regiment Armory,
New York, Oct. 29 to Nov. 12, 1921), ff. dramatics, Boston Mss.

was Dorothy Spicer, who became "Secretary for Nationality
Customs and Folklore" of the Department of Immigration and
Foreign Communities of the YWCA in 1918. Spicer spent the next
decade deepening her knowledge of "the mysticism, idealism and
beauty of other peoples," publicizing her findings in the pages
of Foreign Born, a YWCA periodical, and travelling around the
country helping International Institutes to organize folk festivals,
usually around themes related to the change of seasons.[54] Spicer
saw the folk festival as a means for "bridging the ever widening
gulf between foreign parents and children . . ." and for imparting
to the children "a new reverence and respect for the race, language
and traditional background of their parents . . ."[55] By 1932, as
a result of Spicer's prompting and guidance, more than fifty folk
festivals had already been organized by International Institutes
across the country.[56]

---

[54]Young Women's Christian Association, Annual Report of
the Work of the Department for Foreign Born Women, 1920-1921,
p. 10,in bound volume of documents entitled: "Immigration and
Foreign Community, Reports, 1910-1920," YWCA Mss.; Dorothy G.
Spicer, Folk Festivals and the Foreign Community (New York, 1923),
p. 1; there are numerous articles by Dorothy Spicer on folk festival
themes in the pages of Foreign Born, a newsletter issued by the
YWCA from ca. 1919 to 1922.

[55]Spicer, Folk Festivals, pp. 15-16.

[56]Eaton, Immigrant Gifts, p. 93.

The folk festival attained its peak of grandeur and greatest level of community involvement in three American cities: Cleveland, New York and St. Paul. In Cleveland, under the sponsorship of the City Division of Recreation, the International Institute and the newspaper, The Cleveland Plain Dealer, great city-wide festivals began to be held in 1929.[57] In New York, Florence Cassidy in 1931 joined together with Tom Cotton of the Foreign Language Information Service as well as representatives of seventeen different nationality groups to found the Folk Festival Council. A major aim of the Council was "to conserve the art heritage which the new Americans brought with them out of the Old World creating an incidental respect for these elder traditions in the generation born after the exodus from the old country." Cotton conceived of the Council as the cornerstone of his "Five Year Plan for the Cultural Integration" of the American people. The Council organized festivals in theaters, amphitheaters and parks in the New York City area, published a journal called Folk News and gave courses on folk dancing and folk singing at the New School for Social Research.[58]

---

[57]Mark Villchur, "Conserving Cultural Heritages," Journal of Adult Education, III (June, 1931), 324.

[58]Folk Festival Council of New York, Minutes, Sept. 24, 1931, ACNS Mss.; Thomas L. Cotton, "Folk Festival Council of New York: Report of Activities, Jan. 1 to June 1, 1933," p. 5, ACNS Mss.; Folk Festival Council of New York, "Annual Report of the New School Course Committee of the Folk Festival Council Presented at the Annual Meeting, Feb. 6, 1939," ACNS Mss.

Cassidy's influence was felt by a brilliant and energetic Institute

executive in St. Paul, Alice Sickels, who--after attending a

dress rehearsal of a Council production in New York City in

1931--was inspired to introduce the festival to St. Paul. Sickels

surpassed her tutors in the boldness of her vision for the Festival

and in her attention to detail and authenticity which led her to

do research in Europe on peasant costume and village scenery.

From the first St. Paul "Festival of Nations" in 1932, which

attracted 3000 visitors, to the fifth Festival in 1939 which drew

31,000 visitors, St. Paul became a model city for those reformers

interested in mixing the various cultural strains found within the

American population.[59] Sickels told Louis Adamic, who attended

the 1939 Festival and was delighted by what he saw, that the

Festival was designed to disspell the insecurity and feelings of

inferiority of white ethnic Americans.[60]

Integrationist programs received the strongest support from

------

[59]Alice L. Sickels, Around the World in St. Paul (Minneapolis,
1945), pp. 75-76, 100-103; International Institute of St. Paul, Minutes of the Annual Meeting, May 22, 1939, Records of the International Institute of Minnesota, Immigration History Research Center,
University of Minnesota.

[60]Alice L. Sickels to Louis Adamic, Jan. 2, 1941, Louis Adamic
Papers, Princeton University (Special thanks to Prof. Henry Christian
of Rutgers University for bringing this letter to my attention).

the ethnic groups themselves. Lavish and colorful spectacles such as those staged in St. Paul would not have been possible without the backing and hard work of the ethnic groups. It is not hard to explain the appeal of integrationism to these groups. Cultural pluralism was an untenable position given its association with allegiances to foreign governments and, perhaps, even its connection with caste status in the minds of certain groups. In the short run, the program of the integrationist and that of the cultural pluralist were indistinguishable; integrationism encouraged ethnic education and the temporary maintenance of group ties. Some of the leading advocates of cultural integration: Louis Adamic, Leonard Covello, Arthur Derounian, Mordecai M. Kaplan, Joseph Roucek and Milton Steinberg were spokesmen for ethnic groups. Of these, the most eloquent voice raised on behalf of cultural integration during the inter-war years was that of Louis Adamic.

A true measure of Louis Adamic's overarching contribution to American thought on the minority question has yet to be made. His memory today stands clouded by confusion over the circumstances of his death, suspicion over his political loyalties, and the disrepute into which he has been placed by those who have derided his social philosophy. Yet no man has probably grappled with the ethnic question in American life with such intensity of feeling and fever of commitment; few men have made such an impact on the rank and file of the ethnic groups, and few men have articulated such a vision of national regeneration. Louis Adamic was the pied piper of cultural integration during the Depression; in an outpouring of books, essays, pamphlets and speeches, his ideas reached millions of Americans, including powerful segments of the American elite.

Adamic was a newcomer to the fields of American ethnic history and cultural dynamics in 1934. A young writer of Slovenian birth, he had just taken the American literary world by storm with the publication of his historical treatise Dynamite (1931), his autobiography Laughing in the Jungle (1932) and his poignant travel account Native's Return (1934). His early work had dealt primarily with American working class themes with only passing references to the ethnic dimension of the American proletariat. A trip to his native Slovenia in 1932-33 after an absence of more than a decade made a "deep and lasting impression" on Adamic, reawakened a consciousness of his own cultural roots, and turned him into a passionate advocate of the ethnic cause; yet he did not abandon the radical political and economic posture he had taken in the past.[61] Adamic set out upon the first of his celebrated speaking tours in the early part of 1934, which brought

[61]Carey McWilliams, Louis Adamic and Shadow-America (Los Angeles, 1935), pp. 81-82.

him to ethnic communities in New York, Pennsylvania, Ohio, Illinois and Minnesota. What he experienced on that trip, he reported in an article entitled "Thirty Million New Americans" published in Harper's Magazine in November of 1934--one of the most sensational tracts on the second generation problem to appear during the decade.

The article attempted to explain the emotional malaise and pathological state of the second generation. "The chief and most important fact . . . about the new Americans," wrote Adamic, "is that the majority of them are oppressed by feelings of inferiority . . . ."[62] Unlike their parents, whose cultural formation had taken place in the Old World and whose memories of a secure place in society had helped them to withstand the shock of adjustment of American life, the second generation did not have the ballast of culture and the seasoning of the Old World as part of their psychic armament. The immigrant generation was "too inarticulate" to transmit to their children "a consciousness . . . of their being part of any sort of continuity in human or historic experience." The children are conditioned by "powerful agencies in American life" such as the public schools and the movies to look down upon their

---

[62]Louis Adamic, "Thirty Million New Americans," Harper's Monthly Magazine, CLXIX (November, 1934), p. 685.

parents as "just a Hunky or Polack, a 'working stiff,' a poor, pathetic creature constantly at somebody's mercy and repeatedly stepped upon, and as such not much according to American standards."[63] A large part of the psychological make-up of the second generation, their basic emotional response patterns, their deepest values, were derived from their cultural background; in rejecting that background, Adamic felt, they were also denying themselves and stifling their own creative powers. The symptoms of this unhealthy psychic state were varied and ominous: some tried to compensate for feelings of social rejection by becoming aggressive American nationalists, easy preys, Adamic thought, for demagogues and tyrants; others became anti-social in behavior or turned to lives of crime (although Adamic hastened to add that this group was numerically very small); some totally repudiated their background, changed their names, rejected their families, moved out of their communities and became in the process "hollow, absurd, objectionable persons." The most common reaction was one of apathy, introversion, social withdrawal and spiritual numbness: "They cannot look one in the eye. They are shy. Their limp handshakes gave me creepy feelings all the way from New York to the Iron Range of Minnesota."[64] The few exceptions to

---

[63]Ibid., pp. 686-87.

[64]Ibid., p. 688.

this distressing rule were those children whose parents "were wise and articulate enough to convey to them something of their backgrounds in the old countries . . . make them conscious of their backgrounds and heritage, give them some sense of continuity . . . ." The success of these families pointed the way to a solution to the second generation problem; all institutions of society in contact with this element of the population would have to do all in their power to give the second generation "a knowledge of, and pride in, their own heritage." The ultimate goal should be to nurture "real men and women on the pattern of their own natural cultures."[65]

Adamic did not, however, join the camp of the cultural pluralist. Although he continued to insist upon the importance of ethnic studies and the necessity of ethnic pride, he did not envision, nor could he accept, an America of separate cultural islands.[66] He saw America "in the process of becoming" and the ethnic cultures as the "material[s] out of which the future has to be

---

[65]Ibid., pp. 689-91.

[66]See handwritten comments by Adamic on the following letters: Read Lewis to Louis Adamic, June 9, 1939, and Read Lewis to Louis Adamic, June 12, 1939, ff. Adamic, Louis - Correspondence, Articles, Sept. 4, 1937 to June 19, 1939, ACNS Mss. In the second letter, note how Lewis considered Adamic to be outside the camp of the cultural pluralists.

wrought."[67] He sought "to create a great culture on this
continent; a culture which could approach being universal or
pan-human . . . ."[68] Americanism was not a body of principles
rooted in any one particular ethnic tradition; it was the sum
total of human aspirations for freedom and equality, an openness
to difference and to change. In his famous broadside published
in 1939, Adamic asked all Americans--both old stock and new -
to "become Americanized." Seek out your neighbor, he urged,
understand his background and appreciate his uniqueness; quoting
Emerson, he wrote: "It is the 'not me' in my friend that charmes
me."[69]

Adamic waged a vigorous campaign during the thirties to
popularize his plan for cultural awareness and cultural integration.
He worked in close association with Read Lewis and the Foreign
Language Information Service. Adamic joined the Board of FLIS in
1934 and sought to transform the organization into a spearhead for
his program of American cultural development. Lewis sponsored

---

[67] Quoted in an editorial, The Oregon Sunday Journal (Portland),
Nov. 5, 1939, ff. Adamic, Louis - Correspondence, Articles,
Feb. 10, 1936 to July 22, 1937, ACNS Mss.

[68] Louis Adamic, "Plymouth Rock and Ellis Island" (Summary
of a Lecture by Louis Adamic), n.d., p. 4, ff. Adamic: Plymouth
Rock and Ellis Island, ACNS Mss.

[69] Ibid., p. 12.

and arranged Adamic's speaking engagements throughout the country, helped Adamic obtain subsidies for his literary activities from the Carnegie Foundation, and tried to obtain funding to implement his sweeping vision of American society. So long as cultural integration remained a viable and acceptable alternative to the Melting Pot, the close association between the brilliant writer and the skilled organizer would continue. But as the decade wore on, as cultural integration failed the various tests to which it was put, and as pressures built up to forget differences in the face of the common foreign threat, Adamic's message grew curiously irrelevant to the perceived needs of the times, and led to a falling out between the two men.[70]

The Integrationist Dilemma

Integrationism was a position beset with paradox, and fraught with practical difficulty. It promised to heal a divided nation by hailing its divisions. As Louis Adamic put it, "inviting diversity brings out the basic sameness of people, just as the opposite results only in more and sharper differences."[71]

---

[70]Foreign Language Information Service, Minutes of the Board of Trustees, Dec. 5, 1933, Jan. 31, May 4, 1934, June 8, 1939, ACNS Mss.; Read Lewis to Frederick Keppel, Sept. 28, 1934, ACNS Mss., also see below, pp.

[71]Louis Adamic, "Plymouth Rock and Ellis Island," n.d., p. 12, ff. Adamic: Plymouth Rock and Ellis Island, ACNS Mss.

.he forward march of assimilation in order to begin that

marcn again on a new foundation. Certain questions were left

unanswered: How long, for example, would it take to accomplish

the new fusion of cultural elements in American society? Was

structural pluralism, i.e. the strengtening of ethnic organizations

and communities, a prerequisite for cultural integration? What

aspects of culture were suitable for integration? Part of the

problem was that integrationism meant different things to different

people. For American social reformers, it meant the incorporation

of manual skills, workmanship, artistic abilities--the material

aspects of culture as opposed to the non-material. For people

like Adamic, integration mean a much more profound process of

mutual adjustment involving the substance of culture as well as

its veneer.

The basic dilemma of the integrationists was the potential

conflict between their liberal _methodological_ stance and the

conservative goal which it purported to serve. How far could they

go in activating ethnic pride without subverting the goal of

assimilation? Might not the urgency of dealing with the second

generation problem, of healing the rift that had developed in the

immigrant home, sidetrack the goal of assimilation? At what point

did the program of the integrationists become incompatible with

the goal of assimilation. Could not the means of the reformers

be turned into ends in themselves? The history of the Bureau for Intercultural Education will shed light on these questions,

since the Bureau struggled to apply these principles in the class-

room, and in so doing, revealed in its development the conflict

between practice and goal.

PART II

HISTORY OF THE SERVICE BUREAU FOR

INTERCULTURAL EDUCATION

CHAPTER III

RACHEL DAVIS DUBOIS: FROM PACIFIST TO
ETHNIC STUDIES ADVOCATE

There was one person more than any other responsible for
setting a new agenda for American education. For many years,
intercultural education was virtually synonymous with the name,
Rachel Davis DuBois. The founder and first Executive of the
Service Bureau for Intercultural Education had been seized by an
idea that would become a life-long concern. That idea was
that America, as the meeting ground of the world's peoples,
had been granted a golden opportunity--an opportunity to create
a "cosmic" civilization, one enriched by the talents, traditions,
and collective experiences of the "families of man." Steeped
in the pacifist tradition of the Society of Friends, she tried to
make her life a testimony to the "immanence of the Spirit" and
the living power of love in human relations. The great irony
was that her "soft approach," as Ira Progoff called it, should
have aroused such intense opposition.

The story of the Service Bureau begins with the early

experiences and struggles of Rachel Davis DuBois. Before the

Bureau came to be, DuBois worked for many long years to test

her theories, refine her methods, and convince others of the

importance of her work. She was single-minded and indefatigable,

a blend of idealist and opportunist, a mystic who knew no detach-

ment. The story of her early years, her roots in the pacifist move-

ment, her domestication of the internationalist point of view, and

her discovery of the second generation problem form an important

backdrop to the history of the Bureau.

Pacifism and the Call to Task for America

Born on a farm near Woodstown, New Jersey, in 1892,

Rachel Davis DuBois was reared in a pious Quaker household,

the second of six children born to Charles Davis and Bertha Priscilla

Haines, sober and hard-working people who "worshipped the land"

and tilled the soil as previous generations of their families had

done. Her childhood spent close to home, caring for younger

children, helping out with household chores, working in the fields,

and attending local Quaker schools, Rachel Davis developed a

life-long sense of rootedness in time and place and in a socio-

religious tradition that reached back to her Welsh forebearers (In

later years, she came to view Quakerism not merely as a religious

tradition but as a form of "cultural particularism" within American society).[1] Like other girls reaching maturity in the early years of the twentieth century, who found that they had little future on the farm and who yearned for something better, Rachel seized upon the new opportunities that were opening up for women beyond the horizons of the South Jersey countryside.

The first in her family to attend college, Rachel was a gawky and socially backward student during her first years at Bucknell University, where she majored in the natural sciences. A Quaker at a Baptist university, she had the feeling of being a social outcast, an experience which she later claimed helped her to empathize with the plight of outsiders in a new society. Overcoming initial handicaps, she gradually impressed her classmates with her humor and verve, became a leader of student government and graduated in 1914. For fifteen years thereafter, Rachel Davis worked either as a high school teacher or as a paid publicist for various Quaker-related causes. From 1914 to 1920, she taught social studies at Glassboro High School in southern New Jersey. In June of 1915, she married Nathan Steward DuBois. Unable to have children, she and her husband agreed to pursue separate careers.[2]

---

[1]Rachel Davis DuBois, Build Together Americans (New York, 1945), p. 12.

[2]Rachel Davis DuBois, "Unpublished Autobiography," Chapter 1, pp. 1-20,28-29,32, DuBois Mss.; Rachel Davis DuBois, interview with the author, New York City, February 26, 1974.

While teaching at Glassboro, Rachel became active in Quaker activities in and around Philadelphia. DuBois was a timid pacifist during the days of the preparedness controversy, refusing for a time to sell government bonds in school, but towards the end, as the nation revelled in the martial spirit, she wavered in her convictions. When the illusions of the war were shattered by the Versailles accords, she reaffirmed her commitment to pacifism and threw herself into the peace movement that was sweeping the country.[3] In 1920, she resigned from teaching to accept an appointment from the Philadelphia Yearly Meeting of Quakers to serve as its representative to the first All-Friends Conference in London, convened to reconsider the peace testimony of the Society of Friends. After her return, she accepted a position with the Women's International League for Peace and Freedom. Her first assignment was to monitor the voting records of Congressmen on peace-related issues. She also worked to secure the release from prison of anti-war agitators, most of whom were members of the Industrial Workers of the World. In company with Jane Addams, Honorary Chairman of the League, and other officers of the League, she attended an international conference at the Hague in 1922 convened to apply pressure on governments to renegotiate the

---

[3]DuBois, "Autobiography," Chapter 1, pp. 29-32, DuBois Mss.

Versailles Treaty. Upon her return she was invited to organize a
youth division of the League. In her new assignment, she spoke
to school and college groups up and down the East Coast. In
late 1923, she set out upon the first automobile "caravan" for
peace in the United States, organized to spread the gospel of
pacifism to towns and hamlets in New York, New Jersey and
Pennsylvania.[4]

Although DuBois never lost sight of the goal of world peace
and international brotherhood, she found a new field for the
application of her pacifist philosophy through a "crisis situation"
into which she was thrown in the year 1924. The Philadelphia
Yearly Meeting, which was considering a campaign to raise funds
for a Negro school in South Carolina, had asked her to visit and
investigate the school before going ahead with the campaign.
Largely removed from, and uninformed about, the racial problem
up to this time, the trip opened her eyes to the wretched conditions
endured by Negroes in the United States. While in South Carolina,
she was invited to attend a special dinner held in honor of
Dr. George Washington Carver. Seated next to Carver on the dais,
DuBois was nonplussed that she could have lived so long in

---

[4]Ibid, Chapter 2, pp. 1-7, 12-14; Rachel Davis DuBois to
Nathan Steward DuBois, Dec. 11, 1922, John Turner to Rachel Davis
DuBois, April 27, 1933, Amy Woods to Rachel Davis DuBois,
Oct. 10, 1923, ff. Correspondence, General, 1917-1929, DuBois Mss.

America and not known of the genius of this man, and that--as

her silence at the dinner table made clear--she could be so

ignorant of the plight of the Negro race in America.[5] About the

same time, she read an article by W. E. B. DuBois[6] that made

a very deep impression on her life and reinforced her quickening

resolve to do something about the racial problem. In that article,

the Negro historian and social critic argued that wars were the con-

sequence of intergroup hatreds, that a potentially explosive

situation was brewing in the United States, as blacks adapted to

the system of segregation, developed their own separate institu-

tions, and came to feel a "fanatic" pride in race that ruled out

fellowship with whites. "Where are the pacifists?" asked

W. E. B. DuBois, after describing the incidents of discrimination

that were infuriating Negroes; "The damned fools do not even know

what's going on!"[7] W. E. B. DuBois' criticism of American

pacifists was taken to heart by the young Quaker activist. She

---

[5]DuBois, "Autobiography," Chapter 2, pp. 17-21; Rachel Davis DuBois, "Adventures in Intercultural Education" (Unpublished Ph.D. Dissertation, School of Education, New York University, 1940), p. 135.

[6]W. E. B. DuBois was not related to Rachel Davis DuBois.

[7]W. E. Burghardt DuBois, "The Dilemma of the Negro," The American Mercury, III (October, 1924),179-84; DuBois, "Autobiography," Chapter 2, pp. 21-23.

herself had been disturbed by the "lip-service" being given to the ideal of peace, especially by the leaders of unlikely groups like the American Legion, who, she felt, despite their public posturing for peace, would never refuse the call to arms. It was easy to give verbal assent to pacifism, harder to make pacifism a rule for daily living. "Peace is not a system of dogmatic principles," DuBois wrote, "but simply a condition and habit of co-operation in home, school, nation and the world."[8] If the primary cause of war was inter group misunderstandings, then what better way to build peace than to start on the local level, building harmony and mutual respect among Americans of different racial, religious and ethnic backgrounds. The way Americans related to each other would have an important bearing on how America related to the other nations of the world.

Having found her "concern," the cause to which she, as a conscientious Quaker, could devote her life, she threw herself into the struggle for enlightenment on the racial question. Within the Quaker group she became identified as a gadfly for interracial understanding. She organized interracial understanding committees and edited a special newsletter containing excerpts from the Negro press. She also effortlessly crossed the color line. She joined

---

[8]Rachel Davis DuBois, "The Value of Keeping Peace," Friends Intelligencer, June 11, 1927, p. 473.

the National Association for the Advancement of Colored people,

became identified with a militant, labor-oriented wing, and became

a friend and confidant of both W. E. B. DuBois and

A. Philip Randolph. At a time when taboos against race mixing were care

fully observed, she scandalized both whites and blacks by her

unstudied disregard of such rules. Exploiting her dark complexion,

she was frequently able to "pass" in reverse, intermingling with

blacks both in social and residential situations. Negroes who

ordinarily viewed white liberals with suspicion or condescension

were impressed with her apparent sincerity and conviction.[9]

Return to the Classroom

It was in education that DuBois made the most effective

application of the newly-discovered equation between international

peace and intergroup understanding. Returning to the classroom

in September, 1924, as a social studies teacher at a high school

in Woodbury, New Jersey, she was asked to assume responsibility

for the required assembly programs at the school. There had

---

[9]Raymond Wolters, Negroes and the Great Depression (Westport, Conn., 1970), pp. 313-30; Rachel Davis DuBois, Personal Log, May 27, 1933, Jan. 4, 1934, Jan. 3, 1936, July 4, 1938, DuBois Mss.; A. Philip Randolph to Rachel Davis DuBois, Nov. 7, 1930, March 22, 1930, ff. Correspondence, General, 1930-39, DuBois Mss.; W. E. B. DuBois to Rachel Davis DuBois, May 18, 1949, ff. Correspondence, W. E. B. DuBois, 1948-60, DuBois Mss.; DuBois, "Autobiography," Chapter 3, p. 24, DuBois Mss.

been some dissatisfaction with student reaction to these
assemblies; when guest speakers spoke over the students'
heads, as they often did, students grew restless and teachers
nervously policed their charges.[10] Given a free hand to arouse
student interest in unconventional ways, DuBois set about to
turn the required assembly period into an exciting spectacle and
a platform for the exposition of her views on interracial harmony.
The assembly was an effective vehicle for such purposes: it
brought together the entire student body; permitted actual
demonstrations of the artistic achievements of ethnic groups;
provided a forum for visiting ethnic group leaders, and permitted
an appeal to the students' emotions as well as to their intellects,
a feature of the program that DuBois came to insist made it
pedagogically superior to strictly intellectual approaches. With
the assistance of a student-faculty committee, she planned a year-
long series of assemblies, held at two to six week intervals, each
devoted to the history, achievements and contributions of a
particular ethnic group. At first, only one assembly was arranged
for each group, but later two were scheduled, one at which guest
speakers and performers appeared, and a second which was entirely
student-run--the product of the research and rehearsal done by

[10]DuBois, "Autobiography," Chapter 3, p. 4, DuBois Mss.

the students after exposure to the guest assembly.[11] Assemblies
were usually timed to coincide with a holiday associated with a
particular group, as for example, the Italians in October because
of Columbus Day and the Negroes in February because of Lincoln's
birthday.

Each assembly was a melange of oratory, drama and performance. A typical assembly, such as the one presented at
Woodbury High School on the Jews, featured a Jewish rabbi who
spoke on Jewish religious ideals, records of "Hebrew music, from
'Eili, Eili!' to Irving Berlin," and a talk by a member of the Jewish
Fine Arts Club of Philadelphia. Student participants in the program
made a dramatic presentation of Jewish contributions to ancient
and modern civilizations, delivered speeches on Jewish influence
on American literature and theatre, and presented a short skit
depicting Jewish immigrants arriving on "an improvised gangplank
while the Statue of Liberty greets them with a speech."[12] During
the course of the year, students were feted to performances of
Italian opera and Negro spirituals, German folk dances and Indian

[11]Rachel Davis DuBois, The Contributions of Racial Elements
to American Life (2nd ed.; Philadelphia: Women's International
League for Peace and Freedom, 1930),.; DuBois, "Autobiography,"
Chapter 3, pp. 9-11, DuBois Mss.

[12]DuBois, The Contributions, pp. 11-12.

war chants, demonstrations of Galileo's experiments with falling

bodies, the procedure for making peanut bread using actual flour

sent by Dr. Carver of Tuskegee Institute, recitations of Negro

poetry and German "Tales of the Black Forest."[13] Prominent

individuals such as William Pickens of NAACP, Chih Meng,

Director of the China Institute of America, and Judge Alessandroni

of Philadelphia, accepted invitations to appear at the school.[14]

As innocuous as these programs appear today, they managed

to stir up a storm of criticism against the dynamic, young teacher.

By the end of her first year as assembly moderator, she was under

attack from the local American Legion and under pressure to resign

her teaching position. DuBois was charged with Bolshevik learn-

ings, refusal to salute the flag, belief in interracial marriage and

support of the "cult of nakedness." Owing to the wild and baseless

nature of most of the accusations, the support of the local

superintendent, Malcolm Thomas, the backing of local Quaker

groups, and a New Jersey tenure law that make her ouster difficult,

she survived these attacks and retained her position.[15] During

---

[13]Ibid., pp. 1-20, passim.

[14]DuBois, "Autobiography," Chapter 3, pp. 9-11, DuBois Mss.

[15]Rachel Davis DuBois, Personal Log, April 17, 1927 to
June 5, 1927, DuBois Mss.; DuBois, "Autobiography," Chapter 3,
pp. 11-18, DuBois Mss.; further documentation for this incident may
be found in ff. Correspondence, American Legion Affair, 1927-1928,
DuBois Mss.

the next year and a half, DuBois arranged the publication and distribution of a pamphlet describing the Woodbury Assemblies by the Women's International League and experimented with assemblies on other themes.

The Columbia Connection, 1929-1934

DuBois left Woodbury High School in 1929 in order to study for a doctorate at Teachers College, Columbia University. The move brought her closer to the great immigrant communities of New York City, gave her ready access to the staffs of national organizations with home offices in New York, and exposed her to the exciting atmosphere of educational innovation at Teachers College, where progressive educators such as William H. Kilpatrick and George S. Counts held sway. Her mentor, Daniel Kulp II, had recently steered to completion a doctoral dissertation by George Neumann which struck DuBois with its bearing upon her work.[16] Neumann had argued that attention to attitude formation was at least as important as instruction in facts or skills, and had devised a set of questions, known as the "Neumann Attitude Indicator," to test the "international attitudes" of high school students. This test became a widely-used measuring instrument in the years

---

[16]George Bradford Neumann, A Study of International Attitudes of High School Students (New York: Bureau of Publications, Teachers College, Columbia University, 1926).

ahead. DuBois saw her project as the "next step" after Neumann's work. She had developed a program designed to favorably alter international attitudes, and the test would permit her to measure the impact of her program on student attitudes. As the test was used in field situations, it would lead to necessary "refinements" of the test itself.[17]

Under Kulp's direction, DuBois began working in high schools in and around Philadelphia, organizing assemblies, guiding teachers, and administering the Neumann test both before and after the year's program in each school. The objective of the first year's work (1929-30) was to measure the impact of the assembly program in different types of school settings.[18] A more ambitious experiment, which DuBois planned for her doctoral thesis, was launched a year later involving nine schools, most of which were located in the suburbs of Philadelphia. The purpose of this experiment was "to determine the relative efficacy of the assembly program versus incidental classroom teaching in developing

---

[17]Rachel Davis DuBois to Daniel Kulp II, Nov. 17, 1928, ff. Correspondence, General, 1917-1929, DuBois Mss.

[18]Schools in large urban areas, middle-sized industrial cities, and private schools were used in the experiment. Students were tested for the "liberality" of their international attitudes. See Rachel Davis DuBois, "Measuring Attitudes," Friends Intelligencer, June 14, 1930, 467-68. Also Daniel Kulp II and Helen H. Davidson, "Can Neuman's 'Attitude Indicator' be used as a Test," Teachers College Record, XXXII (January, 1931), pp. 1-6.

tolerant attitudes . . . ."[19] Educational theory at that time

stressed the advantage of emotional over mental appeals in changing

attitudes, and this experiment was designed to test the validity

of that assumption. The assembly program, through its combination

of song, dance, drama and oratory, was considered an ideal form

of emotional conditioning. Of the nine schools participating

in the experiment, three were used as control schools, three relied

exclusively on the assembly program, and three used only factual

materials about the history and contributions of different ethnic

groups. The need to test systematically the effectiveness of the

two approaches, requiring as it did the preparation of written

materials for classroom use, brought home to DuBois both the biases

and distortions in current textbooks and the woeful lack of

curriculum materials on the role played by racial and ethnic groups

in the development of American society.[20]

To correct this situation, DuBois threw herself into the task

---

[19]Rachel Davis DuBois to School Principals, n.d., ff.
Correspondence, General, 1930-39, DuBois Mss.

[20]With the help of students from Temple University, DuBois
surveyed the content of American history books held in the libararies
of the nine schools. The results showed a dearth of information
about ethnic contributions to American civilization and abundant
evidence of bias and distortion in these works. This may have been
the first such survey ever conducted in the United States (Rachel
Davis DuBois, "Autobiography," Chapter 4, pp. 4-5).

of ferreting out information about the history and contributions
of various ethnic groups, which could be introduced into already
existing courses of study, such as history, science, and art.
Although she had begun this work at Woodbury, she now resolved
to do a more thorough and systematic job. She appealed for, and
received, help from a number of ethnic organizations in New York
City such as the China Institute, the Japan Institute, the Block
Publishing Company, the NAACP and the Urban League.[21] She
visited libraries and read voraciously on the subject of ethnic
history and "immigrant gifts." The product of her labors was a
series of mimeographed pamphlets dealing with the historical
development, cultural traits, and individual accomplishments of
each group. These pamphlets were used by the students in the
schools participating in the experiment. The upshot of all this
experimentation, based on test results from 4,000 students in
nine schools, was that the assembly was a more effective method
for changing attitudes than the strictly intellectual approach
represented by the written materials, but that the latter was significantly better than nothing at all, and that to attain the best results,
both should be used at the same time.[22]

---

[21]Ibid., p. 5.

[22]Ibid., pp. 6-7; Rachel Davis DuBois, "Building Tolerant
Attitudes in High School Students," The Crisis, XL (October, 1931),
334,336.

In the years ahead, the number and variety of curricular units offered to the schools were increased. In the summer of 1932, the New York Foundation allocated $500 to enable DuBois with two assistants from Teachers College, Mildred Dougherty and Ruth Davis, to do reasearch for two months at the New York Public Library.[23] After the founding of the Service Bureau for Intercultural Education, the WPA provided funds to permit the hiring of a staff of part-time research workers, at times numbering as many as twenty, to carry forward the pioneering work begun by DuBois. DuBois was probably the first American educator to develop ethnic studies curriculum materials for the public schools.

By violating the taboo against spotlighting ethnicity in public, by attacking directly the prejudices that existed within society, by daring to rekindle pride in what many people assumed to be outmoded traditions, DuBois had fashioned a program that was foreordained to attract criticism. To fend off that criticism, DuBois insisted on certain safeguards being built into her ethnic studies program. In effect, she sanitized the presentation of ethnicity, both in the assemblies and in the curriculum materials,

---

[23]Daniel H. Kulp II to David Heyman, July 8, 1932, Oct. 14, 1932, ff. Teachers College, No. 337, Records of the New York Foundation, 4 West 58th Street, New York, N.Y. (Hereinafter referred to as "NYF Mss"); Rachel Davis DuBois, "Autobiography," Chapter 4, p. 6.

to minimize the possibility of offense or ridicule.

The most controversial aspect of the assembly program was the singling out of particular groups for presentation in separate assemblies. When the group under consideration was not held in high esteem in the local community, as was most often the case with the Negro, or when it included significant numbers of students and teachers within the school, discretion had to be exercised in presenting the topic. For example, the most misunderstood group, the one which might arouse the most antipathy in the audience, was always saved for late in the year, so that students would not realize that a deliberate attempt was being made to alter their attitudes. In the East, the blacks came last; in the West, the Asians.[24] The cast of each assembly was always deliberately integrated, and the master of ceremonies chosen from outside the group, to prevent the isolation of any one group on the stage.[25] Only differences likely to win approval from outsiders were spotlighted on stage; no attempt was made to interpret differences viewed with disfavor by the majority. Great care was taken to invite guests who would not reinforce the stereotype of a particular group:

The first visiting rabbi in the Woodbury School was a young man who looked and acted like a YMCA secretary whom the

---

[24]DuBois, "Adventures in Intercultural Education," pp. 69-78.

[25]DuBois, Build, p. 59.

students greatly admired. Mr. Dipeolu, who was from Nigeria and was dark-skinned, spoke beautiful English. Louise Chin, a third generation Chinese-American girl, was a typical American college girl. [26]

Not only had they to be inoffensive in appearance but safe in philosophy: all speakers recommended by ethnic community leaders had to be screened in advance to make sure they "held a view consistent with the aims of the project." [27] Daring in concept, the assembly programs were extremely cautious in execution.

The curriculum materials that supplemented the assembly programs also carefully treaded in safe waters. Most tried to show that ethnic aspirations and achievements were congruent with the professional and technological thrust of American civilization. Units such as "German Contributions in Physics," "Italians in Chemistry and Physics," "Orientals in Science and Invention," "Poles in American Agricultural Life," "Heinrich Wilhelm Stiegel and Caspar Wistar (Two Glassmakers from Germany)," tried to demonstrate the contributions of minority group members to the advancement of science and industry. Units such as: "Jewish Orchestra Conductors in American Life," "Jewish Violinists in American Life," "Lue Gim Gong (A Chinese American Horticulturalist)," and "Giannini" featured prominent Americans of foreign birth or

---

26Ibid., p. 100.

27Ibid., p. 58.

ancestry. The desire to find pre-Revolutionary ancestors as
a way of legitimizing the presence of an ethnic group in American
society was reflected in such units as: "Italian Immigration:
A Brief Survey of the Italians in Colonial America, and Since,"
"Jewish Participation in Colonial America," and "Irish Immigration."
Of those units which highlighted specific cultural traits of ethnic
groups, most dealt with arts and crafts, with heavy emphasis on
cooking. Among the cuisines given separate coverage in classroom
units were German, Italian, Mexican, Armenian, Japanese,
Scandinavian and Pennsylvania Dutch. Other units on the arts
included: "Mexican Mural Painters and Their Influence in the
United States," "The Negro Contribution to Folk Music in America,"
"Oriental Art and American Homes," and "Japanese Flower
Arrangement." Few of the curriculum units dealt with values that
deeply divided Americans and which entered into the core of human
identity.[28]

During the 1932-33 academic year, DuBois brought her
crusade for brotherhood to the schools of Washington, D.C.,

---

[28]Service Bureau for Intercultural Education, "List of Publica-
tions" (Mimeographed List of Classroom Materials), n.d. and
Publications: Books, Reports of Projects, Classroom Units, Teachers'
Plans, Bibliographies, Plays, n.d., ff Service Bureau, Publication
Lists, 1937-1939, DuBois Mss. An incomplete set of the actual
classroom units is on file in the DuBois Mss.

suburban Boston and Englewood, New Jersey. Subsidies for these

programs came from The American Association of University Women

(Washington), the New Jersey Race Relations Survey Committee

(Englewood), and the Boston Chapter of the National Conference

of Christians and Jews.[29] The National Conference had been an

important "silent partner" of DuBois since 1930, at which time

the National Board of the fledgling good-will organization had

voted to assist DuBois in whatever way possible, short of formal

alliance. It was Everett Clinchy, director of the Conference, who

had secured an invitation to DuBois from Boston University to

teach, what may have been, the first course in the country in the

field of intercultural education. The course was given during the

Spring term of 1933.[30] This was the beginning of a long academic

career that brought her into contact with thousands of teachers and

teacher-trainees in such institutions as New York University,

[29]See document entitled "History of Work" enclosed with letter from William F. Fuerst to Mrs. Sidney C. Borg, Nov. 13, 1935, ff. Progressive Education Association, No. 391, NYF Mss.

[30]Everett R. Clinchy to Prof. John J. Mahoney, Nov. 23, 1932, Everett R. Clinchy to Rachel Davis DuBois, Oct. 5, 1932, ff. Correspondence, General, 1930-1939, DuBois Mss.; National Conference of Jews and Christians, Minutes of the Steering Committee, Dec. 17, 1930, Microfilm Records of the National Conference of Christians and Jews, Reel 1, Library of the National Conference of Christians and Jews, 43 West 57th Street, New York, N.Y. (Hereafter referred to as NCCJ Mss.); Rachel Davis DuBois, "Autobiography," Chapter 4, pp. 9-10.

Temple University, Brooklyn College, San Francisco State
College, Columbia University and The New School. DuBois
courses were a far cry from standard academic fare. They usually
included an array of outside speakers from different ethnic groups
as well as interracial and interethnic social gatherings at the homes
of students or friends. "Interracial teas" were becoming a fad
of the times as small groups of social dissenters tried to break down
the wall of segregation between the races, but DuBois tried to
turn such events into productive learning experiences by probing
into the cultural identities of all participants.[31]

International Education: The First Matrix of Multi-Cultural Education

The educational approach that Rachel DuBois developed
during the twenties and early thirties was marked by a strong
international focus, immediate antecedents in the pacifist movement, and a concern to change the attitudes of the majority rather
than alter the self-concept of minorities. The DuBois high school
assembly program was part of a broader movement of educational
reform known as "international education" that rippled across the
western world partly at the inspiration of certain social and educa-

---

[31]Much later in her career, she developed a technique known
as "group conversation" for exploring the personal histories and
identities of participants in such groups. The technique is fully
expounded in Rachel Davis DuBois and Mew-Soong Li, The Art of
Group Conversation (New York, 1963) and Rachel Davis DuBois and
Mew-Soong Li, Reducing Social Tension and Conflict through the
Group Conversation Method (New York, 1971).

tional agencies of the League of Nations. This movement grew

out of the mood of bitterness and disillusionment that had been

left as an aftermath of World War I; millions had perished for no

apparent reason, and the fruits of struggle for both victor and

vanquished had been so meagre. Many searched for an answer

to the ultimate question: why? Historians looked back on the

years preceding the outbreak of World War I and identified one

demon in particular that had set the nations on a collision course:

the demon of nationalism that had corrupted the educational process

and warped the minds of millions. People had been taught to

worship the state, to nurse old wounds, to identify with national

destiny, and to hate their neighbors. Nationalism had become

"the religion of the schools," as pernicious an association of

dogma and education as that developed by the old theistic schools.[32]

War had been the direct result of such a twisted education. But

if people could be helped to rise above ethnocentrism, identify as

world citizens, understand the cultures and civilizations of other

nations, then a new age of international cooperation and pacific

relations between the nations would dawn for mankind. War or

peace depended on the state of mind of the people, and education

was the most important way to influence that state of mind.

----

[32]Thomas Woody, "Nationalistic Education and Beyond,"
Educational Review, LXXVI (September, 1928), 100.

One way to mold the "new mind" of the future was to break down the physical barriers that separated people. To achieve this end, a number of educational innovations were made in the post-war period, most of which found ready acceptance and became established procedures in international relations. European governments and major foundations in America began to offer scholarships for travel and study abroad; private agencies were organized to promote educational travel; universities permitted students to gain academic credit by study overseas. The Institute for International Education, founded in New York City in 1919, arranged professorial exchanges and administered various scholarship programs for overseas study. Universities such as Stanford and Harvard established Centers of International Study, a new academic concept that spread to other universities. International conferences of educators began to be held on a regular basis. These programs were not the inevitable outcome of improved world communications but owed much to the yearnings for peace that followed World War I.[33]

Another way to shape the attitudes of future generations was to thoroughly reform school curricula, ridding textbooks of

[33]Ibid., p. 107; Edmond A. Meras, "World-Mindedness," Journal of Higher Education, III (May, 1932), 247, 249; Spencer Stoker, The Schools and International Understanding (Chapel Hill, 1933), pp. 56-60.

nationalistic distortions or falsehoods, introducing the study of

modern international problems and developing appreciation for

the contributions of other nations to world civilization. Both the

Carnegie Foundation for International Peace and the Institute of

Pacific Relations appointed commissions to study the prevalence

of historical distortions and national glorification in textbooks

used throughout the world. The results of these investigations

were given wide publicity and as a consequence, new textbooks

were written that reflected the internationalist point of view.

Teachers were urged to make their disciplines relevant to the

modern world by being more issue-oriented and present-minded

in the classroom. Various techniques were suggested for broaden-

ing the horizons of American students. Folk dancing, for example,

became a popular activity in school physical education departments

as a way of "cultivating emotional sympathy between nations and

cultures." Foreign language teachers were urged to instill in

children knowledge and respect for the culture as well as for the

language. Even advocates of progressive education tried to

capitalize on the popularity of internationalism by arguing that

the child-centered approach eased the repression that caused

children to turn their hostilities toward other peoples.[34]

---

[34]Stoker, The Schools, pp. 185-86, 199; Daniel Prescott,
Education and International Relations (Cambridge, 1930) pp 10-23;
Mary Effie Shambaugh, Folk Festivals for Schools and Playgrounds
(New York, 1932), p. v.; Walter V. Kaulfers, "Orientation Courses

It was in the spirit, and as an extension of this effort to develop a fraternal and planetary consciousness that Rachel DuBois undertook her early work in the schools. The term "international education" was used to describe the DuBois approach into the middle thirties. The early curriculum materials sought to develop "world-mindedness" not ethnic consciousness. Some of the first members of the Bureau's Board of Directors, including its first Chairman, Heber Harper, were leading advocates of the internationalist point of view. The original series of ethnic assemblies were part of a three-year sequence of assemblies, of which the second year was devoted to the interdependence of the world's peoples in such fields of endeavor as science and invention, the fine arts and literature, and the third year to the role of pioneers in "building New Frontiers of Civilization."[35] The focus of her concern during the early years was the children of the majority, whose need to understand the strangers in their midst was more apparent to her than the strangers' need to understand themselves. Looking back after forty years, DuBois admitted to being unaware at the time of the psychological implications of cultural studies for the minority child. "College courses in those

---

in National Cultures," Progressive Education, XIV (March, 1937), 195-198; R. B. Raup, "Progressive Education and International Good-Will," Progressive Education, VIII (May, 1931), 376-78.

[35]DuBois, Build, p. 51.

days," she recalled, "were not teaching the value of self-identity
and the blight of alienation."[36]

DuBois Discovers the Problem
of Ethnic Alienation

Although DuBois never lost sight of the global implications
of her work, she came to realize in the thirties that her program
had special relevance for the children of immigrants and blacks.
Once this linkage was made, it tended to overshadow her other
concerns and to provide the principal rationale for her "separate
approach" to intercultural education. How did DuBois acquire
this new perspective? Through her association with Evelyn Hersey,
Director of the Philadelphia International Institute, she had already
felt the heartbeat of a movement that had given high priority to
the second generation issue since 1924. Hersey was in the forefront of those calling attention to the intensity of "bi-cultural
conflict" in the lives of second generation children.[37] After moving

---

[36]DuBois, "Autobiography," Chapter 3, p. 6.

[37]Hersey, "The Emotional Conflicts," p. 84. The very first
assembly programs DuBois ran at Woodbury High School were
modelled on performances of folk music and dances she had witnessed
at the Philadelphia International Institute. Two of the first guest
speakers invited to Woodbury: Judge Alessandroni and Aurora Unti
were recruited from the circle of ethnic-Americans that met at the
Philadelphia Institute (DuBois, "Autobiography," Chapter 3, p. 9;
Rachel Davis DuBois, "My first contact with the International
Institute," [Short Memoir written at the request of the author],
Nov. 21, 1974). DuBois was one of the two guest speakers from outside the Institute Movement (Florian Znaniecki was the other) invited
to address the 1932 National Conference of International Institutes

to New York City in 1929, DuBois began to form close professional

ties and friendships with black leaders and spokesmen for recent

immigrant groups. She was a frequent visitor, for example, at

the Casa Italiana Educational Bureau at Columbia University

where Leonard Covello, Director of the Bureau and a leading inter-

preter of the second generation problem, assisted her in obtaining

factual information about Italian contributions to American life.

She developed close ties to members of the Jewish Reconstructionist

movement, who were waging a campaign to combat the alienation

of Jewish youth.[38] She also met Louis Adamic, whom she

considered a "great influence" upon her and with whom she would

consult frequently in the years ahead.[39] Adamic not only defined

the issue of alienation but proposed a solution to the problem.

In Adamic's provocative 1934 article, he had called for the

---

in Philadelphia. She reported on her experimentation in Philadelphia-
area schools and discussed her techniques for building good-will
between races and nationalities (Twelfth National Conference of
International Institutes, Report of Proceedings [Philadelphia, 1932],
pp. 32-33 [Copy found in Boston Mss.]).

[38]See Chapter 7, pp.179-187, for extended discussion of the
Reconstructionist movement.

[39]DuBois, "Autobiography," Chapter 4, p. 19; descriptions of
her meetings with Adamic are contained in her intermittent log
entries for the period: see, for example, her personal log entries
for June 11, 1940, and Nov. 18, 1941, DuBois Mss.

creation of an "XYZ" organization to undertake "a great educational-cultural work," that of teaching second generation Americans about their history and heritages and of imparting to old-stock Americans an appreciation of the cultural contributions of the newer Americans.[40] Adamic also felt that such an organization should attempt to educate and enlighten public school teachers, whose strong influence on the second generation could bode well or ill for the future of American society. The Service Bureau, as will be discussed in the next chapter, was born the same year that Adamic made this appeal and DuBois and her co-workers saw the organization as the fulfillment of Adamic's wish. Adamic was only "dimly aware" of the existence of the Bureau when he wrote his article and in fact had in mind the transformation of the Foreign Language Information Service into a new agency that would assign higher priority to education.[41] However, when he became better-acquainted with the new organization, he welcomed the Bureau as an ally to his cause. The Bureau was dedicated to the same ultimate goal: as Adamic defined it, "to harmonize and integrate, so far as possible, the various racial and cultural strains in our population without suppre-

[40]Adamic, "Thirty Million," 692-93.

[41]Louis Adamic, "Preface" to reprint of his article, "Thirty Million New Americans," by the Service Bureau for Education in Human Relations, ff. Louis Adamic, Writings, DuBois Mss.

ing or destroying any good qualities in any one of them . . . ."[42]

After 1934, DuBois joined Adamic in calling for a return to ethnic roots.[43] The first question she posed to teachers enrolled in her in-service courses was: "What are you trying to do to develop enough pride in boys and girls of minority culture groups so that they will try to share their cultural heritage with others?"[44] To counteract the deadly poison of Nazi-style race hatreds, she felt it would be necessary to satisfy the need for security of minority group members and restore their pride in group identity: "If normal people were given legitimate ways of feeling adequate they would not seek depraved and sadistic ways of self-assertion."[45]

---

[42]Adamic, "Thirty Million," 692.

[43]DuBois repeatedly cited Adamic in her articles and speeches from 1935 to 1941. As examples see: Rachel Davis DuBois, "Practical Problems of International and Interracial Education" (abstracts of address before Annual Conference of the Progressive Education Association, Feb. 23, [1935]), pp. 2-3; Rachel Davis DuBois, "What American Culture Might Become" (draft of speech before the League of Women Voters, San Francisco, 1935), p. 8; Rachel Davis DuBois, "The Need for Sharing Cultural Values" (talk on Radio Station WEVD, July 26, 1938), p. 1, ff. Rachel Davis DuBois, Speeches and Radio Talks, 1934-1945, DuBois Mss.

[44]Rachel Davis DuBois, "Some Questions to Guide our Discussions on Intercultural Education" (mimeographed notes distributed to teachers enrolled in in-service course at Textile High School, New York City, Feb., 1939), p. 1, ff. Miscellaneous, #1, DuBois Mss.

[45]Rachel Davis DuBois, "What American Culture Might Become" (draft of speech before the League of Women Voters, San Francisco, 1935), p. 7, ff. Rachel Davis DuBois, Speeches and Radio talks, 1934-1945, DuBois Mss.

DuBois was certain that the assault on minority cultures had already taken a devestating toll: the second generation had contributed "a disproportionate share to the asocial and criminal elements"; they had comprised, she believed, "a disproportionate number of our problem children: the shy, sullen, the non-cooperative and the aggressive . . .";they were proving especially vulnerable to manipulation by foreign governments intent on undermining the unity and resolve of the American people.[46] She believed that "creation demands an energy which comes from a faith in one's self." In order to free the imprisoned spirit of the second generation, a new emphasis would have to be placed upon "being what we are," on the confident expression of ourselves as group-defined persons.[47] Progressive educators interested in the rounded development of their students, interested in social and emotional as well as intellectual growth, would have to both accept and teach the cultures of the immigrants.

There were two aspects of DuBois' personality that were imprinted upon the early movement for multi-cultural education:

_____

[46]Rachel Davis DuBois, "Danger or Promise?"(speech delivered at San Francisco State College, 1936),p. 8, ff. Rachel Davis DuBois, Speeches and Radio Talks, 1934-1945, DuBois Mss.

[47]Rachel Davis DuBois, "The Need for Sharing Cultural Values" (talk on Radio Station WEVD, July 26, 1938),pp. 2, 4, ff. Rachel Davis DuBois, Speeches and Radio Talks, 1934-1945, DuBois Mss.

one was her religious outlook, which shaped her perceptions of
reality; the other was her commitment to pacifism, which gave
a distinct direction to her efforts. DuBois sought to achieve
that degree of unity necessary to maintain civil and international
peace. She did not think that it was necessary to steamroll
cultural differences in order to achieve peace, for cultural
differentiation was the end product of an evolutionary process and
the expression of a basic human need. Moreover, people had a
great deal in common beneath the surface differences of culture.
Her mission was to help people see their shared humanity and
understand the valuable contributions of all groups toward the progress
of humanity. The kind of fellowship which she sought to bring about
was foreign to the experience of many people, for it rested on a
philosophy of human interaction that was essentially religious in
nature. Quakerism (for DuBois a way of life and not simply a
Sunday observance) taught her to appreciate the infinite worth
of the individual, each person's capacity to incarnate the supernatural, and the duty of sharing one's light with others. The same
variety of spiritual manifestations could be seen in human cultures.
Each group had its unique gifts and treasures, which held meaning
for mankind only to the extent that they were bound together in an
organic whole.

The image of a lost and deracinated generation so vividly
impressed upon her mind through her contacts with ethnic leaders

during the early thirties, led her to widen her efforts. Not only

would the children of the majority have to be taught to appreciate

differences but the children of the minorities would have to be

taught to confidently express those differences. Only in this

way could the problem of "wounded personalities," as she put

it, so widespread in the second generation, be resolved and the

creative energies of these individuals be released and directed toward

the revitalization of American civilization.

CHAPTER IV

THE SERVICE BUREAU: "SPECIALIZED WORK
FOR THE SECOND GENERATION"

The future in 1934 seemed bleak and uncertain. Across

the seas, forces of barbarism had been unleashed with what

ultimate consequences few could foresee, and at home, social

and economic ailments lingered on and resisted cure. Recently

installed as Chancellor of Germany, Adolf Hitler set about to

rid German society of "traitorous" elements and "inferior racial

stocks." In the United States, manifestations of anti-Semitism,

feeding upon a still smoldering domestic tradition of hate, became

more frequent despite the strenuous efforts of many groups to

contain the new contagion from abroad. The Depression wore on

despite Herbert Hoover's predictions of an imminent upturn and

unresponsive to the New Deal's programs for economic recovery.

The extremes of American politics, both left and right, showed new

signs of vitality and growing popularity. Alien-baiting again became

a common indulgence of many Americans frustrated with the hardships

and insecurities of life in an unpredictable economic system. As the outcry against aliens hogging jobs or padding relief rolls grew

louder, bills were introduced in Congress and in state legisla-

tures calling for the deportation of indigent aliens and the denial

of New Deal benefits to the foreign-born. The flare-up of nativism,

after a few years of relative dormancy, gave evidence of the linger-

ing anxiety felt by many Americans over the presence of minorities

in American society. In the midst of these troubled times, and

in an attempt to repair the dangerous fissures that had appeared in

American society, a new organization was created in New York

City, that aimed to restore social order and unity through educational

means.

The first major step in the formation of the Service Bureau

for Intercultural Education[1] was a luncheon meeting at Town Hall

in New York City on October 27, 1933, attended by sixteen people,

including Benson W. Landis of the National Conference of

Christians and Jews, William Pickens of the NAACP, Chih Meng of

the China Institute, and Louis Posner of the New York City Board

of Education. The participants lamented the "tragic ignorance" of

minority achievements and cultures and endorsed a campaign to

overcome this ignorance by providing "content materials" to

---

[1]The original name of the organization was Service Bureau
for Education in Human Relations. That name was changed in
1936 (See Chapter V,p.132).

teachers and students.[2] The meeting paved the way for the

selection of a National Advisory Committee and the opening up

of an office in February of 1934. There were two important factors

which permitted the organization to be launched at this time: first,

the availability of manpower through the newly-created Civil Works

Administration, and second, the interest of the American Jewish

Committee in the work of DuBois.

To stave off starvation, misery and mass unrest, millions

of unemployed--including white collar workers, artists, and

intellectuals--were put to work by the federal government during

the winter of 1933-1934. Universities such as Columbia were

asked to develop and oversee research-related projects that

could be staffed by unemployed graduate students. By now, DuBois

was well-entrenched at Columbia. Dean Russell of Teachers College

had appointed a special faculty committee to guide her work in 1931,

and she was now offering extension courses to teachers under

---

[2]Service Bureau for Education in Human Relations, Minutes
of Luncheon, Town Hall Club, New York City, Oct. 27, 1933,
ff. Intercultural Education, Agencies and Organizations, Service
Bureau for Education in Human Relations, Box 16, Leonard Covello
Papers, The Balch Institute, Philadelphia, Pennsylvania (henceforth
referred to as Covello Mss.).

University auspices.[3] One of the strongest faculty supporters

of DuBois was Mabel Carney, a professor of rural education

at Teachers College and a woman closely identified with desegre-

gation and black educational aspirations.[4] It was Carney who

served as faculty sponsor for a CWA project that recruited twelve

individuals to do part-time research work for the new organization.

They began work in February of 1934 and were commissioned to

continue the research into ethnic history and cultural contributions

which DuBois had begun earlier. By the end of the year seventy-

four different pieces of classroom material had been developed by

these workers. Plans were formulated with Thomas Nelson and

Company for the publication of ten booklets, each on the contribu-

tions of a different American ethnic group.[5]

---

[3]Mabel Carney to Mrs. Samuel A. Lewisohn, January 13, 1932,
William F. Russell to Felix M. Warburg, April 14, 1931, ff. National
Conference of Jews and Christians, No. 341, NYF Mss. Also see:
"A Brief History of the Service Bureau for Intercultural Education,"
p. 4, Records of the Bureau for Intercultural Education, Immigration
History Research Center, University of Minnesota (hereafter referred
to as BIE Mss.).

[4]Walter G. Daniel, "Negro Welfare and Mabel Carney at
Teachers College, Columbia University" The Journal of Negro
Education, II (October, 1942), 560-62.

[5]These developments are mentioned in the following documents:
Service Bureau for Education in Human Relations, Minutes of the
National Committee, May 8, 1934, Reel 1, NCCJ Mss.; and Service
Bureau for Education in Human Relations, "Sub-Project 17 a and b,"
(report apparently prepared for members of the National Committee,
[1934]), p. 9, ff. Intercultural Education, Agencies and Organizations,
Service Bureau for Education in Human Relations, Box 16, Covello Mss.

Although this plan was never fully executed, the development of curriculum materials became a major emphasis of the new organization.

The Bureau also operated a "Clearing House" for the dissemination of current literature in the field of intergroup education. The organization's interest in the second generation was clear from the titles selected for reprinting and distribution. Of the twenty-five or so publications (mostly articles) selected for distribution during 1934-1935, two were lengthy publications of the YWCA dealing with the second generation: Florence Cassidy's report of the Second Generation Commission and the proceedings of a 1935 YWCA conference on second generation youth.[6] The Bureau also secured Adamic's permission to reprint his controversial article on the second generation to which he contributed a short preface giving his blessings to the new organization. Four thousand copies of the article were printed, almost all of which were distributed during the next year; 900 copies were mailed to secondary school principals across the country.[7] The Bureau, however,

---

[6] A full list of "Clearing House" materials appears in the following pamphlet: Service Bureau for Intercultural Education, Publications: Books, Reports of Projects, Classroom Units, Teachers' Plans, Bibliographies, Plays (New York, c1939), pp. 16-20 (found in ff. Service Bureau, Publication Lists, 1937-1939, DuBois Mss.).

[7] Service Bureau for Education in Human Relations, "Progress Report - Project 89Fb1190-X-15," [1935], p. 7, Reel 2, NCCJ Mss.

advertised a much broader range of services than just the development of curriculum materials and the dissemination of current
literature in the field. To actually gain entry into the schools,
raise the consciousness of teachers and administrators, organize
assembly programs, bring in guest speakers and artists, required
a major investment of money and manpower. The funds to make
this comprehensive program possible came from the American
Jewish Committee.

How did DuBois and leaders of the American Jewish Committee
first cross paths? According to DuBois' memoirs, Theresa Mayer
Durlach, member of the wealthy Mayer family with extensive real
estate holdings in New York City, heard DuBois speak at a NCCJ
conference at Columbia University. Of German Jewish ancestry
and like DuBois, an activist in the peace movement, Durlach
was so impressed with the report of her work and with the promise
it held out to immunize American young people against the Hitler
contagion, that she asked to observe the program in actual operation
at the Englewood public schools. Her reaction to the program
was favorable, so much so that she made a commitment to finance
a much more ambitious experiment and apparently brought the
project to the attention of the American Jewish Committee in New
York.[8] A short time later, Rabbi Jacob Weinstein, then on the

---

[8]DuBois, "Autobiography," Chapter 4, p. 13; Theresa Mayer
Durlach, interview with the author, June 24, 1974.

staff of the Committee, had lunch with DuBois and informed her
that the Committee, through a special sub-committee known as
Information and Service Associates, was ready to finance a one
year experiment in a number of different metropolitan area schools.
A sum of $5,000 was allocated to the Bureau for the purpose
of hiring two field workers to conduct the project during the 1934-
1935 academic year. Miriam Ephraim, Director of Extension
Education at the Central Jewish Institute, and Ione Eckerson, a
teacher at a New Jersey high school, were tapped for this assignment. Fifteen schools in the New York metropolitan area were
selected for participation in the project. Perhaps the most
ambitious ethnic studies experiment in the schools during the decade,
the project was carried out under the careful scrutiny of an organization with both a financial stake in the outcome of the experiment
and a strong concern to control the disease of anti-Semitism. The
project revealed the potential conflict in purpose between those
whose primary concern was the change of majority attitudes and
those who coupled such a concern with a strong desire to change the
self-perceptions of minority students.[9]

The project was an extension of the approach that DuBois
had worked out at Woodbury High School, but with the sophistica-

---

[9]See Chapter VII for an extended discussion of AJC involvement with the Bureau.

tion and refinements that had been added during the preceding

five years of experimentation. In each school, Bureau staff

members called together committees of teachers, students,

community, and ethnic leaders to assist in planning and executing

the program. Two hundred teachers from the participating schools

enrolled in nine separate in-service courses given by DuBois. The

usual assemblies were held at regular intervals during the academic

year with the Bureau handling arrangements for outside speakers

and guest performers. Factual materials were handed out to students

and homeroom discussions were scheduled around the theme of

ethnic cultural contributions.[10]

For the first time since DuBois began her experimentation

with ethnic assemblies and ethnic studies materials, close

attention was paid to the impact of the project on minority children.

Heretofore, only "the attitudes of the young people of one cultural

background toward another" were closely watched; now "the

attitudes of the people within a group toward their own background"

were also carefully scrutinized.[11] The anecdotal records kept by

---

[10]DuBois, Build, pp. 58-59, 62-68; "History of the Service Bureau for Education in Human Relations," [1936], pp. 3-4, ff. Intercultural Education, Agencies and Organizations, Service Bureau for Education in Human Relations, Box 16, Covello Mss.

[11]Miriam R. Ephraim. "Service for Education in Human Relations," p. 22, in Selected Writings of Miriam R. Ephraim (New York: National Jewish Welfare Board, 1966).

the field workers reveal the sharp interest in second generation

and minority cultural awareness. They cite numerous instances

of how young people had acquired more positive attitudes toward

their own ethnic background after having been exposed to the

program. Children at Tenafly High School, for example, were

less fearful of being identified as members of a minority group;

after the German assembly, "children flocked to the stage--

some just to express their appreciation, others to admit their

German ancestry . . . ."[12] After the Jewish Assembly at

Englewood High School, Jewish young people were eager to learn

Hebrew and deepen their knowledge of Jewish history. Similar

results were reported for Italian, Negro and Polish students.[13] By

working to enhance the self-esteem of minority children, the

program also achieved some success, according to the reports, in

raising the academic motivation and improving the deportment of

minority children. The field workers observed remarkable trans-

formations of character and blossomings of hidden abilities as

outgrowths of the program. It was "noticeable that the Italian

---

[12] "Field Notebook," (Section on Tenafly High School), p.6, ff. Intercultural Education Programs, Fifteen Schools in the New York City Metropolitan Area, 1934-35, DuBois Mss.

[13] Ephraim, "Service for Education," pp. 22-23.

students studied much better than they did before" the program

began. A "shy" Jewish girl became more out-going; a "reticent"

Negro girl participated more actively in classroom activities.[14]

The program also seemed to tame the wildness of second generation

students. A Jewish boy was "not nearly as aggressive as he used

to be"; an Italian boy was "less a problem."[15] The apparent

benefits of the program for minority children may not have been

very well appreciated in most of the schools, situated as they were

in suburban, middle class communities with few minority or second

generation students.

The only inner-city school participating in the project was

Benjamin Franklin High School, a school in a working class

neighborhood of East Harlem with a heavy enrollment of second

generation Italian and Puerto Rican students. Leonard Covello,

the newly-appointed, Italian-born Principal of Franklin, was himself

a leading proponent of multi-cultural education for the second

generation. An original member of the Bureau's Advisory Board, he

would write a brilliant and lengthy treatise on the social background

[14]"Reports of Interviews: General Comments," pp. 3, 5, ff.
Intercultural Education Programs, Fifteen Schools in the New York
Metropolitan Area, Reports of Interviews, ca. 1935, DuBois Mss.

[15]Ibid., p. 6.

of the Italo-American school child.[16] Through direct experience--

growing up as an immigrant boy in New York City--Covello was

sensitive to the problem of cultural conflict in the lives of immigrant

children.[17] Although he believed very strongly in the conservation

of cultural heritages and in the responsibility of the public schools

in this regard, Covello was not a cultural pluralist. Instead, he

favored "a BLENDING of different cultures into one basic American

culture - a reconciliation of conflicting heritages . . . ."[18] He

is a prime example of the compatibility of the cultural integrationist

position with a pedagogy calling for bi-lingual and multi-cultural

education. The demonstration project at Franklin, to which the

Bureau attached great importance, was carried out during the Spring

term of 1935. Bureau personnel hoped that the success of the

project would lead to system-wide introduction of the program into

the public secondary schools of New York City. These hopes

proved illusory, but the program endeared itself to Covello and his

teachers, and collaboration between Covello and the Bureau

---

[16]Leonard Covello, The Social Background of the Italo-American
School Child: A Study of the Southern Italian Family Mores and
Their Effect on the School Situation in Italy and America. (Totowa,
N.J., 1972).

[17]Covello relates his autobiography in: The Heart is the
Teacher (New York, 1958).

[18]Leonard Covello, "Intercultural Understanding Among Young
Adults," (typescript), ff. Service Bureau, Reports and Documents,
1932-1935, DuBois Mss.

continued for many years.[19]

The Bureau program at Benjamin Franklin was seen as therapy for the second generation as well as an answer to the problem of intergroup tensions. The teachers agreed that the Bureau program had made second generation children "more interested in and proud of their background."[20] Field Secretary Eckerson was elated that the children "seemed to have gained a new conception of American culture and what their people have contributed to it"; she predicted that their "inferiority complexes, sublimated in bravado and mischief, will gradually fall away and become a normal sense of equality when a feeling of status in the

---

[19]References to on-going negotiations with the New York City Board of Education are made in the following documents: Leonard Covello to James Marshall (drafts of letter prepared by the Service Bureau and attached to Rachel Davis DuBois to Leonard Covello, May 9, 1935), Ione Eckerson to Leonard Covello, June 21, 1935, "History of the Service Bureau for Education in Human Relations," [1936], p. 8. All of the above documents may be found in ff. Intercultural Education, Agencies and Organizations, Service Bureau for Education in Human Relations, Box 16, Covello Mss. A "Committee for Inter-Racial Cooperation," composed of teachers at Benjamin Franklin High School, continued to promote ethnic studies and intergroup education projects at the school throughout the thirties. Covello remained on the Board of the Service Bureau during the period DuBois served as Director (until 1941). After her resignation from the Bureau, Covello joined the Board of the Workshop for Cultural Democracy, the new organization she set up to carry forward her approach to intercultural education.

[20]Rachel Davis DuBois, "Intercultural Education at Benjamin Franklin High School," High Points in the Work of the High Schools of New York City, XIX (December, 1937), p. 29.

community is developed."[21] In a letter to the President of the

New York City Board of Education, Covello urged system-wide

introduction of the program and stressed the mental health

benefits of the Bureau program: "Such a program would . . . help

to overcome the strains of adjustment for the hundreds of thousands

of children of foreign parentage who are to be found in our city

schools . . . ."[22]

The program of the newly-established Bureau was intended

to alleviate the problem of second generation and minority aliena-

tion. While the Bureau never forsook its primary aim of promoting

pacific relations and productive intercourse among ethnic groups,

concern for the second generation became so pronounced that

outside observers such as Read Lewis saw the program of the

Bureau as an instance of "specialized work for the second genera-

tion."[23]

By associating the reestablishment of social harmony

---

[21]Ione Eckerson, "Human Relations Project in Benjamin
Franklin High School" (Mimeographed Report), c1935, pp. 7-8, ff.
Intercultural Education Programs, Benjamin Franklin High School,
DuBois Mss.

[22]Leonard Covello to James Marshall (attached to Rachel Davis
DuBois to Leonard Covello, May 9, 1935), ff. Intercultural
Education, Agencies and Organizations, Service Bureau for Education
in Human Relations, Box 16, Covello Mss. This letter was drafted
by the Service Bureau for Covello's signature.

[23]Read Lewis, "Immigrants and Their Children," Interpreter
Release, XII (April 30, 1935), p. 177.

and the building of a richer American culture with the elimination of the second generation problem, DuBois made a linkage with important bearings upon the history of the Bureau. She found new justification for the "separate approach" to intercultural education that she had developed earlier. This approach called for the separate treatment of ethnic groups in assembly programs, curriculum units and lesson plans--directing the attention of students to one ethnic group at a time. It was at variance with an approach that tried to instill a generalized form of tolerance based on respect for the individual (ethnicity being considered a minor or superficial component of personality), or an approach that examined the contributions of various ethnic groups to various fields of endeavor, such as music, art, science, etc. The most powerful argument she had for the separate approach was that it was the only effective way to favorably alter the self-image of minority students. Since ethnicity, she believed, was a basic force in American society,it would be necessary to confront the issue of ethnicity boldly and directly, in a way that left an unmistakable and lasting impression on students. Only if these students affirmed their past and accepted their heritage could they lead productive and fulfilling lives, could they reach out to others with attitudes of love and appreciation, and could DuBois' dream of cultural integration be realized.

The separate approach, however, was a controversial

one. Some questioned the wisdom of rekindling pride in ethnic

heritage among those whom they considered to be culturally

assimilated. Others were so imbued with the values of American

industrial civilization and so convinced of the universal validity

of those values that any accommodation to small community and

traditional culture seemed retrogressive. There were those who

worried about the political repercussions of such a program; i.e.

that identification with cultural heritage could not be easily

divorced from feelings of allegiance to foreign governments.

And there were those from within the ethnic groups who worried

that accentuation of group divisions within the school curriculum

might place these groups in an exposed and precarious position,

and postpone their entrance into the mainstream of American life.

During the next few years, the separate approach came under

increasing fire. The story of these attacks is the story of how a

nascent ethnic studies movement was challenged and undermined.

CHAPTER V

JOINING THE VANGUARD FOR EDUCATIONAL

REFORM: THE PROGRESSIVE EDUCATION

ASSOCIATION, 1936-1938

By the mid-thirties, interest in ethnic diversity had become
intensive and widespread. In Washington, John Collier, new
Commissioner of Indian Affairs, was carrying out plans to
revitalize tribal arts, language and culture through the medium
of the reservation school.[1] In Pittsburgh, the seventeen Nationality Rooms in the University of Pittsburgh's "Cathedral of Learning" had just opened. They were not intended to be museums,
but rather "classrooms, to be used regularly and there to be a
constant influence in building up respect for the historic
traditions . . ." of the major groups residing in the Pittsburgh
region.[2] The nation was in the midst of a "renaissance of folk

---

[1]Margaret Szasz, Education and the American Indian: The
Road to Self-Determination, 1928-1973 (Albuquerque, 1974), pp. 67-74.

[2]"Overture to Parents," New York Times, Dec. 20, 1934,
sec. 8, p. 4.

dancing" as Boston and Buffalo joined New York in organizing folk festival councils.[3] The Communist Party called for "self-determination" for the black majority in the South.[4] In Washington, Martin W. Royse, along with folklorist Ben Botkin, appointed consultants to the WPA Federal Writers Project, were planning and partially executing an ambitious series of local ethnic studies to be called "Composite America."[5] According to John Bodnar, there seemed to be as many Slavic young people across the country reasserting their ethnic identity as denying it.[6]

---

[3]See article entitled: "Renaissance of Folk Dancing," The International Beacon (Newsletter of the Boston International Institute), II (Dec. 15, 1934). An interesting report on the upsurge of interest in folk dancing appears in an editorial written for an early issue of: Educational Dance, I (October, 1938), p. 2. Mention of the formation of a Folk Festival Council in Buffalo appears in: Florence G. Cassidy, "Adult Education in International Institutes," (Mimeographed Report of the Laboratory Division, National Board, YWCA), April, 1934, p. 8, untitled ff., Boston Mss. The establishment of a Folk Festival Council in Boston is reported in: The International Beacon, IV (Nov. 15, 1936), p. 1.

[4]The Communist Party position on the Negro question is explained and defended in: James S. Allen, The Negro Question in the United States (New York, 1936). See also: William Z. Foster et al., The Communist Position on the Negro Question (New York, 1947).

[5]Jerre Mangione, The Dream and the Deal: The Federal Writers' Project, 1935-1943 (Boston, 1972), pp. 277-85.

[6]John Bodnar, "Materialism and Morality: Slavic-American Immigrants and Education, 1890-1940," Journal of Ethnic Studies, III (Winter, 1976), 13-14.

Taking advantage of the upsurge of interest in minority problems and of the headstart she had acquired over the previous ten years, DuBois during the next four years was able to lead her intercultural brigade into national organizations from which the message of brotherhood and ethnic consciousness was broadcast far and wide. But she now exposed her program to the scrutiny of a wider circle of people, many of whom did not share her ideals and priorities. Her career had indeed blossomed; she had gained the ear of some of the most powerful individuals in American education, but she now faced the difficult task of defending her methodology to those who claimed to be converts to her cause. Not all of those who considered themselves liberal and open-minded on the minority question shared DuBois' desire to intensify ethnic consciousness; hence they were not disposed to employ the method of separate study which her philosophy dictated.

The first organization with which DuBois came into contact was the Progressive Education Association. The principal organized expression of the progressive impulse in American Education, the PEA had been founded by Stanwood Cobb in 1919. At first, an organization comprised primarily of parents and laymen whose base was the elite private schools of the East, the PEA had undergone during the early years of the Depression a number of wrenching changes that had seen the eclipse from power of the "child-centered" wing of the Association and its replacement by

a more professional, socially-concerned leadership with a keen

interest in the reform of public education.[7] These changes had a

salutary affect. Money flowed into the coffers of the Association

from major foundations, and the PEA attracted thousands of new

members and devotees. In 1936, 4,500 people attended the annual

conference of the PEA in Chicago. In 1938, the Association

attained its peak membership of 10,000, and Time Magazine ran

a cover story on the Association which remarked how progressive

education had grown from "a crackpot movement quarantined in a

handful of private schools," to the stature of "a dominant influence

on U. S. Education."[8] The major tenets of progressive education are

well-known: concern for the development of the individual child,

stimulation of the creative impulses and unique capacities of each

child, and the development of a curriculum relevant to the needs and

---

[7]Patricia Albjerg Graham, Progressive Education: From Arcady to Academe: A History of the Progressive Education Association (New York, 1967), p. 100. Graham's book is the most comprehensive analysis of the history of the Progressive Education Association. The story of the struggle for power within the Association between the "social reconstructionists," or activist left-wing of the Association and the older, child-centered wing is told in: C. A. Bowers, The Progressive Educator and the Depression: The Radical Years (New York, 1969).

[8]Graham, Progressive Education, p. 87; "Progressives' Progress," Time Magazine, Oct. 31, 1938, p. 31.

problems of the times. In realizing these objectives, the Progressive Education Association was responsible for some of the most important experimentation and educational innovation during the thirties. The celebrated "Eight-Year Study" was a cooperative venture of some thirty high schools and three hundred colleges the purpose of which was to release students from the tyranny of college entrance requirements and thereby permit the introduction of progressive ideas into secondary education. In 1936, under PEA auspices, the first summer "workshop" for teachers was held at Ohio State University. The purpose of these workshops -- which would become popular and proliferate all over the country in the years ahead -- was to encourage and partially subsidize teachers to make the necessary overhaul of their courses and reexamination of their teaching strategies in the light of progressive educational philosophy and the needs of their particular students.[9] Progressive education was in its heyday in the thirties; the conservative attacks which would later make progressive education synonymous with needless frills and permissiveness had not yet come. DuBois' association with the PEA came at a most propitious moment.

---

[9]Lawrence Cremin, The Transformation of the School: Progressivism in American Education (New York, 1961), pp. 251-53; Paul B. Diederich and William Van Til, The Workshop: A Summary of Principles and Practices of the Workshop Movement (New York, 1945), pp. 1-2.

Although the exact sequence of events leading up to the temporary absorption of the newly-formed Service Bureau by the PEA is not known, the major circumstances contributing to the merger are clear. A self-professed progressive educator in her own right, DuBois was well-known to the Teachers College group that dominated the affairs of the Association. The influence of this group was increased by the transfer of the Association head-quarters from Washington to New York in August of 1935. A number of those who joined the Bureau's Board in 1934; George Counts, F. C. Borgeson and Willard W. Beatty, were influential members of the Association. Prior to formal affiliation with the PEA, DuBois had been asked to speak at a number of PEA conferences. In February of 1935, for example, she and Louis Adamic exhorted the membership of the PEA, convened at their annual conference in Washington, to take vigorous action in the intercultural field. Spurred on by these two dynamic speakers, the Association passed a resolution at its business meeting stating:

> that there is no more important or appropriate task for this
> association than that suggested by Mr. Adamic, not only for
> the education of our thirty million "new Americans" and other
> minority groups, but also for the enlightenment of the children
> of the "old Americans" whose ignorance of other cultures is an
> equally great menace to our community life.[10]

---

[10]Progressive Education Association, Minutes of the Annual Business Meeting, Feb. 23, 1935 (A microfilm set of the minutes of the Association is on file at the library of Teachers College, Columbia University - hereinafter referred to as "PEA Mss., TC"). DuBois also spoke before a regional conference of the PEA in the Fall of

The resolution then called upon the Executive Board to explore the possibility of publishing a "Racial Encyclopedia for the use of the educators of the country." In March of 1935, the PEA's journal, Progressive Education, devoted an entire issue to the subject of "Minority Groups and the American School."[11] A wave of interest in minority problems seemed to be sweeping over the Association.

The most important reason for the link-up with the PEA seems to have been the chronic financial problems of the Service Bureau. The decision of the American Jewish Committee not to renew the grant to the Bureau made during the academic year 1934-35 led to a desperate search for alternate funding.[12] The New York Foundation, to which DuBois appealed for funds in June of 1935, apparently insisted that its grant of $2,500 (not appropriated until November

1934 (Service Bureau, "Sub-Project 17 a and b," mimeographed report, [1934], p. 8, ff. Intercultural Education, Agencies and Organizations, Service Bureau for Education in Human Relations, Box 16, Covello Mss.). Abstracts of DuBois' address before the Annual Conference of the PEA in Feb., 1935, are contained in the DuBois Mss. (See "Practical Problems of International and Interracial Education," ff. Rachel Davis DuBois, Speeches and Radio Talks, 1934-1945, DuBois Mss.).

[11]Progressive Education, XII (March, 1935), 139-213. A wide range of views were represented in this issue, not all of which were supportive of the cultural maintenance position. See, for example Rev. Walden Pell II, "Manners, Morals, and Minorities," 151-55, and Henry C. Fenn, "Educating for a Melting-Pot Culture," 198-201.

[12]For a full discussion of the relations between the Service Bureau and the American Jewish Committee, see Chapter VII.

of 1935) be "supervised" by a reliable, independent agency.[13]
How and why the PEA was chosen for this task is not completely
clear. Willard W. Beatty, Superintendent of Schools in Bronx-
ville, New York, and Board member of the Bureau, was president
of the PEA at that time. He apparently worked to acquaint the
Executive Secretary of the PEA, Frederick L. Redefer (a Quaker like
DuBois), with the DuBois project.[14] It is also clear that the NCCJ,
the unofficial sponsor of the Bureau, had requested Redefer to take
over administration of the enterprise.[15] The relationship offered
potential advantages to both organizations. The Bureau was
probably eager to join forces with the advance guard for educational
reform in the United States and saw its chances for long-range
solvency enhanced through such association. The PEA probably
sensed the growing concern to alleviate intergroup tension and
hoped that a formal program, such as the one developed by the
Bureau, might prove attractive to the foundations. The PEA had

---

[13]Rachel Davis DuBois to William Fuerst, June 4, 1935;
Everett R. Clinchy to David Heyman, Sept. 14, 1935; Everett R.
Clinchy to David Heyman, Oct. 9, 1935; ff. Progressive Education
Association, No. 391, NYF Mss.

[14]See "Survey Report" enclosed with Everett R. Clinchy to
David Heyman, Oct. 9, 1935, p. 3, ff. Progressive Education
Association, No. 391, NYF Mss.

[15]Progressive Education Association, Minutes of the Meeting
of the Board of Directors, Oct. 12, 1935, PEA Mss., TC.

also worked out--through its "Committee" and "Commission"
system--an administrative formula for sponsoring new educational
programs.

The vote to establish a "Committee on Intercultural Education"
took place at a meeting of the PEA Board of Directors on
December 7, 1935. According to Rachel DuBois, the term "intercultural Education" was coined--and first entered the professional
educator's lexicon--at the time the Committee was established.
The original name of DuBois' organization was "Service Bureau for
Education in Human Relations." The term "human relations"
had to be abandoned because it was already being used by another
PEA Commission established a few months earlier (The Commission
on Human Relations), the concern of which was the psychological
and interpersonal development of the child.[16] Emma Schweppe,
a Texas-born teacher at the experimental Lincoln School in New York
City (with whom DuBois was co-editing a book entitled, The Germans
in American Life), was appointed chairperson of the Committee. A
special committee to evaluate the past work of the Service Bureau
was also appointed under the chairmanship of W. Carson Ryan. The
formation of the Committee on Intercultural Education did not mark
the immediate demise of the old Bureau. Committees were set up

---

[16]Progressive Education Association, Minutes of the Meeting
of the Board of Directors, Dec. 7, 1935, PEA Mss., TC.; DuBois,
"Autobiography," Chapter 4, p. 26, DuBois Mss.

quite frequently by the PEA; they were considered temporary

bodies created to test the financial waters for new programming

initiatives. If the program evoked a favorable response, full-

scale commissions were set up.[17] For one year, the old Service

Bureau co-existed with the new Committee and awaited news of

the fate of the Committee. The verdict was favorable. The PEA

had succeeded in raising a modest budget of $8,000 for the new

program and at the expiration of the experimental year agreed to

upgrade the Committee to the status of "Commission on Inter-

cultural Education."[18] The new commission became the twelfth and

last commission set up by the Association during the thirties.

F. C. Borgeson of New York University was appointed Chairman

of the new Commission and Rachel Davis DuBois was made its

Director. The members of the Commission were: Ruth Benedict,

William D. Boutwell, Mabel Carney, William Cherin, Everett Clinchy,

Theresa Durlach, Alice V. Keliher, F. Tredwell Smith, Frederick

Thrasher, and Max Yergan.[19] However, even after the

---

[17]Graham, Progressive Education, p. 92; Progressive Education Association, Minutes of the Meeting of the Executive Board, Feb. 27, 1936, PEA Mss., TC.

[18]Frederick L. Redefer to William Fuerst, Jan. 8, 1937, ff. Progressive Education Association, No. 391, NYF Mss.; Progressive Education Association, Minutes of the Meeting of the Board of Directors, Jan. 10, 1937, PEA Mss., TC.

[19]Rachel Davis-DuBois, Adventures in Intercultural Education: A Manual for Secondary School Teachers (New York: Progressive Education Association, 1938), pp. a-b.

establishment of the Commission, the old Bureau did not disband

completely. One-third of the Commission members were selected

from the Bureau's Board of Directors, and the old Board did not

legally dissolve itself--a decision which DuBois was thankful

for later on.[20]

Despite auspicious beginnings and strong convictions

about the need for the new program (Executive Secretary Redefer

had declared "that there is no more important program to be

initiated during the coming decade."[21],the Commission on Inter-

cultural Education did not live up to the expectations of the PEA.

The PEA did not reap the financial harvest it had forecast for the

Commission, nor was the program of the new Commission acceptable

to influential members of the Association. During the trial year,

1935-36, the Association had drafted ambitious plans to raise

$36,400 per year for the work of the new Commission. Most of

this money, it was hoped, would be raised from the PEA's major

[20]Executive Committee of the Service Bureau for Education in
Human Relations (Mabel Carney, F. Tredwell Smith, F. C. Borgeson)
to Frederick L. Redefer, Dec. 23, 1936, PEA Mss., TC (This letter
follows minutes of the PEA Board of Directors, Jan. 10, 1937); DuBois,
"Autobiography," Chapter 4, p. 32, DuBois Mss.

[21]Frederick L. Redefer to William Fuerst, Nov. 17, 1936, ff.
Progressive Education Association, No. 391, NYF Mss.

financial supporter, the General Education Board (GEB). The

GEB was a philanthropic agency founded by John D. Rockefeller

in 1902, which for more than fifty years endeavored to improve the

quality of education in the United States, especially in the South

and in the field of medical education. During the Great Depression,

the Board, responding to burgeoning enrollments in the nation's

secondary schools, inaugurated a program of financial assistance

to state and national agencies endeavoring to make the secondary

school curriculum relevant to the needs of a rapidly changing and

less academically-oriented school population.[22] The PEA was a

major beneficiary of the new program. Between 1933 and 1941, the

Board channeled more than a million and a half dollars to the PEA,

most of the money going to Commission programs, such as the

Eight-Year Study of the Commission on the Relation of School and

College and experimentation with the educational uses of the motion

picture conducted by the Commission on Human Relations.[23]

Naturally, the PEA hoped that Mrs. DuBois' intercultural program

would have the same appeal to the GEB. It did not.

In April of 1937, Commission Chairman Borgeson met with

John Marshall, an official of the Board, and outlined the financial

needs of the Commission. Borgeson confided to Marshall that some

---

[22]General Education Board, Review and Final Report, 1902-1964
(New York, 1964), pp. 49-51.

[23]Cremin, The Transformation, p. 257.

PEA members were dubious of the separate approach favored by

DuBois and more disposed to support a topical approach, one

which would not require the separate treatment of ethnic groups in

the curriculum. Borgeson went on to suggest that a GEB grant should

be earmarked for an evaluation study of various approaches to

intercultural education.[24] The GEB did not look with favor upon

such a study, but instead preferred to entertain a proposal for

direct support. For the rest of the year, the PEA considered various

options and continued discussions with PEA officers.[25]

The misgivings which Borgeson mentioned in his interview with

Marshall were echoed elsewhere. The emanated from various sources

and took a number of different forms. The report of the Evaluation

Committee set up at the time of the formation of the Committee

on Intercultural Education--although generally favorable to the

work of the Service Bureau--did acknowledge that the DuBois approach

had been attacked "in some quarters" as a "distortion" of the American

[24]Internal Memorandum by John Marshall, Interview with
F. C. Borgeson, April 6, 1937, ff. Progressive Education Association,
Commission on Intercultural Education, 1937-38, Series 1, Subseries II,
Box 284, Records of the General Education Board, Rockefeller Archives
Center, North Tarrytown, New York (henceforth referred to as GEB
Mss.).

[25]Progressive Education Association, Commission on Intercultural Education, "Report of Work during 1937" (mimeographed),
Microfilm Reel 5, NCCJ Mss. For the full record of Commission
negotiations with the GEB, see ff. Progressive Education Association,
Commission on Intercultural Education, 1937-38, GEB Mss.

past. The author of the report, W. Carson Ryan, dismissed these charges as baseless, suggesting that there was "historical as well as social justification for [her] separate accounts of racial and minority groups in American life."[26] Similar reservations were expressed by Margaret Harrison, hired by the PEA as a consultant on potential radio adaptations of PEA curriculum materials. In her report to the organization, presented in 1937, she expressed fears that radio broadcasts based on curriculum materials used by the Commission on Intercultural Education, borrowing the DuBois philosophy of treating each ethnic group separately, would result in an "unwarranted cultivation of group pride"-- an outcome that would be undesirable from the PEA point of view.[27] The Commission had also made plans to publish a series of books, each on the history and contributions of individual ethnic groups. These were to be prepared from the research and curriculum materials gathered by DuBois and her corps of WPA research workers. Two

[26]"The Service Bureau for Intercultural Education: Report of an Evaluation Committee" (Mimeographed), March 9, 1936, pp. 4-5, ff. Progressive Education Association, Commission on Intercultural Education, Documents, 1936-1938, DuBois Mss.

[27]Margaret Harrison, The Progressive Education Association-- Its Possible Contribution to Radio Education through its Philosophy, Organization and Research (New York: Progressive Education Association, 1937), pp. 81-82.

of these books had already been published, and two additional

manuscripts were ready for publication.[28] The project, however,

was discontinued in the early part of 1938. According to DuBois,

it was Ruth Benedict's opposition that doomed the project.[29]

Benedict could not sanction a program that attempted to promote

immigrant cultural conservation. She felt that Old World "idiosyn-

cracies" were given up voluntarily by most groups and that second

and third generation students resented being singled out for special

attention in the curriculum.[30] While it was important, she wrote

later, to "keep alive our pupils' pride in their fathers' people,"

---

[28]The two published volumes were: Rachel Davis DuBois and Emma Schweppe, eds., The Jews in American Life (New York, 1935), and Rachel Davis DuBois and Emma Schweppe, eds., The Germans in American Life (New York, 1935). Manuscripts on the Negro and the British in American Life were near completion toward the end of 1937 (See "A Petition for Support of the Commission on Intercultural Education of the PEA," n.d., attached to internal memorandum by Robert J. Havighurst, Interview with Frederick L. Redefer and Carson Ryan (PEA), Dec. 3, 1937, ff. Progressive Education Association, Commission on Intercultural Education, 1937-38, Series 1, Subseries II, Box 284, GEB Mss.

[29]Rachel Davis DuBois, draft (fragment) of her "Autobiography," untitled ff., DuBois Mss. DuBois has repeated this observation in conversations with the author.

[30]Ruth Benedict, "American Melting Pot, 1942 Model," p. 21, in the yearbook of The Department of Supervisors and Directors of Instruction of the National Education Association, Americans All: Studies in Intercultural Education (Washington, D.C., 1942).

this could best be done by firmly integrating intercultural content
into existing course sylabbi. The chief thrust of an intergroup
relations prcgram, she thought, should be emphasis upon standards
of fair play and according full opportunity to members of all groups.
It was also necessary to concentrate attention upon children "on
the hill," rather than children "across the tracks."[31]

Benedict's preoccupation with children of privileged groups
is indicative of the social forces at work within the Progressive
Education Association. The Association catered to an upper
middle class clientele which counted few immigrants or children
of immigrants within its ranks.[32] Frederick Redefer, Executive
Secretary of the Association, saw this as a basic weakness of
the PEA. The seminars arranged by the Commission on Intercultural
Education at regional PEA conferences, Redefer recalled in later
years, failed to draw large crowds--even when they featured such
high-powered speakers as Louis Adamic or Alain Locke.[33] The
published proceedings of PEA annual conferences for 1936 and 1937

---

[31]Ibid., pp. 22-23.

[32]This observation was made by Frederick L. Redefer in a
letter to the author, Feb. 7, 1974.

[33]Ibid.

reveal little interest in the social class problems or special

educational needs of minorities. The interests of most members

lay elsewhere. As one of the stark realities of America during

the Depression era, ethnic diversity cried out for attention from

progressive educators, but attention was not the same as approba-

tion. For many progressives, the persistence of ethnicity was

symptomatic of a social ailment and assumed significance only

insofar as it threatened social stability and national unity.

In recent years, the progressive education movement has

been reexamined and reassessed by a group of revisionist

historians.[34] They contend that the movement had a clear class

bias and was fully consistent with the basic values of American

capitalism despite the call for "social reconstruction" that echoed

through the left wing of the movement. As part of this examination,

unknown aspects and hidden implications of the thought of John

Dewey, the revered philosopher and leader of the movement, have

been resurrected and analyzed. Charles Tesconi and Van Cleve

Morris, for example, accuse Dewey of abetting "the submission of

the individual" to the will of the majority; this deplorable consequence,

they feel, was an offshoot of "his emphasis on the scientific method,

---

[34]For a review of this literature, see: Christopher J. Lucas, "Historical Revisionism and the Retreat from Schooling," Education and Urban Society, VI (May, 1974), 355-62.

which by definition is a search for social consensus."[35]

Walter Feinberg attacks Dewey's position on race and ethnicity by drawing attention to an early episode in his career. Analyzing a confidential government report written by Dewey in 1918 (entitled "Conditions among the Poles in the United States"), Feinberg sees the philosopher who extolled "community" as deeply hostile to certain expressions of community identity among Polish-Americans. In the report, Dewey censured those Poles who resisted Americanization, expressed his displeasure with the influence of the Catholic Church over Polish-Americans, and appeared to strongly identify with the interests of American foreign policy.[36]

If the current revisionist critique is correct, when progressive educators called attention to the importance of "community," they did not have in mind the sinews of culture and tradition that bound together the ethnic communities of America. Rather they meant a

[35]Charles Tesconi and Van Cleve Morris, The Anti-Man Culture: Bureau-Technocracy and the School (Urbana, Ill., 1972), p. 152.

[36]Walter Feinberg, "Progressive Education and Social Planning," Teachers College Record, LXXIII (May, 1972), 491-95. Feinberg's findings have been vigorously challenged by Charles L. Zerby ("John Dewey and the Polish Question: A response to the Revisionist Historian," History of Education Quarterly, XV [Spring, 1975], 17-30). In this same issue, J. Christopher Eisele also comes to the defense of Dewey (See "John Dewey and the Immigrants," 67-86).

form of education "relevant" to the needs of those communities as

perceived from the outside. For one progressive teacher in a Native-

American community, that meant discarding the traditional curriculum

in order to instruct students (and parents) in the proper use of

flush toilets and in the procedure for white-washing Indian

shacks.[37] For another teacher working with the Cherokee nation,

that meant providing a new vocational education that would train

Indian children for the manual tasks that had been assigned to

them by the American economic system.[38] If indigenous culture

was mentioned at all, an important motivation was to bolster

teacher authority and maintain school discipline by lifting the morale

of the student body.[39] The community-centered school of the

Depression era, the highest expression of the progressive impulse

in education, was not identical with the community-controlled

school of the sixties; the latter attempted to extend community

control over the school; the former frequently attempted to extend

[37]Pedro T. Oralo and Associates, "An Indian School Serves its Community," Progressive Education, XV (February, 1938), 153-55.

[38]Carson V. Ryan, "Science with the Eastern Cherokee Indians," Progressive Education, XV (February, 1938), 143-46.

[39]Such a motivation can be clearly seen in a report of curriculum modifications made in a Phoenix, Arizona, school (See: Eddie Ruth Hutton, "Mexican Children Find Themselves," pp. 45-51, in National Education Association, Americans All).

school control over the community. When progressives spoke about "respect for individual differences," they did not usually mean the varying lifestyles and values of ethnic communities. If they were referring to immigrants or their children, Blacks, Indians or Chicanos, they meant scaling down levels of aspiration within minority communities to the limits imposed by the class structure of American society. If they were referring to upper middle class children, they meaning exempting these children from the regimentation and deadening environment of the public school.

Why did progressive educators devote so much attention to ethnic diversity if they were basically hostile to it? The late thirties were an anxious time in America as the sound of war drums came closer to American shores. As World War II approached, progressives retreated from the harsh social criticism that had characterized the early Depression years and became preoccupied with upholding the "democratic way of life."[40] As was the case during World War I, the prospect of war created greater awareness of the presence of minorities in our midst. Minorities called for

---

[40]This ideological transformation has been recently documented in the career of one of the leading progressive educators, George S. Counts. See: Ronald K. Goodenow and Wayne J. Urban, "George S. Counts: A Critical Appreciation." The Educational Forum, XLI (January, 1977), 167-74.

careful policy planning <u>not</u> because they were exploited by the American economic system, <u>not</u> because minority group members were torn by cultural conflict, <u>not</u> because they were losing touch with wellsprings of creativity, but because they posed a threat to national unity. In her approach to intergroup relations, Ruth Benedict sought to "lessen the psychological civil wars between ethnic groups that have weakened our nation," and to instill "a primary loyalty of the whole community to the whole community."[41] On the eve of American entrance into World War II, Frederick Redefer delivered an eloquent address to the PEA's Board of Directors in which he praised progressive education, with its strong belief in democratic living and community involvement, as the paramount educational philosophy for a nation at war. Progressive education, declared Redefer, is fully committed to "those things for which we will sacrifice our lives." Moreover, it broadens the awareness of American students; they are led to understand the interdependence of all Americans, the contributions of farmer, factory worker and craftsman, the specialization of regions, the weave of ethnic groups. By stressing the "unity of the community," progressive education, said Redefer, will make

---

[41]Ruth Benedict, "American Melting Pot, 1942 Model," p. 19, in National Education Association, <u>Americans All</u>.

"a major contribution to national defense."[42]

The program of the cultural integrationists addressed a set of problems not clearly perceived by, nor consonant with the interests of, professional educators. Problems of social growth within a multi-ethnic society, emotional conflicts arising from assimilationist pressures, mobilization of group resources to attain a more equitable distribution of wealth, and general cultural revitalization were not high on the agenda of social concerns felt by the Association. DuBois' program went too far. What progressives wanted could be gained at far less risk by opening a few doors for the advancement of minorities into white collar and professional employment, by giving minorities a greater feeling of identification with the national culture, and by preventing an outbreak of nativist hysteria. Progressives loathed base and blatant forms of racial and ethnic prejudice because they set group against group, polarizing Americans rather than uniting them. Equally repugnant to progressives was the "compensatory idealized tradition" of minority groups which Donald Young saw as the

---

[42]Frederick Redefer, Democratic Education: Suggestions for Education and National Defense by the Progressive Education Association (Washington, D.C.: American Council on Public Affairs, 1940), pp. 6, 9, 17.

obverse of Anglo-Saxon nativism.[43] Cultural pluralism, to the

extent that it was embraced by progressives, meant a _tolerance_

for diversity, not an acceptance of it. The condition of cultural

diversity during a period of continuing adjustment of immigrant

peoples to technological society was not to be deplored, but to

be understood and dealt with. DuBois, however, represented a

program that went "beyond tolerance." She called for positive

appreciation of immigrant cultural "gifts," both by newer and older

Americans, intensive study of ethnic culture by ethnics themselves

(to overcome alienation and release creative energies), and

incorporation of these gifts into the national patrimony. For those

who saw American culture as the highest embodiment of "world

civilization," such views were naive and foolhardy. DuBois and

her supporters were also treading in dangerous waters. They could

only postulate, not guarantee, that programs to expand conscious-

ness of ethnic cultures would lead to more frequent and more

creative interchanges among the peoples of America and would

build a new unity on a firmer foundation. It was entirely possible

that such a program, especially if captured by parasitical elements

within the ethnic community or foreign interests hostile to the

---

[43]Donald R. Young, Research Memorandum on Minority
Peoples in the Depression (Social Sciences Research Council,
Bulletin No. 31) (New York, 1937), p. 141.

United States, could lead to a hardening of ethnic and racial

divisions and the possible Balkanization of the United States.

By early 1938, DuBois' services were considered expendable

by leaders of the Association. Her moralizing tone probably

grated on the sensibilities of the professional educators and

social scientists who dominated the affairs of the Association.

DuBois was criticized for her deficiencies as an administrator,

and negotiations with the GEB had proved fruitless.[44] Some erst-

while supporters of the Commission on Intercultural Education

urged transfer of the entire enterprise to the jurisdiction of the

Commission on Human Relations, which had a psychological

approach to the elimination of prejudice that seemed an attractive

alternative to the intellectual approach of DuBois.[45] At a meeting

---

[44]Internal Memorandum by Robert J. Havighurst, Interview
with Frederick L. Redefer and Carson Ryan, Dec. 3, 1937, ff.
Progressive Education Association, Commission on Intercultural
Education, 1937-38, Series I, Subseries II, Box 284, GEB Mss.
Negotiations with the GEB dragged on into 1938. The final
version of the proposal submitted by the Commission, a request
for $10,000 annually for two years to pay DuBois' salary as well
as the salary of a supervisory fellow, who would be assigned the task
of integrating the work of the Commission with that of other
Commissions and Committees of the Association, was apparently
never formally acted upon and was withdrawn after DuBois' dismissal
(W. Carson Ryan Jr. to Robert J. Havighurst, Jan. 12, 1938, Flora M.
Rhind to W. Carson Ryan, Jr., Jan. 13, 1938, Internal Memorandum
by "KEO," April 28, 1938, GEB Mss.).

[45]Progressive Education Association, Minutes of Meetings of
the Board of Directors, Feb. 23, 1938, April 22, 1938, PEA Mss. TC

of the Board of Directors of the Association in April of 1938,

Commission Chairman Borgeson was "instructed to inform Mrs. DuBois

that in the process of developing a broader and more comprehensive

program on intercultural education, her services will no longer be

needed after September 1, 1938 . . . ." Borgeson was also asked

to express the Board's appreciation for "the pioneering and

splendid contributions that she has made in this field . . . ."[46]

The "broader and more comprehensive program" to which this

resolution refers never did materialize. The Commission on Inter-

cultural Education was downgraded to the status of Committee

with Borgeson staying on as Chairman; the Committee lingered on

for another two years, long enough to produce a source book on

intercultural relations edited by Alain Locke and Bernhard Stern.[47]

DuBois' effort to marry intercultural education to the progressive

education movement had failed.

---

[46]Progressive Education Association, Minutes of the Meeting of the Board of Directors, April 22, 1938, PEA Mss, TC.

[47]The book was entitled: When Peoples Meet: A Study in Race and Culture Contacts (New York: Progressive Education Association, 1942). The Committee on Intercultural Education was kept alive solely for the purpose of assisting with the preparation of this study (See: PEA, Minutes of the Meeting of the Board of Directors, May 5-7, 1940, PEA Mss., TC).

CHAPTER VI

THE BUREAU BROADCASTS TO THE NATION:

AMERICANS ALL--IMMIGRANTS ALL,

1938-1939

Although deeply hurt by her dismissal from the PEA, DuBois
was now free of the suspicious and skeptical voices that dogged
her path in the Association and soon found an opportunity to
engage in "one of the most far-reaching efforts in [the] general
field of intercultural education that [had] ever been undertaken
in this country.[1] The Federal Radio Project of the United States
Office of Education, a controversial New Deal program designed
to educate and uplift the American people by airing educational
programs on network radio stations, was considering a new series
on the contributions of immigrant groups to American development.
In July of 1938, after funds had been made available by the WPA

---

[1]This was the opinion of Elizabeth Campbell, Executive
Secretary of the International Institute of Pittsburg (Elizabeth
Campbell to Rachel Davis DuBois, Dec. 29, 1938, ff. Service
Bureau, Americans All-Immigrants All, Listener Response, Corres-
pondence and documents, 1938-39, DuBois Mss.).

for the Project, DuBois was asked to serve as consultant for the

series. The invitation came from William D. Boutwell, Director

of the Radio Project, who had been a member of the PEA's Commission

on Intercultural Education and who thus was familiar with DuBois'

experience and expertise in the field.[2] The series--given the

fortuitous title, "Americans All--Immigrants All"--consisted of

26 half hour programs that were broadcast on Sunday afternoons

from November 13, 1933, to May 7, 1939, over more than 100 CBS-

affiliated radio stations. DuBois was called upon to supervise

research activities for the programs and to take charge of the

"educational follow-up" for the series.

Educational radio was in its infancy at this time. Much

was expected from the government program, still in its experimental

stages; some foresaw a new age of civic enlightenment that would

justify a federally-owned radio station; some expected the radio

receiver to join the blackboard and eraser as standard classroom

equipment in the schools of the nation. Conservatives, on the

[2]William D. Boutwell to William A. Wheeler, Jr., May 13, 1938, William D. Boutwell to Sidney Wallach, June 27, 1938, ff. Correspondence, William D. Boutwell, January to June, 1938, Box 202, Subject File, Office of the Director, Radio Education Project, Records of the U. S. Office of Education, Record Group 12, National Archives Building, Washington, D.C. (hereinafter referred to as REP Mss.). See also: the letters of Philip L. Green to Rachel D. DuBois during the months of July and August, 1938 (especially July 29, 1938), ff. Service Bureau, Americans All-Immigrants All, Correspondence. Phillip L. Green, 1938-39, DuBois Mss.

other hand, quaked at the new program, detecting propaganda,

not enlightenment, from the Roosevelt Administration and trying

to cripple the program in Congress.[3] "Americans All," one of the

most successful educational programs (at least from the viewpoint

of audience popularity) was something of a milestone in the history

of educational radio. The series broke new ground both in production

techniques and in arrangements for widespread distribution. A

major innovation was the use of dramatization and live orchestral

music for the series; previous educational programs had been

criticized for their dry, dreary quality; "Americans All" was to be

an exception to this. The series represented "the first big-scale

application of the first principle of radio education . . . that

radio is basically a medium of entertainment, and that in order

effectively to teach by radio one must entertain as well."[4]

---

[3]Raymond B. Fosdick, Adventure in Giving: The Story of the General Education Board (New York, 1962) p. 254; Jeanette Sayre, An Analysis of the Radio Broadcasting Activities of Federal Agencies, Studies in the Control of Radio, No. 3 (June, 1941), Published by the Radio Broadcasting Research Project at the Littauer Center, Harvard University, pp. 89-90; Memorandum, William D. Boutwell to John Studebaker, May 17, 1938, William D. Boutwell to William A. Wheeler, Jr., May 18, 1938, ff. Correspondence, William D. Boutwell, January to June, 1938, Box 202, Subject File, Office of the Director, REP Mss.

[4]"Uncle Sam Schoolmaster," Radio Guide Weekly, Dec. 10, 1938, p. 1 (A re-print of this article may be found in ff. Service Bureau, Americans All-Immigrants All, Brochures, Announcements and Clippings, DuBois Mss.).

Careful plans were made to assure the high quality of program

content. Experts in the field of intercultural education, such as

Louis Adamic, Edith Terry Bremer, Everett Clinchy and Read Lewis,

were invited to serve on a panel of advisors for the series.

Committees of ethnic groups representatives were formed to review

the content of each ethnic program.[5] The series was advertised

widely both in the English and foreign language press. Twenty-five

thousand brochures advertising the series, along with letters

from Commissioner of Education John Studebaker, were sent to high

school principals across the country.[6] The series was the first

educational offering of the Radio Project to be recorded for future

sale or rental to schools and other educational institutions. A

grant from the Carnegie Foundation helped to defray the cost of

recording, at the time a very expensive and unrefined process. A

120 page handbook was prepared for distribution with the recordings,

and mimeographed copies of the scripts were made available upon

---

[5]Minutes of the Meeting of the Advisory Committee for "Americans All-Immigrants All," Sept. 28, 1938, p. 1, ff. Service Bureau, Ammericans All-Immigrants All, Memoranda and Reports, 1938-39, DuBois Mss. Minutes for the meetings of the Italian, Negro and Oriental culture group committees are in the DuBois Mss.

[6]Rachel Davis DuBois, Memorandum entitled "Summary of Washington Visit," Dec. 15, 1938, ff. Service Bureau, Americans All-Immigrants All, Washington Visits, Reports and Memoranda on, 1938-39, DuBois Mss.

request from the Office of Education.[7]

The enlistment of DuBois was a master stroke and was but
one indication of the careful preparations being made to assure
the success of the series. Few individuals had spent more time
studying the history and achievements of ethnic groups in American
society and could provide as wide a range of factual materials
with the mythic and heroic quality so conducive to dramatization.
DuBois, however, probably would not have been given a salaried
position were it not for the willingness of the American Jewish
Committee to provide supplemental funding for the proposed series.
Apparently getting wind of the series from DuBois, Sidney Wallach
of the AJC wrote the Office of Education in June of 1938, offering
to pay DuBois' salary as special consultant as well as to provide
funds for the production of "listener aids"--leaflets to be distributed
to listeners requesting additional information about particular groups.[8]

_____

[7]William D. Boutwell to Paul Kellogg, April 6, 1939, ff. Correspondence, William D. Boutwell, Jan. to June, 1939, Box 203, Subject
File, Office of the Director, REP Mss. Written by J. Morris Jones,
the handbook was entitled: Americans All . . . Immigrants All: A
handbook for Listeners (Washington, D.C.: The Federal Radio Educa-
Committee in cooperation with the United States Office of Education,
[1939]).

[8]Sidney Wallach to Chester Arthur, June 14, 1938, ff. Americans
All--Correspondence with Service Bureau for Intercultural Education,
Box 221, Records Relating to Radio Programs, 1935-1941, Office of
the Director, REP Mss.; Memorandum, William D. Boutwell to
Dr. Klinefelter, June 23, 1938, ff. Correspondence, William D. Boutwell,
Jan. to June 1938, Box 202, Subject File, Office of the Director, REP
Mss.; J. W. Studebaker to Frank N. Trager, March 28, 1939, ff. Corres-
pondence, William D. Boutwell, Jan. to June, 1939, Box 203, Subject

The financially-ailing project had little trouble accepting the offer. Most of the AJC money was channeled to the newly-resuscitated Service Bureau, which resumed operations in the fall of 1938. Approximately $12,000 was allocated to the Bureau during the 1938-39 year, a sum sufficient to hire DuBois as Director (her services were lent to the Radio Project for the duration of the series), Edward Ashley Bayne as Executive Secretary (January to June of 1938), Stanley Walker to work on educational promotion and liaison work with Washington, and Arthur Derounian to handle promotion of the series in the nationality group media.[9]

DuBois took on her new assignment after having been given assurances that her work for the Office of Education would continue after the completion of the series. A "permanent division of intercultural education" within the Office of Education would be set up with DuBois in charge. This division,taking advantage of "the tremendous stirring up of interest among millions of people, which the

---

File, Office of the Director, REP Mss.

[9]A history of AJC financial Support for the Bureau may be found in: M. Jelenko, "American Jewish Committee Relationship with the Bureau for Intercultural Education" (Mimeographed Report), March 29, 1944, ff. Service Bureau for Intercultural Education, 1944-1945, Records of the American Jewish Committee, American Jewish Committee Archives, 165 East 56th Street, New York, N.Y. 10022 (Hereinafter referred to as AJC Mss.). Official notification that the Service Bureau would lend out DuBois' services to the Office of Education was given in the following letter: Vice-Chairman (of the Service Bureau for Intercultural Education) to John Studebaker, Oct. 5, 1938, ff. Service Bureau, Americans All--Immigrants All, Correspondence, John W. Studebaker, 1938-39, DuBois Mss.

'Immigrants All' series would initiate," would carry on the work

begun by the "Americans All" series.[10]

The government's motivation in producing the series is open

to conjecture. According to Louis Gerson, the series was intended

"to avert a unity-destroying explosion of the ethnic 'dynamite.'"[11]

Whether true or not, there was an undercurrent of anxiety that the

nation's enemies would exploit ethnic divisions within American

society. As a committee of the National Education Association

pointed out, "Nazi and Fascist leaders have bragged that because

of the many different groups within our borders and of the resent-

ments which past injustices have bred, it will be easy for them

to create chaos here."[12] It seems apparent that the gathering

storm in Europe was on the minds of government officials and that

the danger was thought to be especially acute in the case of German,

Italian and Japanese Americans. The determination of government

officials to immunize against an outbreak of the anti-immigrant

hysteria that had occurred during and after World War I led to some

disagreement over the content and tone of the "Americans All"

---

[10]Philip L. Green to Rachel Davis DuBois, Aug. 26, 1938, ff.
Service Bureau, Americans All-Immigrants All, Correspondence,
Philip L. Green, 1938-39, DuBois Mss. (See also Green to DuBois,
Dec. 7, 1938, in the same ff.)

[11]Gerson, The Hyphenate, p. 132.

[12]National Education Association, Americans All, p. vi.

programs. Should the programs, as some government officials
wanted, contain explicit appeals for tolerance? Such "sermonizing"
was strenuously opposed by CBS script writer, Gilbert Seldes,
who considered such an approach both self-defeating and "dangerous."
Seldes apparently convinced project officials that his factual,
"straightforward" approach, which steered clear of appeals to
conscience, was the preferable one.[13]

Besides healing divisions at home and preventing a reoccur-
rence of the anti-immigrant hysteria that accompanied World War I,
the series may have been designed to create a favorable climate
of opinion for the admission of refugees from Europe. The refugee
question had assumed increasing importance in domestic American
politics, both with the stepped-up campaign of the Nazis against
the German Jewish community, culminating in the infamous "Night
of the Broken Glass" in November of 1938, and the crushing of the
Spanish Republic by Falangist forces under Generalissimo Franco.
American public opinion, however, seemingly deaf to the pleas
of the fallen and persecuted of Europe, refused to sanction any
relaxation of rules governing the admission of refugees, and this

[13]Gilbert Seldes to William D. Boutwell, Jan. 12, 1939;
William D. Boutwell to Gilbert Seldes, Jan. 13, 1939, ff.
Gilbert Seldes, Box 208, Subject File, Office of the Director,
REP Mss.

sentiment was reflected in Congress, where the majority stood

adamantly opposed to special legislation opening the doors to

the endangered millions of Europe.[14] Unwilling to provoke a

political storm in Congress, President Roosevelt tried to side-

step Congress by authorizing administrative reforms to aid the

refugees and by engaging in behind-the-scenes maneuvering.[15]

In April of 1938, the President set up an "Advisory Committee on

Political Refugees," composed of representatives of American

charitable and religious organizations. The ostensible purpose

of the Committee was to coordinate the activities of American

social service agencies with a proposed Intergovernmental Committee

on Political Refugees scheduled to meet for the first time in Evian,

France, on July 14, 1938.[16] James G. McDonald, Chairman of the

American Committee, was a member of the eleven - member Advisory

Committee for "Americans All." The presence of McDonald on the

---

[14]David S. Wyman, Paper Walls: America and the Refugee
Crisis, 1938-1941 (Amherst, Mass., 1968), pp. 210-211.

[15]Samuel McCrea Cavert, Memorandum on White House Conf-
erence on Refugees, n.d.,ff. Refugees, President's Advisory Commit-
tee on Political Refugees, 1938, Box FCC 103 I4, Records of the
Federal Council of Churches (now National Council of Churches),
Archives of the National Council of Churches of Christ in the U.S.A.,
Presbyterian Historical Society, 435 Lombard St., Philadelphia, Pa.

[16]Ibid.; Minutes of the meetings of the Advisory Committee
may be found in the above file folder.

Advisory Committee, as well as the timing of the series, suggests

that "Americans All" was part of the government attempt to

soften public opinion on the refugee question. This motivation is

also suggested by the involvement of the American Jewish Committee

with the series. Frank N. Trager, who oversaw AJC expenditures

in support of the series, recalled in later years that the refugee

issue weighed heavily on the minds of Committee leaders and

probably accounted for their willingness to support the series.[17]

It is, indeed, possible that the government, as well as the

Committee, may have had a number of purposes in mind in produc-

ing the series.

The Series revealed the conflict of purpose between govern-

ment planners and advocates of cultural integration like DuBois.

For the former, the celebration of diversity was intended to achieve

certain limited objectives, such as the softening of American

attitudes toward the admission of refugees and the popularization

of a cosmopolitan definition of American nationality which would

make nativism unpatriotic. For the latter, the celebration of

diversity was intended to achieve much more: lifting the spirits

and stirring up pride in ancestry among ethnic-Americans in order

to preserve ethnic cultures and accentuating the special gifts

---

[17]Frank N. Trager, taped interview with the author, New York
City, August 5, 1975.

and aptitudes of ethnic groups in order to promote their more general appropriation by the larger society. These additional objectives mandated an effort at cultural maintenance to which government planners would take exception. "Americans All" provided the occasion for the clash.

The question of separate treatment of ethnic groups again created the liveliest controversy. Should separate programs be produced for each of the major ethnic groups in American society, or should each program be devoted to a particular period in American history or to a particular field of endeavor, into which the various group contributions could be woven? The question was taken up for consideration by the Advisory Committee on September 28, 1938. According to the original prospectus for the series, twelve programs (out of twenty-six) were to be devoted to individual ethnic groups. Edith Terry Bremer of the International Institute movement expressed dismay that only one program had been assigned to the Slavic peoples and that the Greeks had not been given a separate program; she insisted that the number of group programs be increased.[18] The justice of her complaint, within the context of the original format of the series, was conceded by other members of the Committee, but

_____

[18]Minutes of the Meeting of the Advisory Committee for "Americans All-Immigrants All," Sept. 28, 1938, p. 11, ff. Service Bureau, Americans All--Immigrants All, Memoranda and Reports, 1938-39, DuBois Mss.

they were unwilling to sacrifice any of the general programs
to achieve a more equitable distribution of air time. The general
programs told the story of the mingling and integration of peoples
in America, the rise of a new civilization in America, and the
disappearance of cultural and social divisions. William Boutwell,
Director of the Radio Project, suggested a way out of the dilemma:
abandon all of the group programs, he advised, and add new
general programs on such themes as agriculture, architecture,
music and medicine.[19] The Committee engaged in a prolonged
discussion of Boutwell's suggestion, but finally decided to retain
the original format for the series. They were persuaded by DuBois'
argument that the only way to dislodge a negative stereotype was
to deliberately create a positive one, and by script writer
Gilbert Seldes' observation that a degree of separation was
inevitable even if Boutwell's suggestion were followed, since
certain groups excelled in certain fields of endeavor, such as the
Irish and Italians in highway building, and the Scandinavians in
agriculture. [20] In order to meet Mrs. Bremer's criticisms, the
committee decided to combine a few smaller groups into one program
and add a second program on the Slavic peoples.

The decision to go ahead with the group programs was a

---

[19] Ibid., pp. 13, 17.

[20] Ibid., pp. 15, 17.

161

reluctant one and based on pragmatic considerations. These

programs would make a direct assault on prejudice in America

and overcome the propaganda of bigots and hate-mongers. However,

as the committee discussion revealed, there was an obsessive

fear that the group programs would be misused for the purpose of

"glorifying" ethnicity.[21] In order to prevent such a distortion of

the purpose of the series, caution was taken in presenting the

story of each group. Instead of treating the totality of a group's

contributions, each program concentrated on a single outstanding

contribution, such as the Scandinavian "gift for cooperation," or

the German contribution to the growth of democracy in the United

States.[22] Although later modifications were made in this original

design, the basic intention was to develop appreciation for the

contributions of ethnic cultures to American culture, not appreciation

for ethnic cultures per se. Lest people miss the point, the

"interdependence" and "inter-relationships" of all groups was to

---

[21]Gilbert Seldes, "General Statement on Approach to Writing of Script for Immigrants All-Americans All," (mimeograph), n.d., p. 1, ff. Service Bureau, Americans All-Immigrants All, Memoranda and Reports, 1938-39, DuBois Mss. (This statement was prepared for, and discussed at the meeting of the Advisory Committee, Sept. 28, 1938); See also Minutes of the Meeting of the Advisory Committee, pp. 6, 11.

[22]Gilbert Seldes to William D. Boutwell, Jan. 12, 1939, ff. Gilbert Seldes, Box 208, Subject File, Office of the Director, REP Mss.

be carefully stressed: "That each group as it came was advantaged

by the work of the group which had come before; and that each

early group had advantage from the coming of later ones."[23] The

goal was to make each listener feel, as Rachel DuBois put it, that

he was "the latest link in the unending chain of a developing

American culture."[24]

DuBois threw herself into the task of research with her

characteristic energy and enthusiasm. Working very often into

the early hours of the morning, she supplied Gilbert Seldes with

a steady stream of research and curriculum materials. She received

able assistance in this undertaking from Ruth Davis, her long-

time associate, whom she succeeded in getting on the WPA payroll.

One of her major responsibilities was to form committees of ethnic

group leaders to review the content of each ethnic program. Some

of the most important ethnic leaders and intellectuals served on

these committees. This effort to guard against misstatements of

facts and distortions of content was not always successful.

---

[23]Gilbert Seldes, "General Statement on Approach to Writing
of Script for Immigrants All-Americans All," n.d., p. 1, ff.
Service Bureau, Americans All-Immigrants All, Memoranda and
Reports, 1938-39, DuBois Mss.

[24]Rachel Davis DuBois, Memorandum to Mr. Seldes,
Sept. 26, 1938, p. 2, ff. Service Bureau, Americans All-Immigrants
All, Memoranda and Reports, 1938-39, DuBois Mss.

Some Jewish leaders were greatly disturbed by the Jewish program.[25] Negro leaders were also unhappy. Roy Wilkins and George B. Murphy, Jr., of the NAACP objected to the emphasis on servile and menial labor in the Negro program; "The script reads," they wrote, "like a history of the progress of white people using the labor and talents of Negroes. It does not read like the history and progress of the Negro himself."[26] After the broadcast of the Negro program, Alain Locke and others vigorously protested against a song sung by black folk singer Jules Bledsoe ("worse than a 'mammy song'") and succeeded in persuading CBS officials to re-record the last fifteen minutes of the program, so that the wax recordings of the program would not carry the offensive song.[27] Yet the series drew less criticism from the ethnic groups, which on the whole welcomed the series, than from those who had a role in developing the series.

DuBois also encountered problems in preparing the leaflets

[25]See Chapter VII, pp.209-212.

[26]George B. Murphy, Jr., and Roy Wilkins, Memo on Script, the Negro, Dec. 9, 1938, ff. Service Bureau, Americans All, Program #6, The Negro, DuBois Mss.

[27]Alain Locke to CBS, Dec. 24, 1938, ff. Service Bureau, Americans All, Program #6, The Negro, DuBois Mss.; Phillip Cohen to William D. Boutwell, Dec. 27, 1938, ff. Cohen, Phil, Jan. 1, 1938, to Dec. 31, 1938, Box 204, Subject File, Office of the Director, REP Mss.

which were supposed to be sent out after each broadcast. When
she failed to supply "satisfactory" copy to the Office of Education,
the plan to distribute weekly leaflets was dropped.[28] It was
decided instead to prepare one over-all leaflet which would be
mailed to all listeners who had requested the weekly leaflets.
Preparation of this over-all leaflet, however, was also taken out
of her hands.[29] Part of the dissatisfaction with her handling of
this task had to do with her insistence that material be organized
according to ethnic group, rather than according to subject matter
(e.g. art, music, etc.) as favored by Project Director Boutwell.[30]
DuBois felt that the "Melting Pot" approach, presumably represented
by Boutwell's plan for the leaflet, "[had] encouraged the second

---

[28]Theresa Durlach to John Studebaker, Nov. 17, 1938,
John Studebaker to Theresa Durlach, Nov. 22, 1938, ff. Studebaker,
Sept. 1938 to Aug. 1938, Box 209; Phil Cohen to William D. Boutwell,
Nov. 17, 1938, ff. Cohen, Phil, Jan. 1, 1938 to Dec. 31, 1938,
Box 204, Subject File, Office of the Director, REP Mss; Rachel Davis
DuBois, Memorandum entitled "Summary of Washington Visit on
Dec. 15, 1938," ff. Service Bureau, Americans All-Immigrants All,
Washington Visits, Reports and Memoranda on,1938-39, DuBois Mss.

[29]John Studebaker to Frank N. Trager, March 18, 1939, ff.
Studebaker, Sept. 1938, to Aug., 1939, Box 209, Subject File,
Office of the Director, REP Mss.

[30]Rachel Davis DuBois, Memorandum entitled "Report on
Washington Interview on Leaflet," Jan. 4, 1939, ff. Service
Bureau, Americans All-Immigrants All, Washington Visits, Reports
and Memoranda on,1938-39, DuBois Mss.

generation to cut off all contact with their cultural past."[31]

Despite these serious problems, the Series turned out to be a huge popular success. Washington was literally deluged with congratulatory mail from listeners; more than 80,000 letters had been received by the end of the series. Never before had an educational program presented on CBS received so much popular acclaim.[32] "Americans All" helped to convince radio network officials that there was a market for educational programs and that they could take the initiative to produce such programs independent of government sponsorship.[33] In April of 1939, the National Radio Women's Committee conferred its annual award for distinction in radio broadcasting on "Americans All." The American Legion Auxiliary awarded the Series its yearly award the following September.[34] As co-sponsor of the Series, the Service Bureau entered the national

---

[31]Rachel Davis DuBois to William D. Boutwell, Jan. 10, 1939, ff. Service Bureau, Americans All-Immigrants All, Correspondence, William D. Boutwell, 1938-39, DuBois Mss.

[32]Memorandum Re: Conference Concerning "Americans All - Immigrants All Radio Series," Feb. 3, 1939, ff. Service Bureau, Americans All-Immigrants All, Washington Visits, Reports and Memoranda on,1938-39, DuBois Mss.; Jeanette Sayre, An Analysis of the Radio Broadcasting Activities of Federal Agencies, Studies in the Control of Radio, No. 3 (June, 1941), p. 87 (Published by the Radio Broadcasting Research Project at the Littauer Center, Harvard University).

[33]Sayre, An Analysis, p. 87.

[34]"'Immigrant' Radio Program Wins Award in Annual Women's Poll," New York Times, April 20, 1939, p. 25. CBS Student Guide, Oct., 1939 (re-print in DuBois Mss.).

limelight and was besieged with requests from all over the country

for curriculum materials and assistance in setting up school

projects in intergroup relations.

Notwithstanding this resounding reception, "Americans

All" proved something of a disappointment to government officials;

the worst fears of those who had warned against the ethnic programs

were borne out. Signs of trouble began to appear as officials

pondered the meaning of weekly fan mail tabulations. It was not

until Program No. 9, the first program (other than the Negro

program) depicting a "controversial" minority (the Irish) that the

Series began to attract widespread interest. Fan mail tabulations,

which had never exceeded 2,000 letters per week for the previous

eight programs, suddenly jumped to more than 6,000 pieces of

correspondence after the Irish broadcast, a level that was sustained

for subsequent programs on the Scandinavians, Germans, Jews

and other recent immigrant groups.[35] Project officials began to

suspect that the target audience--the WASP majority-- was not

[35]See document entitled "Mail Tabulation," Jan. 28, 1939, ff. Service Bureau, Americans All-Immigrants All, Listener Response, correspondence and reports, 1938-39, DuBois Mss.; Also see: William D. Boutwell to Gilbert Seldes, Feb. 18, 1939, ff. Gilbert Seldes, Box 208, Subject File, Office of the Director, REP Mss.

being reached and that the ethnic episodes were being listened

to primarily by the ethnics themselves.[36] This suspicion was

confirmed by a profile done of the letter-writing public. The

profile showed a disturbing number of letters came "from individuals

who show particular interest in the program dealing with their own

nationality" and that an "unanticipated" effect of the Series was

that it gave these individuals "a self-assurance and a sense of

prestige about their own nationality."[37] The pattern of events

became clearer as mail orders began to come in for copies of the

scripts. Commissioner of Education Studebaker complained to

DuBois that the Office of Education was being swamped with requests

from teachers in New York City for copies of scripts on Jewish,

Italian and Irish programs, the preponderant ethnic elements in

that city's population. At DuBois' suggestion, the Office placed a

restriction on single-copy distribution of scripts. Henceforth,

anyone interested in a script about a minority group would have to

purchase a script about a majority group--presumably this procedure

---

[36]Rachel Davis DuBois, Memorandum Re: Conference held Feb. 1, 1939, Feb. 3, 1939, p. 4, ff. Service Bureau, Americans All-Immigrants All, Listener Response, Correspondence and Reports, 1938-39, DuBois Mss.

[37]Memorandum Re: Fan Mail on Americans All (from Dorothea Seelye to William D. Boutwell), n.d., ff. Inter-Office Memos, General, Old, Box 31, Administrative Correspondence, Office of the Director, REP Mss.

would serve as a check against minority chauvinism.[38]

In the adolescent years of radio in America, the series became a classic example of how a program, depending on its thematic content and presentation, "selects," or predetermines, its own audience.[39] The ethnic group format, retained in part at the insistence of cultural integrationists like DuBois and Seldes, had attracted one audience--the ethnic minorities (many of whom were interested only in the programs about their own groups)--and alienated another--the Anglo majority. The "dissatisfaction" with the results achieved by the series led Project officials to plan a new series of programs to be called "United We Stand," which would reexamine the theme of ethnic diversity but avoid the pitfalls of "the separate approach."[40]

The static arising from the series worked to further discredit

---

[38]Rachel Davis DuBois to John Studebaker, March 22, 1939, John Studebaker to Rachel Davis DuBois, March 24, 1939, Rachel Davis DuBois to Leaders of Culture Group Organizations, March 24, 1939 ff. Service Bureau, Americans All-Immigrants All, Script Reproduction and Distribution, Correspondence, 1939, DuBois Mss.; See also list attached to letter from E. Ashley Bayne to William D. Boutwell, April 21, 1939, ff. Service Bureau, Americans All-Immigrants All, Recordings, Sale of, Correspondence and Reports, 1939, DuBois Mss.

[39]This observation is made by Paul F. Lazarsfeld, Radio and the Printed Page (New York, 1940), p. 134.

[40]Sayre, An Analysis, p. 88.

the philosophy of cultural democracy and to undermine DuBois'

position within her own organization. Her approach to intergroup

relations had been borrowed to achieve a limited objective:

namely, to favorably alter the attitudes of the majority toward

ethnic minorities and so prevent a deterioration of the intergroup

situation in the United States. But the "separate approach"

served a dual purpose for its proponents; not only did it promise

to change majority attitudes and thereby protect minorities from

the threat of repression, but also it held out hope of healing the

wounds of ethnic alienation. There is little evidence of any

interest among government officials and top echelons of the

educational bureaucracy in realizing this second objective. Given

their limited vision and scale of priorities, DuBois' critics were

probably right: if the goals were civil peace and national unity,

the separate approach was neither the safest nor the most effective

strategy. It could be misused for nationalistic purposes; the

message took longer to deliver; and it could be misconstrued to

mean that America was—— for the present and for the forseeable

future—— a nation of nations. Among her critics, no one doubted

DuBois' sincerity, her creativity, her rare energies; yet by her

seeming intransigence, her Quixotic attitude, her preoccupation

with considerations of mental hygiene, she grated on the sensibilities

of those less idealistic and less spiritually-oriented than she.

DuBois might have outfought and outlasted the skeptics

and critics if she could have continued to rely upon the support,
both moral and financial, of the ethnic communities. She had
been singularly successful in rallying the moral support of these
communities; in fact, few WASP educators had ever cultivated
such friendly relations with these communities. Her articles had
been given wide circulation in the ethnic press. Ethnic Organizations such as The Italian Teachers Association and the Kosciuzko
Foundation helped her in developing her curriculum materials.
Members of these groups volunteered their services as lecturers
and performers at her school assemblies. But financial support
was another matter. Most of the ethnic organizations were
simply unwilling or unable to provide financial assistance for
her efforts. The one organization that did have the desire and the
means to support such a program: the American Jewish Committee,
had its own reasons for hesitating to fully support such a program
and was in the midst of a major reassessment of the value of ethnic
studies.

CHAPTER VII

INTERCULTURAL EDUCATION AND THE JEWISH
SEARCH FOR SELF-DEFINITION IN
AMERICAN SOCIETY

Better than most immigrant groups, American Jews were
well-acquainted with the dilemma and dangers of minority status.
Uprooted for centuries, frequent victims of persecution in the
lands where they had lived, bearers of a culture that would not
die, American Jews were well-suited both historically and
intellectually to carefully chart their course in American society.
It is not surprising, therefore, that intercultural education was
a matter of vital concern to American Jews. By giving non-Jews
an appreciation for Jewish culture and Jewish contributions to
American society, intercultural education promised to prevent
a mass outbreak of anti-Semitism; it also promised to strengthen
the Jewish identity of the conflict-ridden second generation--a
matter of great concern to some Jews. Advocacy of intercultural
education, however, on the part of American Jews was not
tantamount to an endorsement of "ethnicity." Many Jewish leaders

bridled at the suggestion that Jews were a separate "people";
for them, Jewish studies was not to be confused with "ethnic
studies." Religion was the sole unifying force among Jews,
the only justification for Jewish exclusiveness (just as it was
the only justification for Methodist or Lutheran exclusiveness).
If other Americans misunderstood the true nature of Judaism, they
would have to be enlightened on that score.

The Nazi Threat and the Establishment
of the Service Bureau

It is hard to recreate the heavy atmosphere and capture
the sense of foreboding that were felt by American Jews during
the early thirties. News dispatches from Germany brought endless
tales of horror that chipped away at the security and shook the
complacency of American Jewry. The anti-Semitism that had
surfaced so menacingly in America during the twenties was too
fresh in the mind, and the frustrations of the Great Depression too
real and too intense, to feel safe from the fury of a home-grown
pogrom. If conditions in America failed to spontaneously spawn
such a disaster, Hitler's agents were active in America stirring
up anti-Semitic hatreds. Morris Lazaron, a rabbi who travelled
extensively for the National Conference of Christians and Jews
voiced the anxiety of many Jews when he wrote in 1938 that

". . . anti-Semitism was real and, led by the Nazis, reached out into every corner of the world to destroy the Jew."[1] Evidence was not lacking of the effectiveness of this sinister campaign. Anti-Semitic organizations multiplied in America during the decade to the point where by 1939, AJC estimated that there were five hundred such groups in operation.[2] Mass-circulation newspapers such as The Daily News in New York City spread nasty innuendos about Jewish radicalism and influence on public life.[3] Father Coughlin whipped up feelings against the Jews by his intemperate and vituperative remarks on his weekly syndicated radio program. Even in 1938-39, when thousands of Jewish refugees from Nazi tyranny begged for admission to America, few Americans were willing to relax entry restrictions, as polls taken at the time showed. As James Wyman wrote, anti-Semitism was "hanging heavy in the

---

[1]Morris S. Lazaron, Common Ground: A Plea for Intelligent Americanism (New York, 1938), p. 40.

[2]Naomi W. Cohen, Not Free to Desist: The American Jewish Committee (Philadelphia: The Jewish Publication Society of America, 1972), p. 205.

[3]As an example, see The New York Daily News, Dec. 15, 1938, pp. 1-5. In 1945, the Brooklyn division of the American Jewish Congress condemned the Daily News for printing "innumerous articles and editorials which tend to inflame and incite to acts of anti-Semitism and bigotry . . . ." The resolution adopted by the Congress, as well as other documents pertaining to the alleged anti-Semitic bent of the newspaper, may be found in ff. Racial Discrimination, October - December, 1945, Box 809, Fiorello H. LaGuardia Papers, Municipal Archives, New York City.

atmosphere of the period."[4]

The sudden rise to power of Hitler in 1933 had sent tremors

throughout the American Jewish community. Within six months

of his accession to power, a series of laws were passed by the

Reichstag that spelled the doom of the German Jewish community.

Jews were forced to retire from the civil service; they were barred

from the professions; the admission of Jews to the universities

was severely restricted, and "non-Aryans" were denied the right

to own land within the Third Reich.[5] The implications of this

campaign were not lost on the leaders of American Jewry. As

Harry Schneiderman wrote in the American Jewish Year Book for

1933: "The world-shaking catastrophe which has befallen the

Jews of Germany during the past five months is of such momentous

significance to Jews everywhere, that all other events affecting

[4]Wyman, Paper Walls, pp. 210-11; the evolution of Father Coughlin into an anti-Semite is discussed in: Richard Akin Davis, "Radio Priest: The Public Career of Father Charles Edward Coughlin" (Unpublished Ph.D. Dissertation, History Department, University of North Carolina, 1974), pp. 268-75.

[5]Lucy Dawidowicz, The War Against the Jews (New York, 1975), p. 63.

our people appear to be of comparatively slight importance."[6] Most

American Jews agreed that prompt and concerted action was

necessary to assist their brethren in Germany and to keep the cancer

from spreading to America, but they disagreed over methods to

achieve these objectives. Some like Rabbi Stephen S. Wise of

the American Jewish Congress advocated mass demonstrations and

unequivocal denunciations of the Nazi regime. In March of 1934,

he held a mass rally at Madison Square Garden attended by 22,000

people to protest the treatment of German Jewry. More cautious

Jewish leaders, especially those associated with the American

Jewish Committee and B'nai B'rith shuddered at such tactics,

fearing that they would only play into the hands of the Nazis

and further undermine the position of the German Jewish community.[7]

As pogroms of the past had waxed and waned, so would this crisis

eventually subside. Yet, these leaders realized that there was

something unprecedented about the Nazi attack on the Jews. Never

before had the engines of a modern, totalitarian state been greased

by race hatred. Never before had all the artifices of Nazi pseudo-

science been employed to rationalize such oppression. Never before

had an effort been made to export such hatreds on a world-wide

---

[6]Jewish Publication Society of America, The American Jewish Year Book, Vol. 35 (Philadelphia, 1933), p. 21.

[7]Ibid., pp. 54-55; Milvin Urofsky, American Zionism from Herzl to the Holocaust (Garden City, 1975), pp. 390-92.

basis. Clearly, something had to be done, whether quiet diplo-
matic work, aid to refugees, counter-propaganda, surveillance
of Nazi agents in America, or, as many thought most desirable,
a massive effort at public education.

The Committee's interest in the Bureau and its program
was evidence of a major change of policy on the part of the
Committee. Since its inception in 1906, the Committee had
operated according to the premise that a mass outbreak of anti-
Semitism in the United States was a virtual impossibility; accordingly, the Committee had confined itself to aiding Jewish
communities overseas and to protesting against anti-Semitic discrimination at American hotels and universities. The events of 1933
led to a major reassessment of policy.[8] America could no longer
be considered a sanctuary for world Jewry; the American people
could no longer be considered immune to the virus of religious
prejudice. Thus, the Committee launched a domestic program in
1933. A special unit called the Information and Service Associates
under the direction of Attorney Wolfgang Schwabacher was created to
keep tabs on anti-Semitic agents and organizations in the United
States. This unit was renamed the Survey Committee in 1936 and
stayed in existence as a semi-autonomous entity until 1941. The
Committee was comprised of prominent laypersons within the Jewish

---

[8]Cohen, Not Free, pp. 194-95.

community, some of whom were not even members of the American

Jewish Committee. The Survey Committee had the power to raise

and disburse its own funds, and had by the end of the decade

amassed an annual budget of close to one million dollars.[9]

Undercover work was only a small part of the Survey Committee's

work. Although the Committee continued for the rest of the decade

to aid and abet federal authorities in monitoring the activities

of potentially traitorous elements, the Committee realized from

the start that the Nazi threat could only be undercut by a long-

range educational program. Under the leadership of Sidney Wallach,

the AJC staff person assigned to direct the Survey Committee's

operations in 1933, the Survey Committee therefore undertook to

render all possible assistance, including direct financial support,

to outside organizations that were helping to counteract anti-

Semitic propaganda or that were upholding democratic principles.

Among organizations helped by the Committee were the National

Conference of Christians and Jews, the Foreign Language Informa-

tion Service, the National Council of Churches, and the Service

---

[9]Ibid., pp. 196-97, 207; Sidney Wallach, interview with the author, August 8, 1975 (tape recording on deposit at IHRC, University of Minnesota); Morris Waldman, Memorandum to Staff, May 19, 1941, ff. Survey Committee, Scope and Function, 1940-41, Papers of Morris D. Waldman, Archives of the American Jewish Committee, 165 East 56th Street, New York, N.Y. 10022 (hereinafter referred to as MDW Mss.).

Bureau for Intercultural Education.[10]

The Committee's enchantment with DuBois and her colleagues was not long-lived. Although there was much to admire in her steadfast commitment to the cause of intergroup understanding, although she had devoted years of her life to developing and refining her methods, although she appeared on the scene at a time when the Jewish community was in desperate need of outside allies, DuBois held a conception of Judaism and took an approach to intergroup education with which the AJC could not concur. It took time, however, for the AJC to withdraw its support for DuBois. The Committee, after all, was not of one mind on these controversial questions, and although certain points of view did tend to predominate in the end, the Committee was moving into uncharted territory, groping toward a more sophisticated knowledge of the anti-Semitic mind and how to deal with it. The basic disagreement between the AJC and DuBois was whether Judaism was to be considered a creed only, as most members of the Committee believed, or both a creed and a nationality, as DuBois believed. DuBois had become

---

[10]Cohen, Not Free, p. 199; American Jewish Committee, Minutes of Meetings of the Executive Committee, Vols. 5 to 7 (1923-1943), see entries under "Foreign Language Information Service" and "NCCJ" in index for these volumes, Records of the American Jewish Committee, Archives of the American Jewish Committee, 165 East 56th Street, New York, N.Y. 10022 (hereinafter referred to as AJC Mss.); Frank N. Trager, Report to Heads of Staff Conference (American Jewish Committee), May 12, 1943, pp. 10-11 (copy given to the author by Frank N. Trager).

embroiled in a long-standing controversy within the Jewish
community. By viewing the Jewish group, whether in the assembly
programs or in the curriculum units, in the context of other
nationality groups, she expressed her conviction that peoplehood
was the distinguishing feature of Judaism. DuBois' position on
this issue was not happenstance or a matter of intuition. She
had been deeply impressed with the arguments of a group of Jewish
thinkers known as the Reconstructionists who were attracting many
Jewish adherents with their call for a reinterpretation of Judaism.

The Wedge of Reconstructionism

The Reconstructionist movement appealed to those Jews
concerned to reconcile their socio-religious heritage with the
spirit of modern science and the changing contours of the modern
world. Reconstructionism was an attempt to redefine Judaism as
a collection of customs, traditions, and religious impulses
associated with a particular people--not as a set of unchanging
dogmas and rigid rules for living. The founder of Reconstructionism,
Mordecai Kaplan, was director of the Teachers Institute and
Professor of Homiletics at the Jewish Theological Seminary of
America in New York. Kaplan underwent a "Copernican Revolution"
in his thinking about Judaism when he realized that " . . . the
Jewish religion existed for the Jewish people and not the Jewish

people for the Jewish religion. "[11] The Jewish religion, Kaplan

felt, was an expression of the values, traditions, and experiences

of the Jewish people, and was bound to evolve and take on new

forms as the Jewish people broadened their experience of the

modern world and exposed themselves to the currents of modern

thought. Kaplan did not employ his evolutionary view of religion

and his belief in the primacy of Jewish "civilization" over Jewish

religion to tear down the elaborate edifice of Jewish ritual and

belief. Rather he thought that the orthodox view of Jewish ritual

as supernatural ordinance, unchanged over the generations,

obscured the rational basis for such ritual, and lowered any

incentive to modernize ritual to make it more meaningful to modern

man. Jewish dietary rules, for example, should be considered

"folkways," not divine edicts; they show the distance man has

travelled from the savage state of existence, the spirituality and

self-restraint men are capable of exercising in the act of eating.

Occasional lapses from strict observance, especially when Jews

were invited to dine in Gentile homes, should not be considered

serious sins, but normal adaptations to other styles of living that

need not be followed in one's own home. The same was true for

---

[11]Mordecai M. Kaplan, Judaism as a Civilization: Toward a
Reconstruction of American-Jewish Life (New York, 1934), p. xii.
This book was the first and most complete exposition of the
principles of Reconstructionism.

Jewish Sabbath observance and festivals which should be
strengthened and deepened in significance by being interpreted
in a rational and functional manner.[12]

While Reconstructionists called for full participation of
Jews in modern life and maximum intercourse with other Americans,
they also advocated unceasing efforts to instill in young Jews a
respect for Jewish history, values and tradition. Kaplan and his
followers were concerned about the drift of young Jews away from
Judaism. "How widespread is the disease of self-hate among
American Jews," observed Kaplan, and how damaging, he thought,
to the psychological health and social adjustment of the younger
generation.[13] Rabbi Milton Steinberg of the Park Avenue Synagogue
in New York, an influential member of the Kaplan group, was
especially worried about the problem of alienation. In a series of
books and articles, he warned that "many an American Jew is in
grave peril of losing his sense of worth, his self-respect, his
dignity in his own eyes."[14] Steinberg urged Jewish Center

---

[12]Ibid., pp. 441, 444, 431-59, passim.

[13]Ibid., p. 4.

[14]Milton Steinberg, "To Be or Not To Be A Jew" Common
Ground, I (Spring, 1941), 44.

officials to assume the responsibility of teaching the Jewish heritage to the younger generation.[15] Reconstructionists like Israel Chipkin took the lead in petitioning for the teaching of Hebrew in the New York City public schools.[16] Reconstructionists also gave strong support to DuBois as she sought for ways to ease the burden of minority status through a program of ethnic studies in the public schools.

The impact of Reconstructionism on American Jewry was made less as an organized movement (Kaplan disagreed with those who wanted Reconstructionism to become a fourth branch of Judaism) and more as a popular ferment of ideas.[17] Unlike other movements within Judaism, which had their origins in European societies, Reconstructionism was a wholly indigenous, American phenomenon, a movement which the historian Charles Liebman associated with the second generation of Jews in America.[18] Indeed, Kaplan saw his program of reconstruction as one "calculated to win and hold the youth," and his ability to turn out ardent disciples at

---

[15]Milton Steinberg, "The Jewish Center and Social Change," The Jewish Center, XIV (September, 1936), 15-16.

[16]Kaplan, Judaism, pp. 551-53.

[17]Charles S. Liebman, "Reconstructionism in American Jewish Life," in American Jewish Yearbook: 1970 (New York and Philadelphia: The American Jewish Committee and the Jewish Publication Society of America, 1970), 3-99.

[18]Ibid., p. 4.

the Teachers Institute, most of whom were second generation

Jews, confirmed his estimation of the movement's appeal.[19]

Reconstructionists called for the indefinite retention of Jewish

distinctiveness and Jewish identity, but at the same time urged

Jews to further the process of creative interaction with other people.

Judaism would thrive and provide satisfaction to its members as

it divested itself of outmoded practices, emerged out of the self-

segregation of previous ages, and made its message more relevant

to modern man. Speaking of the changes which Judaism would

have to undergo in order to achieve these goals, Kaplan wrote:

> The individuality of Judaism is maintained so long as the
> newly instituted custom, sanction, idea or ideals helps to
> keep alive the element of otherness in the Jewish civilization.
> Not separatism must henceforth be the principle of living as
> a Jew, but otherness. Separatism is the antithesis of cooperation,
> and results in an ingrown and clannish remoteness which leads
> to cultural and spiritual stagnation. Otherness thrives best
> when accompanied by active cooperation and interaction with
> neighboring cultures and civilizations, and achieves an individual-
> ity which is of universal significance.[20]

This kind of openness to change within the stream of centuries-

old tradition. may have been more characteristic of the children of the

immigrants than the steretypic ambivalence ascribed to them by

many social scientists.

---

[19]Kaplan, _Judaism,_ pp. ix, xii.

[20]_Ibid._, p. 515.

The early Bureau bore the clear imprint of the Reconstructionist movement. DuBois' reading of Kaplan had "opened [her] eyes" to the psychological importance of the philosophy she had already embraced. Seeing in him a kindred spirit, she sought out Kaplan's advice in developing her school programs.[21] Many of DuBois' co-workers were followers of Kaplan. Miriam Ephraim, the first field worker for the Bureau, was an ardent Reconstructionist who had been educated by Kaplan at the Teachers Institute.[22] Rabbi James Weinstein, whom Ephraim called upon to speak to students at her Jewish assemblies, also espoused the Reconstructionist cause.[23] Reconstructionist Dvora Lapson, a leading expert on Jewish dance in America, volunteered her services to organize performances of Jewish dances at DuBois' school assemblies. Rabbi Milton Steinberg, whose radiant personality and driving concern for the fate of young American Jews made him one of the most respected Jewish leaders of his generation, was a life-long supporter

---

[21]Rachel Davis DuBois to Mordecai Kaplan, June 12, 1961, ff. Letters re Work, 1959, DuBois Mss.

[22]Miriam Ephraim, interview with the author, August 18, 1975 (tape recording on deposit at IHRC, University of Minnesota).

[23]Weinstein may have been instrumental in obtaining the original grant from the AJC. He was on the staff of the AJC for a brief period in the early thirties and was given responsibility for overseeing the expenditure of the grant to the Service Bureau.

of DuBois, a friend, counsellor and financial contributor to her cause, and a frequent guest speaker in her in-service courses for teachers.[24] Rabbi Ira Eisenstein, who succeeded Kaplan as Director of the Society for the Advancement of Judaism, the organized voice of the Reconstructionist movement, served as Board chairman of DuBois' Workshop for Cultural Democracy (the organization that DuBois set up after her withdrawal from the Service Bureau in 1941). In the words of Miriam Ephraim, DuBois "represented what we [the Reconstructionists] stood for."[25]

DuBois' ideological kinship with the Reconstructionists served to strain her relationship with her sponsors on the Committee. At that time most members of the American Jewish Committee were third or fourth generation Jews of German Jewish origin whose ideas "reflected the deep inroads of assimilation, as well as the widespread American antipathy to organizations smacking of ethnic separatism."[26] Their ancestors had been given full rights of citizenship in the nation-states of Western Europe, and these leaders had fallen heirs to a tradition that saw Judaism strictly as a religious affiliation which did not preclude full political participation in, and

[24]Rachel Davis DuBois, Personal Log (loose entries), Nov. 1941.

[25]Ephraim, interview with the author, August 18, 1975.

[26]Cohen, Not Free, p. 193.

complete cultural integration with, the larger society. Although

there were some members of the Committee less committed to the

religious view than others, the predominant sentiment, and the

one common to the most influential members of the Committee,

was the soundness of the sectarian view of Judaism.[27] If not

fully convinced of the validity of the sectarian view, Committee

members were conscious of its image-making value. The climate

of the times was not supportive of cultural pluralism; even self-

professed friends of the Jews were critical of the alleged clannish-

ness and superiority complex of Jews. Writing in The American

Hebrew in 1932, George Bernard Shaw implored Jews "to stop being

Jews and start being human beings . . . ." H. G. Wells

thought that Jews were too conscious of their "race"and urged them

to "forget they are Jews and remember that they are men."[28]

---

[27]In an interview with the author, Sidney Wallach referred to
a "shuffling back and forth" on the issue of Jewish ethnicity and
the existence of a "spectrum" of opinion on the question, but he
added that "theoretically . . . the American Jewish Committee
could not condone identifying Jews . . . with a particular culture
which was other than religious culture." (Wallach, interview,
August 8, 1975).

[28]Excerpts from Shaw's article were quoted in a letter from
Louis Rittenberg to Newton D. Baker, Oct. 7, 1932, Reel 1,
NCCJ Mss.; Mrs. Franklin D. Roosevelt, "Mrs. Roosevelt Answers
Mr. Wells on the Future of the Jews," Liberty, Dec. 31, 1938, 5.

The editors of _Fortune Magazine_ wrote: "The quality which makes

them [the Jews] the scapegoats of western history is . . . their

devotion to their cultural tradition under conditions of almost

impossible hardship and the psychological traits which that

devotion has established . . . . All other immigrant peoples accept

the culture of the country into which they come . . . . "[29]

Composed of successful and well-integrated Jews who circulated

freely in Gentile society, the Committee was, perhaps, more aware

of the suspicions and more sensitive to the feelings of other

Americans than other Jewish groups--and more eager to find ways

to make Judaism palatable and inoffensive to the American public.

Capitalizing on America's constitutional guarantee of freedom of

religion and the wide degree of tolerance afforded non-conformist

religious denominations in American society, Committee leaders

tried to convince the American public that credal loyalty was the

sole component of Jewish identity in American society.

---

[29]The Editors of Fortune, _Jews in America_ (pamphlet), n.d.,
p. 5, found in ff. Jews and Judaism before 1939, NCCJ Mss.

Cementing "America's Religious Triangle:"
The AJC and the National Conference
of Christians and Jews

A major role in drafting and implementing the sectarian

strategy was assigned to the National Conference of Christians

and Jews, an organization whose early history is closely intertwined

with that of the Service Bureau. Since the National Conference

operated as the principal ally of AJC in its campaign to win

acceptance for the sectarian view of Judaism and since it aided

as well as circumscribed the growth of the Service Bureau, a brief

consideration of its history may help to clarify an emerging alterna-

tive to the Bureau's philosophy of Jewish peoplehood. Today one

of the largest and most far-flung "good-will" organizations in the

country, NCCJ for many years operated on a shoestring budget and

experienced growing pains that--were it not for the juncture of

circumstance and brilliant leadership--might have doomed the

organization in its infancy. Less by design and more by trial and

error, the National Conference developed a winning combination of

ideology, internal strength, external support and popular programming

that would eventually catapult it to the forefront of the intercultural

education movement. Although the Conference had "several roots,"

including the Rockefeller-funded "Inquiry" movement, the organiza-

tion was an offshoot of the Federal (now National) Council of

Churches. At the Council's Annual convention in 1924, a "Committee on Good Will between Jews and Christians" was established whose mission was to find ways to combat the anti-Semitic menace as posed by the Ku Klux Klan. With contributions from a number of sources, including $6,000 from B'nai B'rith, the Committee embarked on a program of public education under the direction of John W. Herring.. Similarly-named committees were set up by the Central Conference of American Rabbis and other Jewish organizations to map strategy together with the Protestant group.[30] The National Council Committee soon sailed into a storm of controversy between its Jewish constituents and the Protestant fundamentalist wing of the Federal Council, the latter unwilling to abandon the goal of converting Jews to the banner of Christ. Unable to reconcile the differences between the disputing parties, the Federal Council decided to experiment with an organization less tied to official Protestant sponsorship, and in 1926 a rather amorphous, semi-autonomous organization was created called "The National Conference of Jews and Christians" (this order was not changed until 1938).[31] John Herring, a Congregational minister from Indiana, and

---

[30]James E. Pitt, Adventures in Brotherhood (New York, 1955), pp. 13, 26-27; Samuel McCrea Cavert, Church Cooperation and Unity in America: 1900-1970 (New York, 1970), p.284.

[31]Pitt, Adventures, pp. 15-16; Dr. Israel Goldstein to Everett R. Clinchy, Sept. 10, 1952, ff. NCCJ History, Comments on Early days, NCCJ Mss.

Roger W. Strauss, Jewish industrialist and son of Oscar S. Strauss,
were appointed Associate Chairmen of the new organization and
were prototypes of the religious co-chairmen who later would be
selected from the three major religions to oversee the operations
of the organization. The absence of a Catholic co-chairman
until 1930 was indicative of the minor role played by Catholics
in the formation of NCCJ, and portended the "grudging and
qualified support" given to the Conference by the Catholic hierarchy
during the Depression years.[32]

Among the first activities of the new organization was a
membership campaign which netted a first year budget of approximately $10,000 and a search for a director of the fledgling organiza-
tion.[33] The nod for director fell upon Dr. Everett Ross Clinchy, a
youthful and dynamic Presbyterian minister, who--during the period
1923 to 1928--had made a reputation for himself as minister of
the College Church at Wesleyan University and Secretary of the
Wesleyan Christian Association. A man of heterodox religious belief,
Clinchy had organized a number of popular campus programs including intercollegiate forums on controversial public issues to which

---

[32]The quoted phrase is from a confidential memorandum written
by Louis Minsky to Everett R. Clinchy entitled "Subject: Catholic
Support of the NCCJ," n.d. (c1941), Reel 7, NCCJ Mss.

[33]Pitt, Adventures, pp. 24-25.

nationally-known public figures were invited to speak. By stimulating conversations among individuals from a variety of political, religious and philosophic persuasions, including priests, rabbis, and non-believers, Clinchy acquired a fund of experience in the field of intergroup relations and showed himself to be a man open to the winds of conflicting opinion and belief.[34] He took over the directorship of the Conference in the spring of 1928.

During the next three years, with Clinchy at the helm, hundreds of conferences and round tables were held in cities and towns across the United States under NCCJ auspices. Clinchy considered these meetings "a new procedure in human history"; for the first time, the relations between the "three vital cultural groups" in American society were being consciously regulated, and not left to accident or chance.[35] The meetings were not intended to be arenas for theological debate; in fact, such disputation was discouraged. Rather they were seen as forums for the clarification and interpretation of theological or moral positions, and for consideration of ways people of different religious convictions could

---

[34]Everett R. Clinchy, interview with the author, Dec. 10, 1973; Pitt, Adventures, pp. 17-18.

[35]National Conference of Christians and Jews, Report for the Year 1932, rough draft, ff. W2 Annual Reports, 1928-1939, NCCJ Mss.

join together in common pursuits.

In 1933, NCCJ developed its "trialogue" approach to intergroup amity. Clinchy recruited "trios" of minister, priest and rabbi to barnstorm the country for brotherhood. Trio appearances in local communities were used as occasions to organize local committees of support, many of which later grew into local chapters of NCCJ. As a result of the first tour, thirty-five local commities were set up in cities across the country.[36] Appearing before large audiences, each member of the "tolerance trio" took turns asking and answering questions of other members. The trios had something of a theatrical quality to them (one trio member described them as "religious minstrel shows"); the entire exchange was largely prerehearsed even to the jokes that lightened the solemnity of the proceedings.[37] The trio technique was so successful that it was employed on a much more extensive basis in the years ahead. In 1936, twenty-five different trio teams covered 38,000 miles on their tours across the country. During World War II, trios played before some 7,000,000 members of the armed forces of the United States in what was billed as the "Camp Show of

---

[36]Pitt, Adventures, p. 52 (See this book for a narrative account of the first "pilgrimage tour," pp. 40-62).

[37]National Conference of Christians and Jews, Williamstown Institute of Human Relations, Stenographic Proceedings, Aug. 25-30, 1935, p. 129 (A copy of the proceedings is on file at the library of the American Jewish Committee).

Brotherhood."[38] The trios popularized a conception of religious

pluralism that was daring and controversial for their time. Many

Americans were not accustomed to thinking of religion as "hues

in a rainbow in the sky." Those who shared one's religious

belief were numbered among the elect, those who did not were

mired in heresy, or destined for damnation. The trios brought

together individuals who had never before been seen together in

public. Their association together at these meetings bore a hidden

message: that each of the three religious groups was an integral

part of the American social landscape, and that a Protestant concep-

tion of American nationality was erroneous, antiquated and illiberal.

At the same time that trio meetings broadened the concept of

American nationality, they also set limits upon it. Those differences

granted recognition (and deemed legitimate) were religious in nature--

not ethnic; those religions given a special standing were the three

"major" religions: Catholicism, Judaism and Protestantism--not

other great faiths, such as Eastern Orthodoxy, Islam, Buddhism, or

Hinduism.

The mission of NCCJ was formidable and pioneering; it had to

neutralize the forces of anti-Semitism in American society and, at

the same time, legitimate the permanent religious heterogeneity of

American society. However, in order to attain these praiseworthy

---

[38]Pitt, _Adventures_, p. 53.

objectives, NCCJ had to disregard, and at times totally distort,

the realities of American society. While others were associating

the word "culture" with the values and life-styles of nationality

groups in American society, NCCJ leaders and supporters applied

the word to "the three cultures,"[39] or the three organized religions,

which they saw dominating the American social scene. Their

pluralism was neither safe nor fashionable in the early days,

but they settled for something far less than the "cultural," i.e.

ethnic democracy of contemporaries like Adamic, DuBois, etc.

In place of an instrumental cultural pluralism designed to transform

American culture--they promoted a less comprehensive, religiously-

based pluralism that had as its goal a permanent, "tri-cultural

country."[40] The name of the organization was evidence of the

ambitiousness of this goal. Against repeated attempts to change

the name of the organization, made mostly by Jews who cringed

at the prominence of their group in the name, Everett Clinchy

argued:

> By associating Christians and Jews time after time in the use
> of the name of this Conference, we are gradually linking
> these two groups together in the minds of the people so that

[39]The title given to a special issue of The Christian Century,
LIII (January 22, 1936) prepared by NCCJ.

[40]The phrase was used in a 1937 publication of NCCJ.

eventually we will take it for granted in the United States that Christians and Jews are together, work together and will always stand together.[41]

In retrospect, the organization was timid in the application of its humanitarian principles and too willing to forego rigorous analysis of American social conditions as they affected intergroup relations. The reluctance of the organization to speak out against the oppression of American blacks--although characteristic of the times--told an important tale.[42]

NCCJ's religious formula for the future of America was challenged repeatedly in the early days; from within the ranks of the organization came disturbing questions. In 1932, Newton D. Baker, Protestant Co-chairman of NCCJ, got into a lively disputation with Carlton Hayes, the Columbia University historian who had been appointed the first Catholic Co-chairman of the organization. Baker had argued that both "racial" and religious elements were responsible for prejudice, and that for NCCJ to disregard the ethnic question would be a major omission in programming.[43] While

---

[41]Everett R. Clinchy to Hastings Harrison, Dec. 8, 1939, Reel 8, NCCJ Mss.

[42]NCCJ's reluctance to broaden its role as a group defense agency was the subject of the "first and only major internal struggle" in the organization's history (See Pitt, Adventures, pp. 142-54).

[43]Ibid., p. 36.

conceding that Baker's point might be valid with regard to Jews,
Hayes rejected its application to Catholics: " . . . basically,"
he wrote, "the prejudice in the United States against Catholics
is an outcome of ignorance and dislike of the Catholic religion . . . ."
A convert to Catholicism and an authority on modern nationalist
movements, Hayes nevertheless seconded Baker's call for an
investigation to determine whether "the religious element really
is the most fundamental one."[44] Baker's insight into the complex
social forces at work in American society did not imply an endorsement of cultural pluralism: quite the contrary was true. Baker
felt that ethnic diversity, although a basic condition of American
society, was deplorable and dangerous. Those groups that choose
to remain separate and distinct, he felt, must be prepared to suffer
the consequences of their choice. In the case of the Jews, he
believed that a measure of responsibility for the hostile attitudes
of Christians rested on Jewish shoulders. Jews had resisted intermarriage with Gentiles, they had clung to traditional ways, they had
refused to abandon their "romantic" pretensions to the status of
nationality. In blunt language, he declared:

> If they [the Jews] elect to be different in purely doctrinal
> ways about their religion, they are not likely to be much more
> annoying than Christian Scientists or United Brethren, but if

[44]Carlton J. Hayes to Everett R. Clinchy, April 6, 1932,
Reel 1, NCCJ Mss.

they allow the differences which they elect to preserve to
be sufficiently irritating to their neighbors, the consequences
will follow whether they are just or not.[45]

Baker's differences with the leadership of NCCJ were in the realm

of social analysis not ideology. The desire to build a confedera-

tion of organized religions, he seemed to be saying, had distorted

NCCJ's perceptions of the patchwork quality of present-day ethnic

and religious divisions.

Baker's criticisms were expanded upon by others during the

thirties. An NCCJ leader from Memphis, John C. Petrie, questioned

the theory that anti-Semitism was the consequence of Christian

contempt for the Jewish religion. In his view, such local conditions

as the class mobility of Jews in a particular community, their

occupational profile, and their degree of internal cohesion were

the real determinants of anti-Semitic behavior.[46] A Catholic

priest from New Haven, T. Lawrason Riggs, who had represented

the Catholic point of view on the early trio tours, cautioned Clinchy

not to refer to Catholicism as a culture and not to minimize the

importance of "racial and social divisions among Catholics." I

should say," Riggs wrote, "that Catholicism was not so much a

---

[45]Newton Baker to Everett R. Clinchy, March 29, 1933, Reel 1,
NCCJ Mss. For additional insight into Baker's point of view, see
Newton D. Baker to Everett R. Clinchy, July 12, 1933, ff. Newton D.
Baker, 1932-33, NCCJ Mss.

[46]John C. Petrie to Roger W. Strauss, September 29, 1935,
Reel 2, NCCJ Mss.

culture as a religion capable of inspiring and coordinating varied

cultures . . . ."[47] An NCCJ leader from Milwaukee argued that

anti-religious feelings had all but disappeared and that the real

challenge was to rise to the defense of persecuted ethnic minor-

ities.[48] These questionings may have been symptomatic of a

strong current of discontent within the agency; an outside investi-

gator who conducted an evaluation of the organization in 1942

reported that the "central question" faced by the Conference was:

> whether the Conference is essentially an organization of
> religious faiths dedicated to working primarily through religious
> channels for the attainment of ends which most certainly are
> the essence of religious life; or, on the other hand, a movement
> which regards itself as "cultural," with religion as one aspect,
> and which seeks to enlist the cooperation of all possible groups,
> whether clerical or lay, whether religious or secular.[49]

---

[47]T. Lawrason Riggs to Everett R. Clinchy, Sept. 19, 1934, Reel 1, NCCJ Mss.

[48]Member of the Milwaukee Round Table (unidentified) to Everett R. Clinchy, Jan. 6, 1942, Reel 9, NCCJ Mss.

[49]"National Conference of Christians and Jews," ff. Evaluation Study, 1942, NCCJ Mss. In an evaluation study made three years earlier, Clyde R. Miller had written: "It is my conviction that it is not possible to deal effectively with differences in the religious field alone. Many of our present conflicts with which highly emotionalized and dangerous propagandas are associated are in social, political and economic fields" (Clyde R. Miller, "A Report to the Director on Public Relations and Education," p. 3, ff. Evaluation Study, 1942, NCCJ Mss.).

There is little evidence to suggest that NCCJ ever deviated significantly from its initial bias in favor or organized religion, a bias which led the organization to take a myopic view of the inter-group realities of American life.

The history of NCCJ seems to suggest that "the triple melting pot"--that tool of social analysis employed and popularized by Will Herberg - was not the outcome of some inevitable social chemistry.[50] By NCCJ's avoidance of the ethnic question and by its dissemination of a religious view of American pluralism, the organization may have helped to discredit the ethnic group as a source of personal identity, offering the religious congregation as its only alternative. According to Bruno Lasker, an early supporter of NCCJ who later became disillusioned with the organiza-tion, NCCJ worked to "exalt . . . the role of organized religion in

---

[50]Will Herberg, Protestant - Catholic - Jew: An Essay in American Religious Sociology (2nd ed.rev.; Garden City: 1960) The development of NCCJ calls into question the thesis put forth by Will Herberg that social processes beyond the control of the individual account for the substitution of identification with organized religion for identification with the ethnic group. Herberg assumed that "escape" from the ethnic group was the dominant motif of the second generation: "Their language, their culture, their system of values, their outlook on life, underwent drastic change, sometimes obviously, sometimes imperceptibly; they were becoming American, assimilated, acculturated, no longer fully at home in the immigrant family and ethnic group." (p. 28). But detachment from the old ways, according to Herberg, left an unfilled void in the descendents of the immigrants. The third generation, more secure in its Americanism but still unsure of its identity within the larger society, turned to organized religion-- stripped of its ethnic particularities--as a haven from the rootlessness of modern life. It was this generation, less out of spiritual conviction and more for purposes of social orientation, that flocked to the churches

American life" in order to "satisfy the desire of each of the three

faiths to avail itself of the added dynamic of the others in a drive

for greater institutional loyalty on the part of those whom it

regarded as members."[51]

NCCJ's reluctance to alter its religious conception of

American pluralism may have been a consequence of its financial

dependence upon assimilationist elements within the American

Jewish community. For at least the first fifteen years of its

existence, the organization received most of its funds from Jewish

rather than Christian sources--a circumstance that troubled many

Jewish contributors (who would have preferred to give to a truly non-

sectarian organization) and that director Clinchy may have tried to

conceal.[52]   The larger part of NCCJ's Jewish support came--in

---

and synogogues in the fifties. This schema fails to account for
the interventions made by organizations such as NCCJ.

[51]Bruno Lasker to Herbert L. Seamans, Jan. 8, 1941, "Notebooks,"
Vol. XVIII, No. 1, pp. 1-3, Bruno Lasker Papers, Columbia University
(Hereinafter referred to as BL Mss.).

[52]A 1934 summary of the organization's finances, written
apparently in response to an inquiry from Father John Elliot Ross,
Catholic member of the original trio tour, contained the following
statement: "Of the contributors approximately 50% are Jewish and
40% are Christian. The Jewish people, however, are contributing in
larger amounts so that during the years under discussion [probably
1932-34] the proportion has been at least two-thirds from Jewish
sources." (J. Elliot Ross to Everett Clinchy, May 29, 1934, Reel 1;
the untitled financial summary is located at the end of Reel 1, NCCJ
Mss.) Additional evidence of NCCJ's financial dependence on
Jewish sources during the early years appears in the minutes of the
meeting of the National Community Relations Advisory Council,
Sept. 22, 1948 (ff. National Community Relations Advisory Council,

an indirect manner--from the American Jewish Committee. The

Committee had early reached a decision that partnership with the

NCCJ was a key element in its overall defense strategy.[53] Although

the Committee made direct grants to NCCJ, the bulk of AJC-controlled

money took the form of contributions from individuals who followed

the recommendation of the Committee.[54] With a heavy financial

stake in NCCJ, the Committee played an active and continuing role

in the formulation and execution of NCCJ policy. As Jewish Co-

chairman of NCCJ and influential member of AJC's Survey Committee,

Roger Strauss was the most important intermediary between the two

organizations. From a rural Georgia community, growing up outside

the Jewish ghetto, Strauss was an outspoken anti-Zionist whom

---

1948-49). These minutes suggest that the turning point occurred
sometime during World War II. AJC and ADL subventions to NCCJ
had ended by 1945, a year in which 70% of the organization's
national funding came from Christian sources. On the misgivings of
Jewish contributors, see the following letters: Robert A. Ashworth
to Arthur W. Packard, Nov. 6, 1933, Reel 1, Roger W. Strauss to
John D. Rockefeller, Jr., Nov. 21, 1936, Reel 3, NCCJ Mss. The
house history of NCCJ attempts to disguise the extent of Jewish
support during the early years (Pitt, Adventures, p. 135) and argues
the dubious proposition that the organization first arose to defend
Catholics against discrimination (pp. 33, 139). Everett Clinchy
once told Rachel D. DuBois that he didn't know where his organization's money came from (Rachel Davis DuBois, Personal log,
October 15, 1934, DuBois Mss.).

[53]American Jewish Committee, Memorandum from Morris Fine
to John Slawson (Re: The National Conference of Christians and
Jews and the American Jewish Committee"), February 17, 1953, ff.
National Conference of Christians and Jews, 1940-1955, AJC Mss.

[54]Ibid.

Sidney Wallach remembered as the most forceful exponent of the

position that Jews should be considered as members of a religious

congregation, not an ethnic group.[55] Other Jews associated with

the Conference thought along similar lines. Rabbi Morris S. Lazaron,

for example, member of one of the first interfaith teams that toured

the country, was a strong supporter of the American Council for

Judaism, a militantly anti-Zionist organization which favored complete

integration of Jews into "the civic, cultural and social aspects of

life in the United States."[56] Most rabbis active in NCCJ panels

and programs were drawn from the reform wing of Judaism, the wing

least hospitable to Jewish ethnic consciousness.[57]

The Committee attached great importance to the non-sectarian

(but pro-sectarian) image of the Conference. A statement from

the Conference denouncing an anti-Semitic act appeared more potent

and disinterested than a similar statement emanating from a Jewish

agency. Therefore, rather than intervening directly to counteract an

anti-Semitic manifestation, the Committee frequently requested NCCJ

---

[55]Pitt, Adventures, p. 20; Sidney Wallach, interview with
the author, August 8, 1975.

[56]"Rabbi Lazaron, at 70, Recalls Struggle for Interfaith Amity,"
The New York Times, April 16, 1958 (clipping in ff. W History, NCCJ
Mss.).

[57]This was the complaint made by Rabbi Solomon Goldman of
Chicago in a letter to Everett Clinchy dated Feb. 17, 1932 (Reel 1,
NCCJ Mss.).

to intercede on its behalf.[58] AJC also helped to shape the program-

ming policies of NCCJ. The original Brotherhood Day (later

Brotherhood Week) observance, which NCCJ organized in 1934,

owed its inspiration to the fertile imagination of Sidney Wallach

of the AJC. Wallach, who had a flair for public relations, wrote

Robert Ashworth, newly-appointed Educational Secretary of NCCJ, in

1933 that "in order to fight the tide of chauvinism and anti-Semitism,

we must use devices that are as dramatic as those employed by

the protagonists of chauvinism and anti-Semitism."[59] One of

NCCJ's most highly-acclaimed programs, the Religious News Service

(RNS), was heavily dependent during the Depression years on sub-

ventions from the American Jewish Committee.[60] Established in

1934 under the direction of Louis Minsky, RNS was designed to be

---

[58]Morris D. Waldman to Everett R. Clinchy, April 23, 1930,
Harry Schneiderman to Everett R. Clinchy, Oct. 31, 1933,Reel 1,
NCCJ Mss.; Sidney Wallach to Nathan Strauss, October 11, 1938,
Reel 6, NCCJ Mss.

[59]Sidney Wallach to Robert Ashworth, Oct. 11, 1933(see also
Ashworth's response: Robert Ashworth to Sidney Wallach, Oct. 13, 1933),
ff. Brotherhood Day, 1934, NCCJ Mss.

[60]Everett R. Clinchy to Wolfgang S. Schwabacher, May 26, 1934,
Everett R. Clinchy to Wolfgang S. Schwabacher, Oct. 22, 1934, Reel
1, NCCJ Mss; Everett R. Clinchy to Roger W. Strauss, December 16,
1938, Reel 7, NCCJ Mss.; Everett R. Clinchy to Roger W. Strauss,
October 10, 1939, Reel 8, NCCJ Mss.

an "Associated Press of Religion." Feeding weekly (and later daily) religious news coverage to hundreds of religious and secular newspapers around the country, RNS featured religious developments within "the three major faiths," stressed efforts made by Christian groups to counteract anti-Semistism, and made a special effort to reach Catholic Journals of opinion.[61]

It is hard to assess NCCJ's impact upon emerging group patterns in the United States. If the major religious bodies co-exist on a plane of relative equality, if their leaders confer together on a regular basis, if they rise to each other's defense in times of crisis, NCCJ may claim credit for having brought about these wholesome changes. Given the climate of the times, there may have been little more than any organization could have done to extend the horizons of tolerance in the United States, short of a broad and possibly self-defeating attack on the institutional roots of racism and group prejudice. Nevertheless, NCCJ did exceed its mandate, by obscuring the ethnic dimensions of American society and by misinterpreting the true nature of some of the most acute divisions and critical tensions in American life. The gains for Judaism, as a result of these policies, were considerable. Judaism became part of the trinomial "religious equation" of American Life. Yet there was a price to be paid; Judaism gained

---

[61]Pitt, _Adventures_, pp. 79-80.

respectability at the expense of denying part of itself--the ethnic part. That denial, as subsequent history has shown, could not forever be maintained.

The Service Bureau and the Irritant
of Jewish Ethnicity

The opposing outlooks of DuBois, who adhered closely to the teachings of her Reconstructionist mentors, and the NCCJ-AJC proponents of the sectarian view of Judaism, did not lead to an immediate rupture between her and her uneasy allies. DuBois was working too hard to enhance the image of the Jewish community to dismiss her efforts as a disservice to that community. Yet, she and her associates were deemed suspect when they advanced the notion that nationality was the defining characteristic of the Jewish community, and her continued insistence on that point would eventually lead to an estrangement between DuBois and her former supporters.

It will be recalled that Everett Clinchy had given an important boost to DuBois' career. For ten years after their first encounter in 1930, Clinchy's organization lent both material and moral support to DuBois: typing and mimeographing the early curriculum materials, giving DuBois a platform at NCCJ conferences, and attempting to raise money from the foundations. Indeed at one point in the early thirties, Clinchy advertised the DuBois project as an integral part of the National Conference program.[62] It may

seem odd, given the direction taken by the National Conference,

that Clinchy would have found much to admire in DuBois' philosophy

of cultural democracy. Here it is important to distinguish between

Clinchy's personal philosophy and the momentum acquired by his

organization. An admirer of Horace Kallen and a self-professed

cultural pluralist, Clinchy believed that "cultural pluralism [was]

an essential characteristic of genuine democracy."[63] We can

only guess why that philosophy was not given full expression

by the National Conference. The need to protect the financial life-

line to the AJC may have been one reason. The organization had

reached the nadir of its fortunes during the winter of 1932-33.

Clinchy had taken the extreme step of informing Newton Baker that

he was thinking of resigning from the Conference and moving to

the greener pastures of college administration.[64] It was an act

---

[62]Clinchy, however, feared too close an association with the DuBois enterprise. Formal absorption of the project was considered a risky undertaking at this time. As a religiously-based organization, NCCJ might be accused of meddling in non-sectarian, public education. See Clinchy's remarks to David Heyman in a letter dated September 14, 1935 (ff. Progressive Education Association, No. 391, NYF Mss.).

[63]Everett R. Clinchy, All in the Name of God (New York, 1934), p. 177; Clinchy's admiration for Kallen was expressed in an interview with the author, Dec. 10, 1973.

[64]Everett R. Clinchy to Newton D. Baker, Dec. 1, 1932, Reel 1 NCCJ Mss.; Both Newton Baker and Carlton Hayes asked to be relieved of their responsibilities as Co-Chairmen of the organization around

of fate--the appearance of the Nazi threat in 1933 and the infusion
of funds this brought from Jewish sources--that saved the organization. Even if Clinchy believed that Jews possessed a secular as
well as a religious culture, he may have been hesitant to publicly
sanction such a view for fear of displeasing his assimilationist
benefactors.

Rachel Davis DuBois was less malleable. Her commitment
to a multi-cultural approach became apparent during the fifteen
school project of 1934-35. Funding for this project, it will be
recalled, had come from the American Jewish Committee, which
soon wondered how its money was being spent. Only three of the
twenty-six guest assemblies presented during the fall semester
of 1934 dealt with the Jewish group.[65] When Jews were spotlighted
on the assembly stage, their "cultural," as well as their religious
contributions, were depicted. The Committee was so disenchanted
with the project that it announced its intention to withdraw funding

---

the same time (See Newton D. Baker to Everett R. Clinchy,
Oct. 27, 1932, and Carlton J. Hayes to Everett R. Clinchy
Nov. 3, 1932, Reel 1, NCCJ Mss.).

[65]A list of the assembly programs presented during the fall
semester appears in the Leonard Covello papers (See "Assembly
Programs," ff. Intercultural Education, Agencies and Organizations,
Service Bureau for Education in Human Relations, Box 16, Covello
Mss.).

for the second semester. According to DuBois, the Committee

objected to separate presentations on the Jews in the context of

a series of ethnic presentations. She remembered a representative

of the Committee to say: "You don't have a program on the

Baptists; why one on the Jews when the Jews are only a religious

group."[66] DuBois pleaded with the leaders of the AJC to honor

their commitment to the two field workers, who had taken leaves

of absence for the entire academic year.[67] Acceding to her request,

the Committee agreed to fund the project for the second semester,

even though it had serious reservations over the Service Bureau's

approach.

The Committee did not entirely sever its connection with

DuBois after the expiration of the grant year. Sidney Wallach and

Morris Waldman, Executive Secretary of the AJC, tried to get

money for the Service Bureau from other sources.[68] Wallach seemed

---

[66]DuBois, "Autobiography," Chapter 4, pp. 19-20; Miriam R. Ephraim to Leonard Covello, Jan. 7, 1935, ff. Intercultural Education, Agencies and Organizations, Service Bureau for Education in Human Relations, Box 16, Covello Mss.

[67]DuBois, "Autobiography," Chapter 4, p. 20.

68Morris D. Waldman to William F. Fuerst, June 5, 1935; Sidney Wallach to David M. Heyman, Aug. 15, 1935, ff. Progressive Education Association, No. 391, NYF Mss.; Miriam R. Ephraim to Rachel Davis DuBois, June 25, 1935, ff. Correspondence, General, 1930-1939, DuBois Mss.

optimistic about the Bureau in a report he submitted to the

Committee in 1935:

> We have continued our support of an educational bureau in
> the city of New York that is attempting to provide supplementary
> materials on Jews in American life to various high schools.
> While the Bureau is still in an experimental stage, we have
> reason to expect that a valuable contribution will be made . . .
> and that those features . . . which can properly be incorporated
> in general school systems will be brought to the attention of
> the school authorities.[69]

After the merger of the Bureau with the PEA, the Committee

resumed its financial support of DuBois, albeit at a much more

modest level. This support, according to Sidney Wallach, was

given with a "measure of reservation," the reservation having to

do with DuBois' attachment to an ethnic view of the Jewish community.[70]

The issue of the disputed identity of American Jews surfaced

again during the Americans All--Immigrants All radio series. It

is not certain why the Committee decided to resuscitate the Bureau

after DuBois' departure from the PEA. The possibility of using the

Bureau as a lever to influence government policy may have been

the decisive factor. The presentation of a separate program on

the Jew in a series of programs dealing with nationality groups

was bound to antagonize those Jews who saw their identity

---

[69]Sidney Wallach, "Report of Information and Service Associates,"
May 1, 1935, p. 6, ff. Survey Committee, Educational Department
Survey, 1933-1941, MDW Mss.

[70]Wallach, interview with the author, August 8, 1975.

strictly in religious terms. The liveliest and most prolonged

discussion at the September 28, 1938, meeting of the Advisory

Committee revolved around the question of a separate program on

the Jew. Some members of the Committee, led by Avenire Toigo,

Executive Secretary of the Illinois Committee on Citizenship

and Naturalization, urged the cancellation of the Jewish program.

Toigo argued:

> You handle the Jewish question as you do the Catholic.
> When mentioning Father Marquette mention that he was a
> Catholic. You handle them in this manner not putting any
> greater emphasis on Catholic, Jew or Protestant.[71]

Toigo's suggestion, however appealing as a long-term solution

to the Jewish problem, was not followed by the Committee. Jews

were viewed as members of an ethnic group by the public. The

negative stereotypes that stigmatized the group could not be dis-

spelled unless they were faced directly.[72] This concession to

reality, however, did not rule out efforts to alter the public

conception of Judaism, which was what Toigo was calling for. The

American Jewish Committee, which apparently gave its tacit

approval to the separate program, was especially insistent on this

[71]Minutes of the meeting of the Advisory Committee for "Americans All--Immigrants All," Sept. 28, 1938, p. 14, ff. Service Bureau, Americans All--Immigrants All, Memoranda and Reports, 1938-39, DuBois Mss.

[72]Ibid., pp. 16, 19.

point. The Committee requested that information about Jewish
contributions to American life be woven into the German, Slavic,
and general historical programs. Pressures were brought to bear
upon DuBois to adhere to this line ("My Jewish advisors are asking
me to see that Jews are more and more considered in the category
of religion.")[73] Despite efforts made in this direction, there was
a certain amount of dissatisfaction with the results of the series.
Mrs. Theresa Durlach, the woman who had "discovered" DuBois
(and who was now vice-chairman of the Service Bureau) asked
Studebaker to present separate programs on Catholics and Protestants
in order to disspell "the misconception of the public that the Jews
constitute a separate racial group."[74] A protest against the
Jewish program also came from the wife of the publisher of The New
York Times, Mrs. Arthur Hays Sulzberger, who wrote that "there
is a great mistake being made at the present time in regarding the
Jews as a race, when they are merely a religious group."[75] DuBois

---

[73]Memorandum,Rachel Davis DuBois to Gilbert Seldes,
Oct. 24, 1938, ff. Service Bureau, Americans All - Immigrants All,
Correspondence, Gilbert Seldes, 1938-39, DuBois Mss.

[74]Theresa Mayer Durlach to John Studebaker, Oct. 27, 1938,
ff. Service Bureau, Americans All - Immigrants All, Memoranda
and Reports, 1938-39, DuBois Mss.

[75]Mrs. A. H. Sulzberger to Arthur Derounian, Feb. 24, 1939,
ff. Correspondence, General, 1930-1939, DuBois Mss.

in her memoirs blamed the disruption of her work on those Jews
who opposed her cultural interpretation of American Jewry.[76]
This interpretation may have been exaggerated; she had antagonized
other groups besides assimilationist Jews. Yet AJC controlled
the purse strings, and if they decided that DuBois' approach
rendered a disservice to the Jewish community, she would lose
her only reliable base of support. Throughout most of the thirties,
the Committee and DuBois could live with each other, even though
they did not share the same outlook. The Committee's indulgent
attitude, however, began to dissolve toward the end of the decade.
In part, this change had to do with the removal of Sidney Wallach
for the direction of the Survey Committee in 1938; in part, it also
had to do with a basic change in prescriptions for dealing with anti-
Semitism in American society.

Shifting Ground in the Fight Against Anti-Semitism

So long as AJC leaders believed that anti-Semitism was
treatable using educational means, there was some room for accommodation between DuBois and the Committee. As had been shown
with the radio program, the Committee could condone a separate

---

[76]See the five-page fragment of her autobiography entitled
"Why the Opposition to our Work?" ff. Manuscripts, Rachel Davis
DuBois, Autobiography, 1965-1973, DuBois Mss.

program so long as they were assured that the advantages of such
an approach, in terms of overcoming prejudice and destroying
stereotypes, outweighed its chief disadvantage: supporting the misconception that the Jews were a separate nationality. Confidence in
that assumption began to wane in the late thirties. A growing body of
evidence from the social sciences seemed to suggest that anti-Semitism
was a much more complex and deep-rooted phenomenon than had previously
been thought and that outbreaks of anti-Semitism were closely correlated with dips in the economic cycle and increases in anti-democratic
behavior. A German Jewish social psychologist, Kurt Lewin, who had
emigrated to America in 1932, was a key figure in molding the new outlook on anti-Semitism. Lewin argued that anti-Semitism crested during
periods of economic stagnation and mass hardship. The Jewish
minority, Lewin believed, served as a convenient scapegoat for the
frustrations of the majority. "This is one of the reasons," Lewin wrote,
"why Jews everywhere are necessarily interested in the welfare of the
majority among whom they live." In the light of Lewin's findings, faith
in an educational approach to the problem of anti-Semitism was shaken.
"One cannot hope to combat Father Coughlin effectively," Lewin wrote,
"by telling everybody how good the Jews are."[77]

Anti-Semitism also came to be seen as one of many manifesta-

---

[77]Kurt Lewin, Resolving Social Conflicts: Selected Papers on
Group Dynamics (New York, 1948), pp.161-63. The chapter from which
these quotations were taken was originally published in 1939 as an
essay in the Jewish Frontier.

tions of anti-democratic tendencies in American society--"a symptom

of a larger evil," as a 1938 Survey Committee report put it, which

would have to be attacked directly.[78] A leading proponent of this

position was Dr. Max Horkheimer of the Institute of Social Research,

Columbia University. Horkheimer, while doing research on

university students in California, had discovered that prejudice

against Jews was closely correlated with prejudice against other

minority groups as well as with certain mental predispositions

that were endemic in authoritarian societies.[79] The implications

behind this research for AJC policy planning were enormous. A

program to educate the general public about Jewish history and

culture, "Jewish apologetics" as it was derisvely called,[80] appeared

---

[78]"Report Given at Annual Meeting," Jan. 16, 1938, ff. Survey Committee, 38 - (48?), Reports, MDW Papers.

[79]Horkheimer's research was cited in the official minutes of the Conference on Research in the Field of Anti-Semitism, May 20-21, 1944 (bound copy of minutes on file at AJC Library in New York). Research projects of the Institute of Social Research had been funded by the AJC (Mention of this relationship appears in: The Report of Frank N. Trager to Heads of Staff Conference [American Jewish Committee], May 12, 1943, pp. 6-7, copy given to author by Frank Trager). In 1944, Horkheimer became the first Director of AJC's Department of Scientific Research.

[80]Morris D. Waldman uses the term in his memoirs: Nor by Power (New York, 1953), p. 162.

diversionary and futile. Jewish leaders could purchase immunity

from anti-Semitism only by championing the cause of democracy

in general. The task of education was to encourage open-mindedness,

critical thinking, respect for the individual, and equality of

opportunity.[81] By turning its attention to the personality make-

up of the anti-Semite, AJC was also opening up an area of scientific

investigation that would take years to complete. In 1944, as an

outcome of an historic, AJC-sponsored scholarly conference on

anti-Semitism, AJC set up a Department of Scientific Research

under the direction of John Slawson. The Department funded the

investigations that led to the publication of the famous "Studies in

Prejudice" Series from 1949 to 1952. The most important of these

studies was the volume prepared by T. W. Adorno and his associates

entitled The Authoritarian Personality.[82] AJC was coming to the

realization that an "indirect" approach to the problem of anti-Semitism:

---

[81]The new educational approaches advocated by AJC members
are discussed in the minutes of a special "Advisory Committee on
Intercultural Education" set up by AJC in 1948. See minutes for
March 3, 1949, April 27, 1949; Oct. 19, 1949; and Jan. 10, 1950, in
ff. American Jewish Committee, Intercultural Education Committee,
Minutes, 1949-1950, AJC Mss. The Committee concluded that the
term "intercultural Education" was obsolete and that a more
appropriate term was "human relations." (March 3, 1949).

[82]T. W. Adorno, Elsei Frenkel-Brunswik, Daniel J. Levinson
and R. Nevitt Sanford, The Authoritarian Personality (New York, 1952).

"sterilizing the soil" in which anti-Semitism grew, was the most
effective self-defense strategy.[83]

As a result of this more sophisticated knowledge of the anti-
Semitic personality, DuBois found herself suspect not only for
her devotion to Reconstructionist principles but also for her faith
in reason to overcome anti-Semitism. The development of the
Service Bureau had been hampered by misgivings of the AJC over
the ethnic categorization of the Jewish community. DuBois'
representation of the Jewish community threatened the delicate
accommodation to American society, based on the sectarian
character of Judaism, that had been worked out by the Committee
in conjunction with organizations like the NCCJ. Nonetheless, so
long as the anti-Semitic mind was considered open to persuasion,
DuBois' pioneering work could not be dismissed. When faith in
the power of reason began to crumble in the late thirties, the cautious
alliance between DuBois and the AJC was undermined. By 1940,
younger members of the AJC were thoroughly disillusioned with the
entire "gifts" or "contributions" approach.[84] DuBois' faith, on the

---

[83]The quotations are from Richard Rothschild, "Report to the
Survey Committee," n.d., ff. Survey Committee, 38 - (48?), Reports,
MDW Papers.

[84]This was reported by Bruno Lasker in a memo to Stewart Cole,
March 14, 1941, "Notebooks," Vol. XVIII, No. 1, pp. 52-54, BL Mss.

other hand, proved to be unshaken by the powerful arguments of the

social scientists. Intergroup harmony was clearly subordinate in

her mind to the task of building a richer American culture, which

could only be achieved if the second generation knew and treasured

their cultural backgrounds. It was paradoxical that AJC, an

organization representing a minority group, was more concerned

with attitudes of the majority, and DuBois, a member of the majority,

was more concerned with attitudes of the minority.

CHAPTER VIII

UPHEAVAL IN THE SERVICE BUREAU, 1939-1941

During the first five years of its existence, the Service Bureau had developed a program designed to attain two basic objectives: maintenance of intergroup harmony and amelioration of minority self-concept. The program stressed the separate study of the history and contributions of ethnic groups to American society. By the late thirties this program came under increasing attack. Those who were committed to the first goal were wary of an approach that accentuated, rather than downplayed group differences. Such an approach, they felt, could easily backfire, fueling nationalistic feelings, erecting barriers between people, and taking unhealthy political forms. The dangers of such an approach had become apparent during the PEA period and amply demonstrated during the Americans All Radio series. Many Jewish leaders, for whom civil peace meant a society emancipated from bigotry, were disillusioned with an approach that appeared both superficial in its treatment of the anti-Semitic problem and defective in its representation of the Jewish community. The concern to develop an educational program for a fragmented society had not abated, but clearly the program of the Bureau--for those unconcerned about personality development and social disorganization within minority communities--was inadequate.

The Bureau had reached an important juncture in its history. The organization had achieved national stature and had reaped a host of new contacts as a result of its collaboration in the Americans All series. After the passage of the so-called "Tolerance Resolution" by the New York City Board of Education on December 14, of 1938, which mandated that each school in the city hold assemblies stressing the importance of "tolerance and freedom for all men," Bureau offices in New York City were besieged by New York City teachers eager to obtain assistance in setting up assembly programs.[1] In early 1939, the Board asked the Bureau to give its first in-service course for teachers in the field of intergroup education. Forty-one high school teachers enrolled in the course which was taught by DuBois at New York University during the spring term of 1939. Repeated during the fall and spring terms of 1939-1940, the course

---

[1]Rachel Davis DuBois to William D. Boutwell, Jan. 10, 1939, ff. Service Bureau, Americans All - Immigrants All, Correspondence, William D. Boutwell, 1938-39, DuBois Mss.; see also: "Petition for Support" (enclosed with letter from Rachel Davis DuBois to John Marshall, March 27, 1939), p. 6, ff. Bureau for Intercultural Education, 1939-1941, Series 1, Subseries II, Box 284, GEB Mss.

drew even larger numbers of teachers.[2] Requests had also come in

from school systems in Philadelphia, Pittsburgh, Cleveland and

Washington for direct Bureau assistance in setting up system-wide

programs in intercultural education.[3]

In this whirl of activity, a chain of events was set in motion

that would rock the organization and lead to the departure of

DuBois and those who sided with her. The American Jewish Committee,

the financial benefactor of the Bureau, had decided that, in return

for a long-term commitment to financially sustain the Bureau, a

major reorganization of the Bureau's operations, and presumably a

reorientation in philosophy, would have to be carried out. The

architect of these changes was Frank N. Trager, who had succeeded

Sidney Wallach as administrative officer of the Survey Committee in

1938.[4] Trained as a political philosopher, Trager came to the

Committee after a stint as National Labor Secretary of the Socialist

---

[2]Committee for Evaluation of the Work of the Service Bureau for Intercultural Education, "Report B and Appendix," 1940, p. 18, GEB Mss. (Mimeographed)

[3]"Petition for Support" (enclosed with Rachel Davis DuBois to John Marshall, March 27, 1939), p. 7, ff. Bureau for Intercultural Education, 1939-1941, Series I, Subseries II, Box 284, GEB Mss.

[4]The following two documents summarize the Committee's relationship with the Service Bureau during this period: American Jewish Committee, Memo, re Service Bureau, May 31, 1939, ff. Bureau for Intercultural Education, 1939-1940; and M. Jelenko, "American Jewish Committee's Relationship with the Bureau for Intercultural Education," March 29, 1944, p. 3, ff. Service Bureau for Intercultural Education, 1944-1945, AJC Mss.

Party and after teaching philosophy for six years at Johns Hopkins.

Trager felt that DuBois was too set in her ways and had not acquired

an adequate grasp of the emerging literature on the origins of

prejudice. He also felt that she lacked the intellectual acumen

to exercise leadership over the organization. As Trager recalled

many years later, he did not intend to oust her but to "demote"

her and turn over executive responsibilities to a person whom he

considered more capable and less volatile.[5] Believing that her

leadership was not being challenged (she was told that she would

continue to function as "Educational Director" of the Bureau)[6]

DuBois apparently did not object to turning over some of her admin-

istrative responsibilities to a recognized educational leader.

Trager's initial choice for the job was a disappointment to DuBois

and ultimately to Trager. In January of 1939, Edward Ashley Bayne,

the son of a well-known district superintendent of the New York

City school system, was appointed Executive Secretary of the Bureau.

During his brief tenure as director, Bayne quarreled with certain

policies that had been followed by the Bureau. Not only did he

object to a separate radio program on the Jew, but he also suggested

that the Bureau soften its position in favor of full equality for blacks

---

[5]Trager, taped interview, Aug. 5, 1975.

[6]DuBois bore this title, as time went by more honorific than
real, from January of 1939 until April of 1940.

lest the radical image of the organization scare away white supporters.[7]

Bayne's views were less of a handicap than his deficiencies as

an administrator. Accordingly, he was released from his responsi-

bilities after only six months on the job.

The Missionary and the Minister:
the Advent of Stewart Cole

During the six months of Bayne's directorship of the Bureau,

the staff of the Service Bureau was expanded and an effort was

made to recruit new members for the Board.   Stanley Walker

assumed responsibility for liason work with Washington and relations

with other educational organizations. Arthur Derounian, who later

would thrill the nation with tales of undercover work in the American

Nazi underground,[8] was placed in charge of publicity for the radio

---

[7]Edward A. Bayne to Jeanette Sayre, Feb. 16, 1939, ff.
Service Bureau, Americans All - Immigrants All, Listener Response,
Correspondence and Reports, 1938-1939; Edward Ashley Bayne,
"Report on National Education Association Convention at Cleveland,
Feb. 23 - March 3," March 13, 1939, (point 6 of this report concerns
the Negro question), ff. Service Bureau, Americans All - Immigrants
All, Washington Visits, Reports and Memoranda on, 1938-1939,DuBois
Mss. DuBois was regarded as a strong advocate of Negro rights. See
the following entries in her Personal Log: Jan. 3, 1936; July 4, 1938,
DuBois Mss.

[8]John Roy Carlson [Arthur Derounian], Under Cover: My Four
Years in the Nazi Underworld of America (New York, 1943).

series. L. Hollingsworth Wood, a prominent Quaker lawyer and

trustee of Fisk University, long associated with black educational

causes, became treasurer of the organization. It was hoped that

Wood would broaden the financial base of the Bureau to include non-

Jewish contributors.[9] On April 27, 1939, the Service Bureau hosted

a conference at Quaker Meeting House in New York City to which

representatives of leading civic, labor, educational and ethnic

organizations were invited. The conference was a rite of passage

for the young organization; it had received acclaim for its achieve-

ment in radio broadcasting; it had been invited by the New York

City Board of Education to provide technical assistance in the field

of intercultural education. Now the Bureau sought to enlist the

cooperation and assistance of other agencies in the long-term

pursuit of its goals.[10] But there were serious problems facing the

----

[9]A biographical sketch of Hollingsworth Wood appears in: The
Friend (London), Feb. 5, 1937, p. 125. The expectation that Wood
would be successful in courting gentile contributors was reported to
John Marshall of the GEB (Internal Memorandum by John Marshall,
Interview with Mrs. Rachel DuBois, Mr. Hollingsworth Wood,
March 21, 1939, ff. Bureau for Intercultural Education, 1939-1941,
Series I, Subseries III, Box 566, GEB Mss.).

[10]See an "Outline for Meeting of Service Bureau for Intercultural
Education, Inc., April 27, 1939," ff. Service Bureau, Americans All -
Immigrants All, Washington Visits, Reports and Memoranda on, 1938-
1939, DuBois Mss. (A press release about the meeting, dated
May 4, 1939, appears in the same file folder).

Bureau. It had yet to resolve the delicate problem of leadership, and it had yet to iron out the philosophical and methodological differences that were ready to erupt into open conflict.

Soon after the conference, a new effort was made to solve the leadership problem. Still convinced that the Bureau needed a more professional and accountable leader, Trager invited a Canadian-born professor of religious education, Stewart Cole, to become director of the Bureau. Cole was an unlikely choice for the position. He had taught at Crozier Theological Seminary from 1924 to 1936 and had been president of Kalamazoo College from 1936 to 1938. In three books published since 1930, Cole evinced little interest in the minority problem. His driving concern had been to demonstrate the compatibility of Christian faith and secular idealism.[11] Cole's friend, Hugh Hartshorne, Professor of Character Education at Yale, had nominated Cole for the position.[12]

---

[11]This theme is stressed in Cole's book: Character and Human Education (New York, 1936). In his History of Fundamentalism (New York, 1931), Cole argued that fundamentalist movements in various Protestant denominations were defensive reactions against the growth of scientific secularism. The third book published by Cole before 1940 was: Leisure in our Time (New York, 1934).

[12]Transcription of Tape No. 1, p. 4, ff. Transcriptions of Stewart Cole Tapes Nos. 1 and 2, BIE Mss. In 1958-1959, two students at Boston University, Shirley Kolack and Olive Hall, undertook a study of the Bureau for Intercultural Education. As part of the study, which was never completed, they submitted questions to Stewart Cole about his role in the history of the Bureau. Cole responded to these questions on tape. Transcriptions were made of the three tapes he recorded. Both the tapes and the transcriptions, as well as other documents collected by these students, are on deposit at the Immigration Center, University

Hartshorne had been invited to serve as a consultant for the Bureau in developing curriculum projects for the New York City schools; later as member of the Bureau's Executive Committee, he would play an important role in redirecting the policies of the Bureau. As with Hollingsworth Wood, it was hoped that Cole would prove to be an effective fund-raiser from non-Jewish sources.[13]

Cole's appearance on the scene sparked a bitter conflict that shook the Bureau for the next two years. As Cole came to consolidate his position as director of the Bureau--making a fiction of the "50-50" division of authority that apparently had been agreed upon at the start--and as he came to question the "pluralist" approach that had become the Bureau's hallmark, DuBois and her supporters fought to retain control of the organization and turn back any challenges to the philosophy of cultural democracy. "The air is thick with fear and suspicion," reported Rose Nelson six months after Cole's take-over.[14] It is hard to untangle the complex of emotions and issues that underlay the upheaval which the Bureau was going through. Much of what was debated and

---

of Minnesota.

[13]Trager, taped Interview, Aug. 5, 1975.

[14]Rachel Davis DuBois, Personal Log, Jan. 29, 1940,DuBois Mss.

argued about was petty or personal in nature. Cole complained

of DuBois' intransigence on certain issues and of her lack of

loyalty to him. He accused her of not comporting herself in a

"professional" manner and of alienating influential leaders in

the field of intergroup education, such as John Studebaker and

Frederick Redefer. He felt her judgment was not sound, she

dabbled in too many things, and she did not attach sufficient

importance to fundamental research, an item high on Cole's agenda

for the Bureau. While recognizing her "genius" and "sensitivity,"

Cole also saw DuBois as an individualist who could not submit to

the discipline of an organization founded on "team-work" and

collective deliberation. Cole was also under the impression that

he was building a new organization, not taking control of an old

one. He referred to the pre-1939 history of the Bureau as Rachel

DuBois' "experimentation" or the "incipient project." Cole's

attitude doubtlessly contributed to DuBois' feelings of anger and

indignation.[15] DuBois, for her part, resented not being consulted

---

[15]DuBois, Personal Log, Jan. 26, 1940, DuBois Mss.;
Transcription of Tape #3 (Reminiscences of Stewart G. Cole),
responses to questions Nos. 1 and 12, ff. Transcription of
Stewart Cole Tape No. 1, BIE Mss.; Stewart Cole to the author,
August 10, 1974, Nov. 21, 1974.

on important policy decisions, and complained that Cole administered

the Bureau in an imperious manner, rarely holding staff conferences

and intimidating the staff into playing a subservient role. DuBois

also brooded about being pushed aside because of her sex. She

saw her displacement from power as in part the result of "the

darker forces . . . of a past era, which do not represent democracy

and love;" one of these forces was that of "the dominance of the

male, the fundamental reason why I was not allowed to be director

last year."[16]

The root cause of the conflict, however, was most likely in

the realm of ideology. This interpretation is supported by statements

of the two adversaries, a close analysis of their writings, and

subsequent developments within the Service Bureau. As a novice in

the intercultural field, Cole may have lacked strong convictions at

the start of his new assignment, but he soon joined the chorus of

critics who were lambasting the Bureau under DuBois' leadership.

Cole was convinced that "something more fundamental" than

personality was involved in their confrontation.[17] He confided to

a foundation official in January of 1940 that he could not continue

in his current capacity unless the Bureau adopted "a program which

[16]DuBois., Personal Log, Jan. 26, April 15, 1940, DuBois Mss.

[17]DuBois, Personal Log, Jan. 29, 1940, DuBois Mss.

he [could] fully believe in."[18] Cole faulted DuBois and her

associates for what he considered their obsession with the "contri-

butions" approach. In a policy memorandum submitted in April,

he called for the Bureau to place "a greater emphasis upon publica-

tions that stress cultural likenesses among the people of America."[19]

In conversations with officials of the Federal Radio Project, he

concurred with their criticism of the Americans All Radio Series.[20]

Cole may have been swayed in his thinking by the tentative find-

ings of a Committee of Evaluation that was in the process of making

a thorough investigation of the Bureau's activities and philosophy.[21]

Cole, however, had ample reasons of his own for questioning the

DuBois approach.

Unlike DuBois, Cole had a greater sense of a "unified

culture" that had developed in the New World - a culture that had

a prior and indisputable claim on the loyalties of minority groups.

As a product of the genius and historical experience of the American

---

[18]Internal Memorandum by John Marshall, Interview with
Stewart G. Cole, Jan. 22, 1940, ff. Bureau for Intercultural Education,
1939-1941, Series I, Subseries III, Box 566, GEB Mss.

[19]Stewart G. Cole, Memorandum to Special Committee Meeting,
April 20, 1940, ff. Bureau for Intercultural Education, 1939-1940,
AJC Mss.

[20]This was recorded by DuBois in her Personal Log, Jan. 29, 1940.

[21]See below, pp. 235-250.

people, this culture had acquired a universal jurisdiction. In Cole's view, it was as important to teach loyalty to American culture as it was to teach respect for cultural differences. Using the standard of a national culture, Cole attempted to set limits upon the expression of cultural differences in American society. Only those cultural differences should be preserved which "are amenable to the spirit and purpose of American democracy."[22] DuBois, on the other hand, saw American culture as raw and incomplete, fluid in nature, a future possibility rather than a present reality. In this view she was influenced by Louis Adamic, who had argued that all Americans (old stock as well as new) should consider themselves "naturalized citizens" of a new nation whose culture has yet to be born. For DuBois, the problem was not to demand the conformity of minority groups to already-established cultural patterns; the problem was to cultivate the soil of cultural diversity, stop the erosion of values and customs, so that the cultural resources of America's varied peoples could be integrated into a new American commonwealth. "Our American culture," she said, "is not a finished and static thing; it is still in the making, and we can each have a part in that making if all of us, no matter

---

[22]Cole's position is outlined in a statement submitted to John Marshall of the GEB (attached to Internal Memorandum by John Marshall, Interview with Stewart G. Cole, Jan. 22, 1940), ff. Bureau for Intercultural Education, 1939-1941, Series I, Subseries III, Box 566, GEB Mss. The quotes are from pp. 4 and 7 of this untitled statement.

what our cultural background, will hold on to what is socially valuable and share it with others."[23]   The anxious years before Pearl Harbor, however, were not supportive of sentiments such as these. William H. Kilpatrick, the influential philosopher of education, who had become chairman of the Bureau's Executive Board in February of 1940, shared Cole's concern to limit this apparent free reign to differences; in his installation address as Board chairman, he observed that one of the basic problems facing the Bureau is deciding ". . . what degree of differentiation is right and proper for any sub-group to maintain within the larger whole."[24]

DuBois' difficulties, however, were not the sole result of her dispute with Cole. Despite her momentary impressions of the situation, which saw Cole as the instigator of her troubles, she had also managed to alienate members of the Board, in particular Clinchy and Trager. The Board could no longer condone her "separate approach" and had reached a decision to place her on the sidelines,

---

[23]Script of radio broadcast entitled "Appreciating Other Cultures," p. 3, ff. Rachel Davis DuBois, Speeches and Radio Talks, 1934-1945, DuBois Mss.

[24]William H. Kilpatrick, "Education and Group Relationships," p. 2 (digest of an address delivered at the Annual Dinner of the Service Bureau for Intercultural Education, April 15, 1940), an insert enclosed with Intercultural Education News, I (April, 1940). The Bureau began publication of this newsletter in September of 1939. A full set of the first eight issues of the newsletter may be found with the papers of George Graff, Immigration History Research Center, University of Minnesota.

if not remove her completely. In January of 1940, Clinchy, who

was now Chairman of the Board, reported to DuBois that the Executive

Committee, which had been called into session without her know-

ledge, had voted to offer her a six month leave of absence.[25] Cole

reassured her that "things would go on us usual" upon her return,

although DuBois later came to believe that the Board's action was

a ploy to ease her out gracefully.[26] The strategy used by the Board

was both peremptory and disingenuous. In reporting the Board's

action to John Marshall of the GEB, Cole mentioned that the leave

was offered "ostensibly to enable her to complete her work for a

doctorate, but probably with the proviso that during her leave she

seek psychiatric advice."[27] Bitterly entering in her diary the news

of her "betrayal," DuBois told Clinchy that she would "think it over"

and left town for one week to see W. E . B. DuBois in Atlanta.

While she was away, the news of her "illness" and "need for a rest"

---

[25]DuBois, Personal Log, Jan. 26, 1940, DuBois Mss.

[26]Ibid., entry for the period April 15 - June 11, 1940.

[27]Internal Memorandum by John Marshall, Interview with Stewart G. Cole, Jan. 22, 1940, ff. Bureau for Intercultural Education, 1939-1941, Series I, Subseries III, Box 566, GEB Mss.

spread rapidly.[28] Upon her return, she wrote Clinchy and--citing

pressing responsibilities to supervise school projects in New York

City and New Rochelle--declined the Board's offer of a leave. She

was now, however, resigned to playing second fiddle to Cole.[29]

Finding herself the center of a storm of controversy, diagnosed as

mentally imbalanced by her adversaries, she received reassurance

from two psychologists that her sanity was unimpared.[30] The Board

would have probably insisted upon the leave were it not for the

firm opposition of L. Hollingsworth Wood, who as a partisan of

DuBois would become a thorn in the side of her opponents.[31] At a

meeting of the Executive Committee on February 13, 1940, Cole's

sole authority as director was affirmed, DuBois was taken off the

---

[28]I have been unable to find any evidence of a mental
disorder affecting DuBois at this time. Both Stewart Cole and
Frank Trager, in interviews with the author, could not recall any
such problem. The only emotional strain which DuBois may have been
suffering from was a marital difficulty which led to her divorce from
Nathan DuBois in 1941.

[29]DuBois, Personal Log, Jan. 26, Feb. 3, Feb. 9, Feb. 13, 1940,
DuBois Mss.

[30]Ibid., April 15, 1940.

[31]Ibid., Feb. 13, 1940. For evidence of Wood's bitter opposition
to the new directions taken by the Bureau, see correspondence in
ff. Fieldston School Project, 1940, BIE Mss.

Executive Committee, and her fate was placed in the hands of a

sub-committee consisting of Clinchy and Trager.

For the next two months, agonizing and tedious discussions

took place over DuBois' future with the organization. Cole resisted

entreaties from DuBois to pray together to resolve their differences;

Trager and Durlach advised DuBois to resign and set up shop in

California or Philadelphia; meanwhile, DuBois sought legal counsel

and weighed a court battle to regain her position. Trying to mediate

the dispute was the new Chairman of the Board, William H. Kilpatrick,

who began to regret ever having gotten dragged into this sorry mess.[32]

Eventually, Hugh Hartshorne was called in to work out a "compromise

plan." His recommendation that DuBois be made "Secretary" of a

semi-autonomous Teacher Education Committee was adopted by the

Board at a meeting on April 29, 1940. The new Committee was made

directly accountable to the Board but responsibility for all initial

contacts with schools and teacher training institutions was placed

in the hands of Cole as Director. At this same meeting, DuBois learned

of Trager's "malevolence" for the first time. Board member,

Eduard C. Lindeman, a DuBois partisan, told her that Trager had been

_____

[32]Ibid., Feb. 15, Feb. 16, Feb. 20, 1940. "Notes from
Kilpatrick's Ledgers," p. 2 (These notes were taken during an interview with Willialm Kilpatrick, Oct. 24, 1958, by Shirley Kolack
and Olive Hall), ff. Bureau for Intercultural Education, Interviews,
1958, BIE Mss.

masterminding her downfall from power.[33] After the meeting, the
DuBois forces did not abandon their fight to retain control of the
Bureau. In June, Wood invited partisans of DuBois to attend a
luncheon conference to discuss "a certain cleavage of opinion
as to method which we all ought to know more about." In a follow-
up letter to Leonard Covello, DuBois disclosed that "our underlying
philosophy of cultural democracy is being challenged more and more
because of the war crisis."[34] DuBois received the Board's authorization to "temporarily" transfer relevant office records and materials
to her home near New York University "as a convenience for her
teaching program during the summer."[35] From this sanctuary, she
continued to fight against the "selfish" forces that had taken control
of the Bureau and in the fall, refused requests to return to the Bureau's
offices.

---

[33]Hugh Hartshorne to William H. Kilpatrick, Theresa Durlach,
Frank N. Trager, Rachel Davis DuBois and Stewart G. Cole,
April 26, 1940; Service Bureau for Intercultural Education, Minutes of
the Executive Committee, April 29, 1940, ff. Bureau for Intercultural
Education, 1939-1940, AJC Mss. Rachel Davis DuBois, Personal Log,
April 29, 1940, DuBois Mss.

[34]L. Hollingsworth Wood to Leonard Covello, June 5, 1940,
Rachel D. DuBois to Leonard Covello, June 7, 1940, ff. Inter-
cultural Education, Agencies and Organizations, Service Bureau for
Intercultural Education, Box 17, Covello Mss.

[35]Service Bureau for Intercultural Education, Minutes of the
Board of Directors, June 9, 1940, ff. Bureau for Intercultural Education, 1939-1940, AJC Mss.

235

The Attack on "Cultural Pluralism:"
The GEB-financed Committee
for Evaluation

During the turbulent months that led up to DuBois' demotion, certain events were taking place that further weakened the position of DuBois and her supporters. A Committee for Evaluation of the Work of the Service Bureau, financed by a grant from the General Education Board, was conducting a thorough examination and evaluation of the Bureau's programs and philosophy. The story of this evaluation adds an important context to the events described above. The results of the evaluation provided the rationale for reshuffling the staff and for the rejection of the "pluralist" approach advocated by DuBois and her associates. It will be recalled that an important reason why the PEA severed its connection with the Service Bureau in 1938 was the failure to obtain funding from the General Education Board. The GEB's rejection of the PEA proposal had apparently been based on doubts as to its administrative feasibility. The rising fortunes of the Bureau after its departure from the PEA probably emboldened DuBois, either on her own initiative or at the suggestion of a member of the Board, to make another appeal for GEB funding. The Bureau was especially hard-pressed to meet the request of the New York City Board of Education for assistance in implementing its resolution that schools in the city hold assemblies showing "the contribution of all races and nationalities to the growth and development of American democracy."

DuBois hoped that the GEB would reverse its earlier decision and

appropriate funds for the direct support of a program in intercultural

education.[36] The GEB, however, had serious reservations over

supporting such a program. Apprehensive about the "dynamite" of

intergroup tensions in the New York City Schools, John Marshall

confided to DuBois: "A primary question for [me] is: Is doing any-

thing better than doing nothing at all?"[37] Albert R. Mann, another

GEB officer, echoed a by-now familiar refrain when he admitted to

Marshall that he was "fearful of procedures which single out the

Jew, as such emphasis is likely to sharpen the target for attack; and

obviously it is the status of the Jew which looms large." The GEB

was also reluctant to undertake a new programming initiative at a

time when pressures were building up to discontinue the program in

general education.[38] As a result, the Board turned down DuBois'

---

[36]Internal Memorandum by John Marshall, Interview with
Rachel DuBois and Hollingsworth Wood, March 21, 1939 (proposed
budgets are attached to this memorandum), ff. Bureau for Intercultural
Education, 1939-1941, Series I, Subseries III, Box 566, GEB Mss.

[37]Ibid.

[38]Memorandum by Albert R. Mann to Members of Staff,
March 31, 1939, ff. Bureau for Intercultural Education, 1939-1941,
Series I, Subseries III, Box 566, GEB Mss.; Fosdick, Adventure,
p. 256.

appeal for direct support but left the door open for an "appraisal

of what the Bureau's work is accomplishing." Such an appraisal,

as Marshall advised DuBois, should explore "deeper levels of

behavior" and should examine the latest "literature on the subject."[39]

DuBois was skeptical of the value of an evaluation that lacked an

experimental base. She tried to persuade the foundation to sponsor

a "demonstration project" in one school district through which an

intensive and comprehensive program of intercultural education would

be tested and evaluated. This plan must have smacked too much of

direct support to be acceptable to the GEB, for by May 17, the

proposal was changed to conform more closely with Marshall's

suggestion.[40] As finally worked out, the plan called for the hiring

of an outside investigator who would look into "the classroom

practices of teachers who are using the Bureau's materials and

---

[39]John Marshall to Rachel Davis DuBois, April 6, 1939, ff.
Bureau for Intercultural Education, 1939-1941, Series I, Subseries
III, Box 566, GEB Mss.

[40]Rachel Davis DuBois to John Marshall, May 1, 1939,
Harold G. Campbell to John Marshall, May 13, 1939, Rachel Davis
DuBois to General Education Board, May 17, 1939, "Appraisal of
Intercultural Education as Carried on in the New York City Schools
by the Service Bureau for Intercultural Education" (proposal enclosed
with Rachel Davis DuBois to John Marshall, May 19, 1939), ff.
Bureau for Intercultural Education, 1939-1941, Series I, Subseries
III, Box 566, GEB Mss.

receiving its advice."[41] This person would work under the super-

vision of a committee of experts which would recommend techniques

of evaluation and review findings. This provision of the plan was

apparently inserted at the insistence of the GEB, whose officers

were concerned that the evaluation plug into the latest scientific

research in the field of intergroup relations. Noting " . . . how

deep the psychological roots of intercultural conflict and how

complicated the forces in society which nourish them" the GEB's

Executive Committee stipulated that a "special advisory committee"

for the project be formed which would include "the best available

people from the fields of psychology, anthropology, and sociology."[42]

The actual selection of committee members was apparently left up

to the Bureau, but the names of prospective members were submitted

to Marshall for his "approval." By the end of June, a committee of

eight members had been organized. It consisted of Hugh Hartshorne

and Leonard Doob of Yale University, E. Franklin Frazier, the black

sociologist from Howard University, Donald Young of the University

of Pennsylvania, the psychologist Harry Stack Sullivan, W. G. Carr

---

[41]General Education Board, Annual Report 1939 (New York, 1939), pp. 109-110.

[42]Internal Memorandum by John Marshall, Telephone Conversation with Rachel DuBois, June 1, 1939, John Marshall to Rachel Davis DuBois, June 21, 1939, ff. Bureau for Intercultural Education, 1939-1941, Series I, Subseries III, Box 566; General Education Board, Minutes of the Executive Committee, June 9, 1939, GEB Mss.

of the National Education Association, Harvey Zorbaugh of New York University,[43] and Otto Klineberg of the Columbia University Psychology Department, who was named Chairman of the Committee.

The Committee worked for the next two months to find a qualified person for Director of Research.[44] By the beginning of September, the Committee had chosen Genevieve Chase for the position, formerly Dean of Women at Kalamazoo College and at the time of her appointment Research Associate at Columbia University. Chase's previous association with Cole (they had both known each other at Kalamazoo College) may have given her an inside track for the job.

Chase and the Committee spent the next year probing the operations of the Bureau. Every crevice and cranny of the Bureau's operations--from office management to basic philosophy--were examined. The curriculum materials were evaluated by a specially-selected group of "experts." Questionnaires were sent to purchasers of these materials to ascertain their reactions to them. A

---

[43]For unknown reasons, Zorbaugh did not participate in the Committee's deliberations and did not afix his signature to the final report.

[44]For a short time in May, Stewart Cole was under consideration for this position. This was before Bayne had stepped down as Bureau director ("Appraisal of Intercultural Education as Carried on in the New York City Schools by the Service Bureau for Intercultural Education" [Proposal enclosed with DuBois to Marshall, May 19, 1939], p. 2, ff. Bureau for Intercultural Education, 1939-1941, Series I, Subseries III, Box 566, GEB Mss.).

second set of questionnaires was sent to purchasers of the

Americans All recordings. The Bureau's program of assistance to

the New Rochelle school system (a program under the direction of

George Graff) was carefully evaluated. Other services provided

by the Bureau were described but not appraised. These included

the "living newspaper project," under the direction of Francis

Bosworth, the radio broadcasting activities of the Bureau, and

DuBois' regular courses at New York University. The Committee

concentrated, however, on the Bureau's program of assistance to

teachers. Since this assistance was mainly rendered through the

in-service course, the Committee spent most of its time investigating

the course and analyzing its impact. Chase attended every session

of the two courses scheduled during the 1939-40 academic year.

She held interviews with, and distributed questionnaires to, teachers

who had enrolled in the courses. She visited their classrooms to

observe the affects of the course on teaching techniques and student

attitudes. She interviewed principals, district superintendents, and

even students. [45]

---

[45]Committee for Evaluation of the Work of the Service Bureau
for Intercultural Education, "Report A--Report of the Committee for
Evaluation to the General Education Board" (mimeographed), 1940,
pp. 17-21, GEB Mss.; Committee for Evaluation of the Work of the
Service Bureau for Intercultural Education, "Report B and Appendix"
(mimeographed), 1940, pp. 18-19. The Report of the Committee was
subdivided into two parts. Report A was signed by the full Committee
for presentation to the GEB and the Service Bureau. It summarized
the findings and contained the major recommendations of the Committee.
Report B was prepared by Chase and Klineberg for other members of the

After a year and four months of study, the Committee submitted
its report to the General Education Board and to the Service Bureau
in January of 1941. Containing over 200 pages of recommendations,
program descriptions, data summaries, and appendix materials--an
intensive and thorough examination of a small, non-profit agency--
the Report praised the work of the Service Bureau as timely, pioneering and "unique." The recommendations of the Committee touched
upon almost every facet of the Bureau's program. One of the
Committee's most important findings concerned the recently-established
in-service course. Because of the "scattered distribution" of the
teachers in the course (never more than three or four from any one
school) and the many obstacles they faced in implementing changes
in their schools, the report concluded that the concentration of
staff time on the course was both inefficient and unproductive of
visible results. The Committee favored a more intensive effort
in one or two schools, such as had been attempted in the New Rochelle
program. Such an approach could be "more flexibly adapted to
individual teachers and local schools."[46] Among other recommendations

Committee (although copies were sent to the GEB and to the Service
Bureau). It explained the research methodology and major findings
in greater detail.

[46]Committee for Evaluation, Report B, p. 35; Committee for
Evaulation, Report A, p. 19, GEB Mss.

made by the Committee were: greater emphasis on pre-service
training of teachers; greater effort to secure the input of "members
of oppressed groups"; diversification of curriculum materials for
different age levels; greater attention to questions of fundamental
research; consideration of class conflict as an important dimension
of intergroup conflict; and further experimentation with the Living
Newspaper Project.[47] The main recommendation, however, concerned
the ideological orientation of the Bureau.

Running like a constant refrain through the Report is the
Committee's skepticism with regard to the "one fundamental assumption" that had guided the Bureau's work over the years; namely,
"that prejudices are dispelled and attitudes of understanding and
appreciation of various cultures are built up through school experiences
around the cultural contributions of these groups."[48] The evidence
that the Committee presented for what amounted to an indictment of
the DuBois philosophy was rather impressionistic and was based on
teacher reactions to Bureau courses and materials. The Report found
that "the teachers [in the in-service course] objected to the emphasis
(as they interpreted it) . . . on the differences between various

---

[47]Committee for Evaluation, Report A, pp. 9, 12, 17, 21-27,
GEB Mss.

[48]Report B, p. 13, GEB Mss.

culture groups."[49] As Miss Chase toured the schools, she heard

"expressions of doubt as to the attitudes resulting from programs

bringing out cultural differences."[50] The testimony of these teachers

was used to cast doubt upon the entire ethnic studies approach.

It seems likely that Klineberg and Chase had certain preconceptions

that colored the report's findings. Even before they had completed

their investigation, they had reported to the GEB that:

> . . . teachers are fearful that programs built on themes of
> cultural contributions of various groups will bring about an
> increased consciousness of differences among children . . . .
> This the teachers feel is contrary to American ideals and encourages
> adherence to old-world habits rather than adaptations to American
> life.[51]

There is little evidence, however, that the majority of teachers, as

opposed to a vocal minority, actually objected to the Bureau's

philosophy of cultural democracy. Sample responses to a question-

naire sent to teachers in the in-service course reveal no dissatis-

faction with the course for the reasons given by Chase.[52] A

---

[49]Report A, p. 5, GEB Mss.

[50]Report B, p. 52, GEB Mss.

[51]Otto Klineberg and Genevieve Chase to John Marshall,
March 27, 1940, ff. Bureau for Intercultural Education, 1939-1941,
Series I, Subseries III, Box 566, GEB Mss.

[52]Report B (Appendix), pp. 16-19, GEB Mss.

second evaluation form used by DuBois, as well as term papers

turned in by her students (copies of which have survived), are

equally unrevealing of any current of discontent.[53] At one point,

the report admits that dissatisfaction with DuBois' approach was

not universal: "Some of the teachers violently disagreed with this

method, while others reported enthusiastically that they had used

it with success."[54] In a program admittedly as "controversial"

and "pioneering" as that advocated by the Bureau, it was probably

inevitable that some teachers would be hostile to the Bureau's

program. Why the "fears" of these teachers should--in effect--

condemn that program is not clear. An analysis of the literature

on the subject might have clarified the issue, but that task was

not undertaken in the report. Although as part of its investigation

the Committee prepared digests of hundreds of articles that had

appeared in the field of prejudice and intergroup relations, no

attempt was made to relate this literature to the Committee's find-

ing that:

> a concurrent emphasis upon essential similarities between
> the culture groups, as well as upon their respective contribu-

[53]The Evaluation forms, as well as the term papers, are found
in: ff. New York City Board of Education, In-service Course, Fall,
1939, DuBois Mss. Only thirteen of the evaluation forms turned in
to DuBois have survived. These are filed alphabetically by student
name from "G" to "M". They most likely constitute a random sample.

[54]Report A, p. 6, GEB Mss.

tions, would be better received, and <u>would in the long run</u>
<u>prove more effective</u> [italics mine]. [55]

The Committee was correct in arguing that the Bureau's efforts to

<u>combat prejudice,</u> relying on the study of cultural contributions,

had been "on a symptomatic and superficial level" and had failed

to take into account the "social and economic forces" that gave

rise to prejudice, but the methods used by the Bureau were designed

to achieve a number of different goals. [56]

The Committee's finding that the Bureau lacked an adequate

grasp of the literature on prejudice was indicative of the Committee's

concern with the problem of conflict resolution. The value of the

cultural contributions approach was appraised according to a single

criteria: how effective was it in eliminating prejudice. The effective-

ness of the in-service course was judged on the basis of "teachers' ef-

forts to break down prejudice" in the classroom, not according to

whether the teachers had achieved success in creating more positive

student self-image or better social adjustment. [57] From the point of

---

[55] Report A, p. 7, GEB Mss.. A copy of Chase and Klineberg's
examination of the literature entitled, "Digests of Books and Articles
on Prejudices and Education for Overcoming Prejudices," n.d., may
be found in the library of the Rockefeller Archives Center.

[56] Report A, pp. 12-13, GEB Mss.

[57] Report B, p. 36, GEB Mss.

view of the Committee, the fact that most teachers enrolled in

the in-service course were Jewish was evidence of a misdirection

of the Bureau's energies. "The responsibility for eliminating

prejudice did not lie with them." It would have been preferable,

argued the Committee, to recruit "teachers who belong to the

relatively 'privileged' groups."[58] The possibility that the Jewish

teachers could better interpret their group's history and traditions

and also serve as "role model ideals" for their students did not

dawn upon the Committee. Failing to perceive the psychological

dimensions of the Bureau's program, the Committee attached greater

importance to teacher education than to instruction of children.

The report recommended that the Bureau work more closely with

teacher-training institutions and thereby assist with the task of

educating "prospective teachers . . . before they have the opportunity

of handing down their prejudices to the children."[59] No attempt

was made in the Report to appraise the value of the Bureau's

approach for overcoming student alienation or "building a richer

American culture." One section of the report--a ten-page history

of the Bureau--[60]completely failed to mention the "mental health"

---

[58]Report A, p. 7, GEB Mss.

[59]Report A, p. 9; Report B, p. 41, GEB Mss.

[60]Report B, pp. 1-10, GEB Mss.

function of the Bureau's cultural studies approach. DuBois, for

her part, was still an ardent supporter of cultural studies for the

minority child. In her articles, speeches and radio talks during

this period, she continually made reference to the second generation

problem.[61] She never failed to schedule at least one session on

this subject in her in-service courses.[62] In the summer of 1940,

with the help of her NYU students, she developed the "festival

approach" to ethnic studies and intergroup fellowship. This

technique called for the open discussion of ethnic identity in a

small group setting and an almost therapeutic effort to reawaken

lost memories of the group past.[63] The children of the immigrants,

she wrote in 1941, "are still wandering, culturally speaking, in a

No Man's Land"; why, she asked, "should 'becoming an American'

---

[61]See transcript of radio interview with DuBois entitled: "Appreciating Other Cultures," April 17, 1940, p. 3; see also plans for second radio broadcast to be called: "Culture Groups in Community Life," November 10, 1940, pp. 5-6, ff. Rachel Davis DuBois, Speeches and Radio Talks, 1935-1942, DuBois Mss. The second generation problem is also discussed in Rachel Davis DuBois, "The Need for Sharing Cultural Values," Friends Intelligencer, Feb. 11, 1939, 84-85.

[62]Report B (Appendix), pp. 13-16. DuBois delivered four lectures during the course (the other sessions were devoted to talks by guest speakers). One of the four lectures dealt with the problem of ethnic alienation (Report B, p. 19).

[63]The technique is discussed in detail in: Rachel Davis DuBois, Get Together Americans: Friendly Approaches to Racial and Cultural Conflicts through the Neighborhood-Home Festival (New York, 1943).

be such a tragic experience for the immigrant and his children. "[64]

Evaluating the progress made by the Bureau in achieving only one

goal was to ignore the other goals it had, perhaps, been more

successful in achieving.

Was the Evaluation Committee interested in the cause of

minorities or in their control? Fear of the dangerous consequences

of the cultural studies approach, rather than despair over its

effectiveness, may explain the Committee's preoccupation with the

question of cultural differences. The Report did not rest its

critique of the pluralist approach with the mere assertion that such

an approach was ineffective; it also implied that such an approach

was dangerous and divisive--a curious charge considering the fact

that the Committee had already argued the futility of intellectual

approaches to intergroup harmony. If the study of cultural

differences did not change attitudes for the better, why should it

change them for the worse? The rumblings of war on the European

horizon may have evoked painful memories of internal strife and dis-

unity a generation earlier. In troubled times such as these, Americans

did not need to be reminded of their differences, but of their unity.

Wrote the Committee:

> In the light of the present crisis in world affairs, and the
> possibility that the United States may become more deeply

---

[64]Rachel Davis DuBois, radio speech entitled: "How Shall we
Fight Intolerance?" April 14, 1941, pp. 3-4, ff. Rachel Davis DuBois,
Speeches and Radio Talks, 1935-1942, DuBois Mss.

involved, it is all the more important that Americans should be
united in defense of their democracy. The ethnic and religious
prejudices which interfere with such union, and divide Americans
into mutually hostile sub-groups, constitute therefore a menace
to American solidarity . . . .[65]

Committee member Hugh Hartshorne was candid in giving his reasons

for condemning the ethnic studies approach. Such an approach

would "keep a particular culture group apart from the total life"

and interfere with the development of "a sense of unity in our

culture." It would also "ally" the Bureau "with the German govern-

ment in strengthening the separativeness [sic] of German Americans."[66]

Perhaps, the apprehension of the Committee was best voiced by two

high school superintendents asked to evaluate the Bureau's

curriculum materials. The materials, they argued, "arouse[d] in

the thinking of so-called minority groups an undesirable emphasis

upon their own importance and a determination to insist upon their

own rights . . . ."[67] The connection between pride in ethnic

identity and political militance was apparently well-understood

during the Depression era.

The GEB report fell short of being an objective analysis of

---

[65]Report A, p. 1, GEB Mss.

[66]Service Bureau for Intercultural Education, Minutes of Meeting of Executive Committee and of Committee for Evaluation of the
Work of the Service Bureau for Intercultural Education, Dec. 13, 1940,
p. 3. "Notebooks," Vol. XVII, No. 3, pp. 128-145, BL Mss.

[67]Report B, p. 67, GEB Mss.

the Bureau's program and goals. Although it made many astute

observations and sound recommendations, the Report failed to

weigh the psychological objectives of the Bureau's program and

criticized the cultural studies approach without presenting

sufficient evidence to support that criticism. The report was

also used for partisan purposes, providing the rationale for a

campaign to dislodge the cultural integrationists from positions

of power within the Service Bureau. About the same time that the

Committee was presenting its findings, so damaging to DuBois

and the philosophy she represented, another attack was launched

against the program of the Bureau. This time the target for attack

was the curriculum materials which DuBois and her colleagues had

labored for six years to develop.

Lasker's Attack on the Curriculum Materials

In the spring of 1940, the Bureau's Board had decided to hire

a "publications expert" who would assume overall responsibility

for the preparation and distribution of printed materials. The man

chosen for this position was Bruno Lasker, who began his assign-

ment in October of 1940. Born in Hamburg, Germany, in 1880,

Lasker served as Associate Editor of The Survey Magazine from 1916

to 1923. He later worked for the Rockefeller-funded Inquiry move-

ment (1923-1930), serving as head of the Committee on Race Attitudes

in Children. Growing out of his work for The Inquiry were the raw materials for his ground-breaking book, Race Attitudes in Children,

published in 1929. The book showed how young children absorb

unfavorable racial stereotypes even before entering school. Just

before joining the staff of the Service Bureau, Lasker worked

for the American Council of the Institute of Pacific Relations.[68]

Despite his long-standing friendship with Rachel Davis DuBois,

Lasker lost no time in mounting a full-scale attack on the

curricular materials developed by DuBois and her co-workers. Within

two months of the start of his new assignment, Lasker implored

Cole to call a "complete moratorium" on the continued dissemina-

tion of these materials. A few days later, he appeared before the

Bureau Board and made the same appeal--arguing his case so force-

fully that he felt compelled to apologize to DuBois "for the extreme

candor, not to say rudeness or brutality" of his presentation.

Lasker's impatience was prompted in part by his desire to get Board

authorization for a "radical change in publications policy."[69]

Although the Board could not sanction the scuttling of a line of

products that had become the Bureau's stock in trade, the gradual

[68]Bruno Lasker to Mrs. Clark, August 23, 1941 (Lasker reviews his career in this letter), "Notebooks," Vol. XVIII, No. 1, pp. 137-139; Bruno Lasker to Mr. Jones, n.d., "Notebooks", Vol. XVII, No. 3, pp. 10-11, BL Mss.

[69]Memorandum from Bruno Lasker to Stewart G. Cole, Nov. 22, 1940, Bruno Lasker to Rachel Davis DuBois, Nov. 25, 1940, "Notebooks," Vol. XVII, No. 3, pp. 115, 118-119; Service Bureau for Intercultural Education, Minutes of the Board of Directors, Nov. 24, 1940, ff. Bureau for Intercultural Education, 1939-1940, AJC Mss.

withdrawal of these materials over the next three years attests in part to the power of his critique. Lasker had discovered serious flaws in the Bureau's literature.

Lasker noted defects that were both technical and ideological in nature, and although extensive tinkering might have removed defects of the former type, piecemeal revisions could never have accomplished the kind of major ideological alterations that Lasker had in mind. Lasker's technical criticisms were generally carping and unmellowed by any appreciation for the obstacles faced by the Bureau in previous years. He thought it irresponsible to compress a complicated subject, like the history or cultural contributions of a particular ethnic group, into units of a few pages in length, containing disconnected and often superficial facts and information. He faulted the Bureau for failing to distinguish clearly between a publication that was experimental in nature, that ought therefore to be limited in distribution and subject to periodic reevaluation and revision, and a publication that was considered a finished product. Most of the Bureau's mimeographed units, he felt, were of the former type though they were being marketed as tested and refined products.[70]   He insisted that the pragmatic test of a unit's

---

[70]Bruno Lasker, "Prolegomena for the Consideration of a Program of Publications," Oct. 21, 1940, pp. 2,4, "Notebooks," Vol. XVII, No. 3, pp. 50-64, BL Mss.

worth, whether teachers and students were satisfied with its

content (Lasker admitted that most teachers were enthusiastic

about the materials) was not adequate, that such a unit must stand

the test of careful scrutiny by the best subject authorities in

each relevant field of study. To achieve this objective, he pushed

through a change in publication policy at the December 13, 1940,

meeting of a special Committee on Publications organized to assist

him with his work. As of that date, all new or revised manuscripts

would have to undergo review by at least two scholars before

Bureau publication would be authorized.[71] Lasker also took excep-

tion to the rationale that seemed to govern the coverage given to

certain ethnic groups to the exclusion or neglect of others. Foreign

policy considerations weighed more heavily on his scale of prior-

ities, i.e. whether an actual or impending entanglement overseas

threatened to involve a minority in this country, than such previous

criteria as the size of the ethnic group or widespread ignorance as

to its role in the development of American society.[72]

---

[71]Service Bureau for Intercultural Education, Minutes of the
First Meeting of the Committee on Publications, December 13, 1940,
p. 1, ff. Bureau for Intercultural Education, 1939-1940, AJC Mss.
For Lasker's rather condescending attitude toward the classroom teacher,
see: Bruno Lasker to Rachel Davis DuBois, Nov. 25, 1940, "Notebooks,"
Vol. XVII, No. 3, pp. 118-119, BL Mss.

[72]Bruno Lasker, "Prolegomena," p. 16, "Notebooks," Vol. XVII,
No. 3, p. 65, BL Mss.

Lasker's methodological objections had less bearing on the ongoing reassessment of Bureau policy than the basic ideological objections that he made, which foretold a growing disenchantment with the romantic view of immigrant contributions. Wishful thinking in this regard--whether as an expression of the status-cravings or filio-pietism of the immigrants or as an expression of the excess zeal of their self-professed advocates--was Lasker's pet aversion. Lasker took exception to two tendencies in the Bureau's literature: first, the attempt to credit ethnic groups for cultural influences exerted upon American society through other means; and second, the attempt to credit ethnic groups for the achievements of individuals who sprang from the ranks of these groups.

In the first instance, Lasker was disturbed by the failure to properly distinguish between the cultural influence of the immigrant and cultural borrowings brought about in other ways. The German Kindergarten, for example, was introduced into American education by American social reformers, not by German immigrants, and the influence of Oriental culture on American life--a subject about which Lasker was especially knowledgeable--had been exerted "hardly at all through Oriental immigrants."[73] In some of

---

[73]Bruno Lasker, A Draft Statement of Certain Principles Affecting Publication Policy, to be submitted to the Board of Directors (Service Bureau for Intercultural Education), March 11, 1941, p. 3, ff. Bureau for Intercultural Education, 1939-1940, AJC Mss. This seven page document is the most detailed and revealing statement of Lasker's position. Bruno Lasker, Memorandum to Stewart G. Cole "Re Suggestions from

the Bureau's units, the cultural traits in question had not yet

been transferred to America but were implied to be a potential

contribution of the members of a particular group given a proper

climate for their acceptance. Lasker argued that such studies were

not relevant to the Bureau's avowed purpose: to show the cultural

processes at work in the actual mingling of ethnic groups in

American society. To the extent that a false inference could be

drawn from some of the curriculum materials, i.e. that ethnic

groups had served as the conduit for cultural borrowings, Lasker's

criticism was justified. But he was incorrect in suggesting that all

of these units coveyed such a false impression. Many of the units

clearly implied that the achievements of foreign cultures had not

yet been transferred to American society, despite the presence of

members of those cultures in America. The purpose of these units

was not to show that the immigrants and their descendents had

already enriched American civilization, but that they were potential

enrichers given the proper set of circumstances.[74] But it was true

---

Frank N. Trager re 'evaluation and publication of plays, etc.'"
Nov. 18, 1940, "Notebooks," Vol. XVII, No. 3, pp. 111-112, BL
Mss.

[74]Among curriculum units of this type were the following:
"British Contributions in Physics," "German Influence in American
Education," "Italians in Chemistry and Physics," "Italian Contributions
to Biology and Medicine," "Japanese Etiquette," "Chinese Shadow
Pictures." Copies of these units may be found in the DuBois Mss.

enough that what was often associated with the immigrants were
the achievements of the "high cultures" of foreign nations, an
inheritance in which the peasant classes often did not share and
which may have rested on their economic exploitation.

Lasker also objected to the Bureau's emphasis on notable
individuals of foreign birth or parentage. That each group had
produced certain exemplary types, be they explorers, scientists,
businessmen or whatever, hardly seemed relevant to an accurate
assessment of that group's history or contributions to American
society. For one thing, such individuals, argued Lasker, were
on the whole definite exceptions to the general rule of poor achievement or mediocrity in most of the recent immigrant groups.[75] For
another, such individuals had bilked their ethnic brethren or turned
their back on communal responsibilities in rising to the top; many
of them he wrote,

> have successfully climbed over the prostrate bodies of their
> countrymen. Others are successful because throughout their
> careers they have disregarded those social obligations that eat
> into the sympathies, the energies and the pocketbooks of the
> great majority and prevent them from putting all they had into
> their personal careers. They are great individualists, not
> representatives of their groups.[76]

[75]Lasker, A Draft Statement, March 11, 1941, p. 3, ff. Bureau
for Intercultural Education, 1939-1940, AJC Mss.

[76]Bruno Lasker, Memorandum Re Culture Map of Council Against
Intolerance, Dec. 11, 1940, "Notebooks," Vol. XVII, No. 3, p. 160,
BL Mss.

Although Lasker may have overstated the degree of group disloyalty involved in mobility American-style, he realized that communal separation and renunciation of ethnic culture were the heavy prices many second generation Americans had to pay for advancement within the American economic and social system. If the purpose of the Bureau's literature was to show how ethnic cultures have produced exemplary social types, then why grant recognition to individuals who fought against their backgrounds in rising to the top.

Although Lasker's criticisms of the Bureau's curricular materials dovetailed with similar objections raised by the GEB Evaluation Committee, and although he paid lip-service to the expressed fears and misgivings of the Committee, his position differed sharply on one very important point with that of the Committee: Lasker was more willing than the other critics to confront head-on the issue of cultural diversity within American society. He repeatedly referred to the importance of "realism" in intercultural education: that no truth--no matter how distasteful or potentially divisive--should be hidden from people; he urged adoption of a rational approach: that people should be helped to deal with this disturbing reality through a clear presentation of facts and a scientific weighing of policy alternatives. His non-evasive and non-sentimental approach set him apart from both warring factions within the Bureau.

It is not easy to pin down precisely Lasker's personal

predilections since he was under pressure from several quarters during his brief period of service with the Bureau and he knew how to twist and turn to please whatever audience he was addressing. During his first few months of service, as he caught the drift of the GEB evaluation, he often echoed the Committee's concern to get away from the separate approach to intercultural education. He busied himself commissioning curricular materials that would integrate the contributions of separate groups within certain fields of endeavor such as science and music. Yet--as is clear from later documents--he was disillusioned with the entire contributions approach, whether organized separately or integrated within certain themes. Privately, he confided to Rachel DuBois that he disagreed with "those who would rule out altogether materials on particular culture groups because they tend to accentuate differences." He realized that what was required was "an entirely new and realistic set of materials, doing greater justice to the masses of often poorly educated immigrants and their children, farmers and laborers in the main."[77]

Lasker's primary concern was "to substitute realism and objectivity for convention and bias" in the study of ethnic interactions.[78]

---

[77]Bruno Lasker to Rachel Davis DuBois, Nov. 25, 1940; Bruno Lasker, Memorandum to Stewart G. Cole "Re Suggestions from Frank N. Trager re 'evaluation and publication of plays, etc.'" Nov. 18, 1940, "Notebooks," Vol. XVII, No. 3, pp. 111-112, 118-119, BL Mss.

[78]Lasker, A Draft Statement, March 11, 1941, p. 4, ff. Bureau for Intercultural Education, 1939-1940, AJC Mss.

The dispassionate intellect guided by the strictest standards of scholarship and applied to the task of devising educational programs for the schools should be the mainsail of the Bureau's work. No valid social purpose was served by praising the glories of ethnic sub-cultures; no legitimate psychological need compelled the Bureau to repair the cultural image of the minority group child. Sentiment, nostalgia for the past, reverence for ancestors, cultural encapsulation of any sort, as well as fear of difference: these were the very things that had blinded and misled people for centuries, that had pitted group against group in recurring conflict and animosity. Only the unadulterated truth, both the twin facts of cultural diversity and the "minor role" played by minority groups in the development of American civilization--however threatening to the guardians of national unity and however disappointing to ethnic apologists--could make the Bureau's program beneficial to the entire society.

The Second Generation as New Americans: The Emerging Individualist Alternative

By now the various gales that had been blowing over the previous two years had reached peak intensity: the report of the Evaluation Committee, highly critical of the Bureau approach, had been turned in; Lasker had ripped into the curriculum materials, and DuBois and her supporters were being moved to the sidelines. The time was ripe for a general stock-taking that would--if not forge a consensus from the conflicting points of view--agree upon a new

policy for the future. Such a meeting, the purpose of which was

to discuss the major recommendations of the GEB Committee, took

place on December 13, 1940, at the home of Theresa Durlach.[79]

No more comprehensive and profound discussion of policy

alternatives in the field of intercultural education had probably

ever taken place in the history of the Service Bureau (nor perhaps

has such a far-reaching and searching discussion taken place since).

Predictably, the issue that evoked the greatest dissension was

whether cultural studies were necessary and desirable for solving

the adjustment problems of minority children. In the discussion

that ensued, the two arch-protagonists, DuBois and Cole, found

themselves in substantial accord--arguing in favor of ethnic studies

for the second generation--with all the other participants in varying

degrees of opposition to this idea. The harshest critics of the

Service Bureau's past approach were the social scientists on the GEB

---

[79]Service Bureau for Intercultural Education, Minutes of Meeting of Executive Committee and of Committee for Evaluation of the Work of the Service Bureau for Intercultural Education, December 13, 1940, "Notebooks," Vol. XVII, No. 3, pp. 128-145, BL Mss. The meeting was called to discuss the recommendations of the GEB Committee for Evaluation. This remarkable eighteen-page document, although not a verbatim transcription, paraphrases the arguments of each participant in the discussion in great detail. The quotations which follow in the text, therefore, are not the actual spoken words of the participants, but excerpts from the minutes. These excerpts probably bear a very close resemblance to what was actually said.

Evaluation Committee: Hugh Hartshorne, Otto Klineberg and

Donald Young. Also opposed was William Kilpatrick, the "dean"

of progressive educators and new Board Chairman of the Bureau.

Each of these individuals brought a theoretical perspective to the

consideration of educational policy that could not accommodate

cultural studies whether for the enlightenment of the majority or

the well-being of the minority. Their attitude was based on certain

assumptions concerning the speed of the assimilation process, the

inevitability of cultural integration, and the cultural roots of group

conflict.

Hartshorne was the leading exponent of the new point of

view. He argued that the elimination of group barriers based on

ethnicity, race or religion would hasten the day when Americans

would judge each other as individuals, not as group members--by

the content of individual character not by the supposed characteristics

of groups. Consciousness of ethnic groups encouraged the habit of

classifying individuals according to erroneous group stereotypes.

He urged the Bureau to take steps to "induce some sort of amnesia"

for all group affiliations rooted in historic traditions, including

both those of recent immigrants and those of old stock Americans.

"Inherited group structures," he declared, "must give way if all

citizens are to live and cooperate on a plane of equality." Once

the group referrant had been forgotten, the way would be cleared for

a radical reordering of society according to which individuals would band together to achieve goals of a rational and socially productive

sort: ". . . new groups could more easily organize themselves

in terms of function and not in terms of tradition. "[80]

Hartshorne was not blind to the skills and creative contribu-

tions of ethnic groups to American society; he sought to develop

"techniques of culture conservation" that did not perpetuate the

ethnic group. He wanted to expropriate cultural traits from the

exclusive possession of the few to the common ownership of all:

". . . We need a different type of cultural education, " he suggested,

"an education that would magnify the inherited resources of ethnic

groups . . . but not as patterns according to which life must be

lived. " Other than to propose that the Bureau "reconceive culture

in terms of individual background, " he did not specify how such an

education could be provided without directly or indirectly legitimiz-

ing the pattern of life out of which such resources had been created.[81]

Perhaps, the most important reason why such a question was

never considered was the reigning orthodoxy of ideas that tightly

constricted the consideration of alternatives for American society.

Parkian sociology predicted the rapid disintegration of peasant

cultures within an urban-industrial milieu; both the inevitability of

the process as well as the unvarying response of the individual to it

_____

[80]Ibid., p. 3.   [81]Ibid., pp. 3, 5.

were assumed without question. A laissez-faire approach was the
only sensible one under the circumstances. Any attempt to intervene
in this process, either to advance or to retard it, would upset the
natural unfolding of a process the outcome of which was irresistable
and as much the desire of ethnic group members as it was the
preference of the social scientists heralding the new order. Any
educational program that tried to reinvigorate or prolong the life of
ethnic cultures, said Klineberg, constituted an "artificial" intrusion
into the process of cultural change; he concluded, " . . . we have
no educational task in that connection."[82] Hartshorne echoed such
views and added that such a program would be resented just as
much by the groups themselves as by outsiders: " . . . why should
we impose on particular groups the duty to hold on to traditions
they would just as well give up?"[83] Genevieve Chase, the research
director of the GEB study, went so far as to suggest that the Bureau
should promote the assimilation of minorities: "There are special
advantages in beginning a program of intercultural education with
emphasis on similarities when assimilation is actually taking place;
it helps assimilation."[84]

The most powerful argument for the separate approach was
its potential to heal the inferiority complex of the minority group

---

[82]Ibid., p. 13.   [83]Ibid., p. 11.   [84]Ibid., p. 1.

child. The critics of that approach had to challenge the premises upon which that argument rested. In defending separate studies, Cole had raised the hypothetical example of the maladjusted second generation Italian boy. Cole argued: "We must help him to make peace with his parents and their way of life by, first of all, insuring that he understands and appreciates what this is."[85] Donald Young retorted that "by stressing the Italianism of the Italian boy, problems of mental adjustment are liable to be increased, even created, not solved."[86] He added:

> The Italian boy comes to school, as we have seen, not as an Italian but with a complex of attitudes . . . . The first and most important thing is the acceptance of that Italian boy by his playmates. He does not want to be accepted as an Italian but comes to school with the expectancy of being accepted as an American. Yet, he is at once labelled a "Dago." Hence, the real task, to start with, is not his reconditioning but theirs.[87]

Kilpatrick carried this argument to its logical extreme. When pressed by Cole and Durlach to be more consistent in his lame defense of the anti-DuBois position, he could only reply: " . . . there is no particular culture they wish their children to hold on to . . .: the parents, too, want their children to become good Americans."[88] In one rash remark, he denied the very existence of conflict between the first and second generation, overlooking the vast literature on the "marginality" of the second generation.

---

[85]Ibid., p. 9.   [86]Ibid., p. 10.   [87]Ibid., pp. 14-15   [88]Ibid., p.

Both sides were arguing from a set of assumptions which had

not undergone empirical verification and which, perhaps, could

never be verified beyond a reasonable doubt. Klineberg and

Hartshorne were perhaps more guilty in this regard, for they rather

carelessly assumed what was open to serious question, i.e. that

the minority child was more "American" than ethnic by the time he

reached school and that the parents of that child were cheering him

on as he embraced a new way of life. These assumptions were a

return to the pre-World War I liberal position on ethnicity. Most

teachers in daily and intimate contact with the second generation

child knew that this was not the case. DuBois' contention that

"a group must be helped to achieve some pride in its own background

before it can function cooperatively,"[89] assumed the opposite to be

true: that the child's group background was a basic component of

his personality. That contention was also difficult to prove. If it

was true, however, as experience with scores of children had

suggested, then it at least had the weight of modern psychology on

its side, for had not Freud taught that self-acceptance was a pre-

requisite for acceptance of others? The crucial word in the DuBois

formulation was "some." Freud had also shown that there were forms

of self-love that were akin to egocentrism, that denied the dignity

[89] Ibid., p. 6.

and worth of others, in order to bolster an insecure or threatened
self-image. DuBois had been less than prudent in differentiating
between the healthy and the neurotic forms of group self-love.
Lasker's critique had been well-deserved in noting the artifice
in some of the curriculum materials. To the extent that DuBois
flirted with self-deception in her quest to affirm the humanity of
cultural groups in American society, she also must be faulted.
Although the xenophobic furies that were whirling across Europe at
the time were repugnant to her, there was always the danger--and
in a few instances it came to pass[90]-that her program could be
exploited by those with different purposes.

The final "break" which DuBois had feared and half-expected
was now imminent. Using the tactics of the pacifist, she had
failed to "wear out" her opponents with what she thought was the
righteousness of her position. The arguments of the cultural
integrationists--so her opponents thought--had been shattered.
Her protests against the "undemocratic" way in which new policy
changes had been implemented had fallen on deaf ears. Most of

---

[90]During the Fifteen School Program (1934-1935), one activity
held during the assembly on the Japanese was the singing of the
Japanese national anthem with students reading the lyrics off an
illuminated screen (DuBois, School and Community Project, p. 11).
On another occasion, her pleas for ethnic consciousness were published
in a pro-Fascist Italian-American newspaper. See the series of
articles written by DuBois in: La Tribuna d'America (Detroit),
February 9 to March 30, 1934.

DuBois' supporters had already been ousted: George Graff (field worker), Rose Nelson (guidance-by-mail and office conferences), Lily Edelman and Ruth Davis (research and writing). In protest against these changes, L. Hollingsworth Wood and Eduard C. Lindeman had resigned from the Board in disgust.[91] If DuBois had entertained illusions of reversing the course of events, her position was now untenable. In the spring of 1941, a special sub-committee of the Board--appointed to decide DuBois' fate--turned in its recommendation. DuBois was asked to submit her resignation "with the best wishes of the Board."[92] Her two-year ordeal had come to an end, and so had a chapter in the history of American education.

---

[91]L. Hollingsworth Wood to John Marshall, July 9, 1943, ff. Bureau for Intercultural Education, 1942-1949, Series I, Subseries III, Box 566, GEB Mss. Rachel Davis DuBois, Personal Log, Oct. 21, 1940, DuBois Mss. Also see the questionnaire filled out by Frank N. Trager in 1958, p. 5, ff. Questionnaires, Bureau for Intercultural Education, BIE Mss.

[92]Service Bureau for Intercultural Education, Minutes of the Board of Directors, May 21, 1941, ff. Bureau for Intercultural Education, 1941, AJC Mss. Transcription of Tape #3 (Reminiscences of Stewart G. Cole, ca. 1958), see response to question #12, ff. Transcription of Stewart Cole Tape No. 3, BIE Mss.

CHAPTER IX

SIGNPOSTS TO THE PRESENT

The departure of DuBois and her associates from the Service

Bureau can be placed into a larger context of events. By 1941,

it was thought harmful to the national interest to stress cultural

differences in American society. Louis Adamic, the most eloquent

voice for cultural democracy in the thirties, abruptly terminated

his long association with Read Lewis of the Foreign Language

Information Service, when he sensed that Lewis was reneging on

his promise to make FLIS a lobbying force for cultural integration.[1]

Lewis knew which way the wind was blowing. Officers of the

Carnegie Corporation, which had bankrolled FLIS since its start,

were becoming uneasy with a program that emphasized cultural

---

[1]See the series of letters between Adamic and Lewis in: ff.
Adamic, Louis--Correspondence, Articles, Nov. 14, 1939 to
May 26, 1940, and ff. Adamic, Louis--Correspondence, Articles,
June 6, 1940 to May 17, 1943 (especially Lewis to Adamic,
June 14, 1941), ACNS Mss.

differences under war-time conditions.[2] Similar misgivings were

had by leaders of the International Institute movement. At the

1940 convention of International Institutes and Foreign Community

Departments of the YWCA, calls were heard to "take youth one

step 'beyond nationality.'" A report, apparently prepared by the

national leadership of the YWCA and submitted to the convention

for its consideration, observed that a "great zeal for foreign

causes . . . [had] been absorbing the interest of our young people

of foreign parentage," and urged the delegates to intensify their

efforts to make the second generation "identify with America."[3]

The Roosevelt Administration which had given aid and comfort to

the cultural integrationists was now reconsidering its position. The

sharp drop in support for Roosevelt's third term candidacy in Italian

and German-American electoral districts was a bitter disappointment.

A report prepared for Roosevelt by Louis Bean in early 1941 warned

[2]Carnegie Corporation, Internal Memorandum, Interview between Frederick P. Keppel and Read Lewis, Sept. 25, 1939, ff. Common Council for American Unity (formerly FLIS), 1932-41, Carnegie Mss. See also comments by Charles Dollard attached to a memorandum from Louis Adamic to Frederick P. Keppel, Oct. 1, 1938, ff. Louis Adamic, Carnegie Mss.

[3]Young Women's Christian Association, Minutes of Meeting of Committee to Plan for Pre-Convention Meeting of International Institutes and Foreign Community Departments of the YWCA, Feb. 21, 1940, and report entitled "How Should the Program of International Institutes be Adjusted to the Changing Community?" n.d., Reel 101 (Section 1), YWCA Mss.

that if such political behavior should:

> develop and spread to other nationality groups, this Nation
> cannot maintain its unity and will be split up into innumerable
> national or racial minority groups each feuding with the other and
> each fighting for supremacy over the other--none of them thinking
> of the American Nation as a unified whole and of the supreme
> loyalty owed to it.[4]

Francis Brown, a New York University professor who had supported

the cultural studies movement and who had co-edited one of its

leading textbooks[5], had by 1940 reversed himself. At a gathering

of the National Council on Naturalization and Citizenship in 1940,

he warned that it was impossible to separate the "sense of cultural

continuity," so carefully nurtured by agencies like the Service

Bureau, from political loyalty to foreign governments.[6] The

grave crisis that faced the nation, added to the suspicions that had

already developed over the dangerous side-effects of the separate

approach, whittled away support for the cultural integrationist

position.

---

[4]Gerson, The Hyphenate, pp. 121-22.

[5]Francis J. Brown and Joseph Slavey Roucek, Our Racial and
National Minorities: Their History, Contributions and Present
Problems (New York, 1937).

[6]Francis J. Brown, "New Tensions and Cultural Minorities"
(Address delivered at the joint luncheon of the Adult Education Division
of the National Education Association and the National Council on
Naturalization and Citizenship, Feb. 28, 1940, St. Louis, Mo.),
p. 4, ff. E-G, Boston Mss.

The impulse to take decisive action to prevent the fragmentation and polarization of American society did not disappear after 1941. If anything, it grew stronger. After the Detroit and Los Angeles race riots in 1943, a veritable explosion of interest in intergroup relations programs occurred.[7] In communities across the country, human relations commissions were set up to dampen the tinderbox of group hatreds. In 1944, the Bureau for Intercultural Education, under the leadership of H. Harry Giles, underwent a tremendous expansion, entering into consultative relationships with school systems in Detroit, Gary and Philadelphia. However, it became almost a central dogma of the burgeoning human relations profession not to expect any general reformation of individual attitudes through the use of ethnic studies materials. In a pamphlet put out by Youthbuilders, the following admonition appeared:

> Don't plan separate units on Jewish history, Negro history, or any other cultural history. Isolating such histories--as though they had taken place in a vacuum without reference to the rest

---

[7]In the field of education, a spate of special issues devoted to the theme of intergroup relations appeared during the year, 1944. As samples of these, see: The American Teacher, XXXIX (April, 1944); Childhood Education, XX (April, 1944); and Educational Leadership, II (April, 1944).

of society—builds a sense of group division rather than of group cooperation. It is <u>segregation</u>, historically.[8]

Among alternatives to the "separate approach" put forth by inter-group relations specialists were the following: the racial integration of teaching staffs, the integration of student government and extracurricular clubs, the elimination of the "undemocratic classroom," the development of critical thinking, lessons in propaganda analysis, etc. With all of these new techniques, a strong emphasis was placed on the notion of human sameness. Wrote a New York City high school principal:

> That intercultural education will be most effective which leaves the students with the convictions and feelings that there are basic similarities in all peoples, that human beings are moved by the same fundamental forces, the same needs and wants, the same aspirations . . . ."[9]

Dan Dodson, a leading expert in the post-World War II intergroup relations movement, summed up the conventional wisdom on what had been attempted in the thirties: " . . . the stressing of our differences, such as we have done . . . has made us more in-group out-group conscious than before and [has done] more harm than good."[10]

---

[8]Youthbuilders, Inc., <u>Methods and Results in Inter-group Education</u>, n.d., p. 5, Box 59, Covello Mss.

[9]Hymen Alpern, "The Role of the High Schools in Improving Intercultural Relations," <u>Journal of Educational Sociology</u>, XVI (February, 1943), 364.

[10]Dan W. Dodson, "Changing Attitudes Through Education" (speech given before the New York Society for the Experimental Study of

The widespread concern to immunize American society against the contagion of intergroup hatreds, which marked the post-war period, was accompanied by a strange silence on the subject of nationality groups in American life. By 1944, the Bureau for Intercultural Education had withdrawn almost all of its units on white ethnic and Oriental groups, leaving only a few units on blacks and Jews. A content analysis of articles appearing in Common Ground magazine, a leading contemporary journal in the field of minority studies and intergroup relations, showed a marked shift around the year 1944 away from nationality subjects and toward racial questions, in particular black and Jewish themes.[11] If white ethnic groups were referred to, they were usually lumped together as "Catholics" or "working class" Americans. Louis Adamic's seething mass of "Thirty Million New Americans" had become the "vanishing minorities" of the post war period.[12]

In looking over the ruins of the DuBois program, Bruno Lasker had noted in 1940 that there was "little room for 'intercultural education'

Education, Dec. 8, 1944), p. 8, Reel 10, NCCJ Mss.

[11]David B. Truman, "A Report on the Common Council for American Unity" (A report prepared for the Carnegie Corporation "to give the officers and trustees of the Corporation a fresh judgment on the value and performance of an organization to which we have given major support over many years . . . ."), August, 1946, pp. 70-71, ACNS Mss.

[12]The term "vanishing minorities" was the title of an essay by Maurice Davie, which appeared in: Brown and Roucek, One America (1945), pp. 540-551.

as that term has previously been regarded."[13] Lasker was right.

Although the term "intercultural education" remained in use for

many years, the growing preference for such terms as "intergroup

education" or the more effusive "human relations" showed the

obsolescence of the term. When "intercultural education" was used,

it meant--as a Bureau survey of 500 cities reported in 1947--"primarily

interracial education."[14] Indeed, the major focus of the Bureau's

program in the years after World War II was in the area of Negro-

White relations. Stewart Cole (who like DuBois believed that it

was important for children to have pride in their ethnic ancestry)

was forced out of the Bureau directorship in 1944. His successor,

H. Harry Giles, had formerly been Director of the Educational

Division of the American Council on Race Relations. Under Gile's

leadership, the Bureau offered its services to school systems in

cities where rapidly-expanding black populations collided with

established white ethnic communities. The invitation to enter into

---

[13]Service Bureau for Intercultural Education, Minutes of Meeting of Executive Committee and of Committee for Evaluation of the Work of the Service Bureau for Intercultural Education, December 13, 1940, "Notebooks," Vol. XVII, No. 3, p. 10, BL Mss.

[14]Victor E. Pitkin, "Intercultural Policies of Selected School Systems," July 18, 1947, p. 18, ff. Bureau for Intercultural Education, Department of Analysis and Research, 1947, BIE Mss.

consultative relations with the Gary, Indiana, school system came

after clashes between Negro and Slavic communities over the

integration of a previously all-white school.[15] The Bureau's relation-

ship with the Detroit school system came as an aftermath to the

bloody disturbances of 1943. Walter Feinberg, who studied the

Bureau's efforts to assist the Detroit public schools from 1945 to

1949, found that the Bureau's recommendations for administrative and

curricular reforms were largely ignored, but that "the Bureau's

staff . . . were as reluctant to leave Detroit as the administration

of the schools was reluctant to have them leave."[16] Feinberg,

who did not have ample documentation available to him when he

undertook his investigation, saw little discontinuity between the

Bureau under DuBois' leadership and the Bureau under H. Harry Giles;

according to Feinberg, "the innate trust that she [DuBois] had

expressed in the good will of school administrators and in their

ability to translate that good will into programs of action persisted."[17]

---

[15]"Report on Activities in the Gary, Indiana, Public Schools,"
1947, ff. Service Bureau for Intercultural Education (Library File),
AJC Mss.

[16]Feinberg, "Progressive Education," 501.

[17]Ibid., 499.

The foregoing analysis of the Bureau's history, however, would seem to suggest that, if she did have such "innate trust," her refusal to capitulate to pressures from powerful professional educators did set her apart from those willing to enter into "marriages of convenience" (to use Feinberg's phrase) with school bureaucrats.

The sudden shifting of liberal concern that occurred during World War II was related to the "epidemic of interracial violence" that broke out during the year 1943. The Social Science Institute at Fisk University reported a total of 242 incidents in forty-seven cities.[18] As Harvard Sitkoff noted, "interracialism became an overnight fad . . . . Scores of liberal organizations that never before cared about the race problem suddenly awoke to the realization that they had to do something."[19] Sitkoff contended that the liberal stratagem had a "stunting effect on Negro militancy"; a nascent, mass-based black political movement was nipped in the bud, thanks in part to the abandonment of radical tactics by "bourgeois" Negro leaders.[20] If Sitkoff's analysis is correct, there

---

[18]Harvard Sitkoff, "Racial Militancy and Interracial Violence in the Second World War," *Journal of American History*, LVIII (December, 1971), 671.

[19]*Ibid.*, 678.

[20]*Ibid.*, 679.

was a consistent pattern to liberal efforts to disarm potentially divisive or uncontrollable forces in American society--whether composed of white ethnics before World War II or blacks after.

DuBois struggled on after her departure from the Service Bureau. In 1941, with a small band of loyal supporters: Eduard C. Lindeman, Leonard Covello, W. E. B. DuBois, and such members of the Reconstructionist movement as Steinberg, Kaplan and Eisenstein, she founded the "Intercultural Education Workshop," later renamed the "Workshop for Cultural Democracy." Working more frequently with adults than with children, she developed a technique known as "Group Conversation" for leading small group workshops. With this technique, she believed she had a formula for "easing tensions" in schools, unions, housing projects and other settings where people of diverse races, creeds, and national-ities met and interacted.

Group Conversation was an extension of her earlier approach in the schools. Alice Chalip, who did an in-depth study of the technique, wrote that a basic principle of Group Conversation was the need to affirm one's own group identity as a precondition for entering into productive and harmonious relations with others.[21]

---

[21]Alice Grace Chalip, "A Descriptive Study of the Group Con-versation Method of Rachel Davis DuBois" (Unpublished masters thesis, California State University, Hayward, 1974), pp. 32-33.

Participants in a Group Conversation were asked to recall the

formative influences and experiences of childhood. By sharing

memories associated with such universal experiences as the change

of seasons, family life, school life, early work experiences, work-

shop participants were expected to develop an appreciation for both

the varieties of human experience and the common feelings and

common longings of all peoples. As DuBois and her colleague,

Mew-Soong Li, explained it, the purpose of Group Conversation

was to enable a "mixed group" to "see and feel the oneness of

the human family and ... gain an appreciation of the beauty,

significance and wondrous qualities inherent in diversity."[22]

DuBois also dabbled in radical politics. In 1941, she prepared

to join her old friend, A. Philip Randolph, on his "March on

Washington." She became a Board member of the "American League

for Puerto Rico's Independence," because she disapproved of "the

economic exploitation of Puerto Rico by certain forces within our

country."[23] After the imprisonment of the President of the Puerto

Rican Nationalist Party, Albizu Campos, in 1950, she joined in

agitation to effect his release from prison.[24] DuBois' heterodoxy

---

[22]DuBois and Li, Reducing Social Tension, p. 23.

[23]Ruth M. Reynolds to Rachel Davis DuBois, July 17, 1949;
Rachel Davis DuBois to Editor of El Mundo, Feb. 6, 1951, ff. Campos,
DuBois, Mss.

[24]DuBois' support of the campaign to free Campos is documented
in letters and flyers found in: ff. Campos, DuBois Mss.

landed her a summons to appear before the McCarthy Committee, but after her first appearance, this "good American and gracious lady," as Senator Stuart Symington called her, was excused by the Committee and spared any adverse publicity from the incident.[25] During the turbulent days of the civil rights struggle, DuBois and her associates helped to establish the "Dialogue Department" of the Southern Christian Leadership Conference. The Department worked to heal divisions between whites and blacks as southern communities adjusted to the ordeal of desegregation. With the rebirth of interest in ethnicity that accompanied the black struggle of the sixties, DuBois took satisfaction in declaring once again that "we are all ethnics now," and became a living link between the old and the "New Ethnicity."

---

[25]Rachel Davis DuBois to "my very special friends," n.d., ff. Correspondence, General, 1950-1959, DuBois Mss. (Symington's comment is quoted in this letter).

CONCLUSION

The "mainstream" liberal position on the minority problem,
which spanned both the pre-World War II and postwar periods
and which we have called "scientific Americanization," was not
intended to promote continued ethnic identification. Instead,
it meant just the opposite: a variety of strategies to encourage
assimilation using non-coercive tactics. Those persons conver-
sant with the contemporary literature on cultural change realized
that assimilation, though gradual and multi-generational, was
inevitable. The only circumstances which might interfere with
the unfolding of this process were a resurgence of Anglo-Saxon
nativism, which could create a backlash of ethnic consciousness,
and a damming up of economic opportunities for ethnic group members.
Until it became apparent that reason did not dissuade and deter
the bigot, scientific Americanizers   might even endorse a program
of ethnic studies. This conditional support for ethnic studies,
which had all but dissipated by the time of World War II, was not
meant to revive ethnic consciousness, but to avert a new wave
of intolerance. No doubt some liberals also saw ethnic studies as

temporary expedient for minority children. The "revolt" of the

second generation, the manifestations of which could be seen

in rising crime rates, juvenile delinquency, and infractions of

school discipline, could be quelled by restoring the social control

function of the immigrant family. Ethnic studies was an image-

repairing strategy which promised to bolster the authority of the

older generation. Despite a kind of rhetorical celebration of

diversity, many liberals saw the ethnic group as a breeding ground

of narrowness and bigotry, and ethnic consciousness as a contaminent

of American individualsim. What apparently motivated the main-

stream liberal position was a desire to maintain national unity and

social control.

Not all liberals harbored motives such as these. Some were

gripped by the vision of a cosmic civilization--the highest potential

of a diversified people. These cultural integrationists, as we

have called them, were drawn from the ranks of the ethnic groups.

They included such ethnic luminaries as Louis Adamic, Leonard

Covello, and W. E. B. DuBois; leaders of the Jewish Reconstruction-

ist Movement such as Mordecai M. Kaplan, Milton Steinberg and

Ira Eisenstein; and the "nationality workers" of the International

Institutes of the YWCA. The ideology of cultural integration also

appealed to a group of American social reformers, e.g. Edith Terry

Bremer, Florence Cassidy, Dorothy Spicer, Alice Sickels and

Rachel Davis DuBois. Although scientific Americanizers sometimes lent support to projects developed by the cultural integrationists, the history of the Service Bureau for Intercultural Education suggests that there was a basic conflict in purpose between the two groups. Unlike the Americanizers, integrationists prized the cultures and artistic achievements of immigrant groups. They were alarmed by the rapid pace of Americanization, which seemed to destroy more than to create, which seemed to rob people of their color and vitality. The supporters of integrationism were not cultural pluralists, however. Instead they envisioned a new America, baptized and reborn in the healing waters of cultural diversity, possessing a cosmopolitan and planetary culture, the shared inheritances of all of its peoples. To realize this dream, America's new immigrant peoples, in particular the pivotal second generation, would have to be taught to know and value their separate cultures. At the same time, all Americans, whether old stock or new, would have to be taught to transcend their differences, to open themselves to new ideas and new values, to appreciate the contributions of others. This formidable agenda was perhaps the purest expression of what was known as intercultural education during the inter-war years.

It is tempting to write off the cultural integrationists of the inter-war years. The inevitability with which they viewed the disappearances of ethnic differences in American society seems to damage their credibility. They tended to romanticize the cultures of the immigrants, blocking out the disharmonies with the larger

culture, and emphasizing the inoffensive and superficial aspects

of culture. They failed to reckon with the range of variations

within particular groups. They thought of culture as a static rather

than a dynamic entity, as an intellectualized construct, not as

the living social fabric of a people. Seeing themselves as the

guardians of a higher morality, they at times adopted a paternal-

istic attitude toward immigrants and their children, which dismissed

self-help efforts at cultural maintenance (parochial schools and

self-segregation). To have considered questions such as these

would have opened up the painful and illusion-shattering reality

of irreconcilable values and conflicting ways of life, a reality

which would have cast doubt upon the attainment of that ultimate

unity to which they all aspired. Integrationists like DuBois also

failed to grapple with the institutional roots of racism and group

prejudice. They were too confident of the reformation of individual

attitudes and of the ability of the school to transform society. This

being said, however, we should not lose sight of their singular

accomplishments. They were sensitive to the ordeal of those whose

traditions were being assaulted and whose values were being

challenged. They rose above their own cultural rootedness to affirm

the dignity of the stranger in their midst and the legitimacy of his

lifestyle and culture. They also set about to achieve their goals

by appealing for the support of all groups and building a broad coalition for change.

It would be a mistake to assume that cultural pluralism was the burning desire of ethnic groups during the period. The split within the Jewish community between reconstructionists and assimilationists may have been mirrored in other ethnic groups. We need to have more studies of the internal history and development of these groups before any answers will emerge. If the Jewish dilemma with intercultural education was not idiosyncratic, it suggests that minority groups have had ambivalent feelings about ethnic studies in the school curriculum. While it is true that the retreat to religion offered a path of least resistance to Jewish leaders eager to legitimize their group's separate identity in American society, other groups may have shown a similar shyness for publicity. With a history of persecution, Jews were well-attuned to the stalking patterns of their enemies; some of their leaders were fearful that a pluralist program in education could easily play into the hands of their enemies--making the Jews more visible as a target for attack. Jews faced a conflict of serious proportions. Two forms of destruction threatened them: the slow extinction of their culture by neglecting the Jewish education of their children, and an external attack precipitated by a too - vigorous effort at cultural maintenance. It is not inconceivable that members of other groups have shown a similar reluctance to publicly identify themselves as "ethnics" for fear of being cast in the role of the pariahs of

American Society.

A lesson to be learned from this study is that there are powerful forces in American society, emanating from the government, industry, foundations, and private organizations that have worked, either consciously or unconsciously, to weaken or destroy ethnic groups. Sometimes these forces conceal their true intentions by patronizing the minority person and posing as his advocate. It cannot be automatically assumed that those who celebrate our diversity are not fearful of it at the same time and would not wish it away if they could. If by "pluralism" we mean promoting the consciousness of differences, then such an approach may serve a variety of purposes. For some, it may serve to rationalize racial segregation;[1] for some, it may serve as a means of social control; for some, it may serve to perpetuate a neanderthal conception of the political process; for some, it may provide a livelihood. As was the case forty years ago, the pluralist movement is split between those who wish to exploit ethnicity and those who wish to tame it. What the "new ethnicity" may really signify is not so much the dawning of a new age of tolerance, but the death of the old sociology. The persistence of our divisions, whether they be regional, class, or ethnic in nature, is still a profoundly disturbing

---

[1]This contention is made by Howard F. Stein and Robert F. Hill in: "The Limits of Ethnicity," The American Scholar (Spring, 1977), 186-87.

situation--a situation which threatens a major disruption of the existing social order. The measure of "pluralism" as a force for human liberation will be made in the quality of our relations with others and in our capacity to build a just and caste-less society. For all their limitations, this was the great insight of the cultural integrationists.

SOURCES CONSULTED

A NOTE ON MANUSCRIPT AND INTERVIEW SOURCES

The story of the Service Bureau for Intercultural education
from 1934 to 1941 has been pieced together from a number of
different sources. One of the most important, the Rachel Davis
DuBois papers (DuBois Mss.), are deposited at the Immigration
History Research Center of the University of Minnesota. The
DuBois papers are especially useful for an understanding of the
intellectual evolution of this pioneer reformer and activist and
of the curriculum and adult education projects she helped to conduct.
Her papers also help to fill the gap left by the destruction of the
primary records of the Bureau for Intercultural Education (reportedly
lost when a building at New York University in which they were
being stored was demolished in the late fifties.) Other smaller
collections at the Immigration History Research Center complement
the DuBois papers. These include: the Stewart Cole papers, the
George Graff papers, and the Bureau for Intercultural Education
research papers (BIE Mss.). The Cole papers, unfortunately,
contain very little documentation for the 1939 to 1944 period when
Cole served as director of the Bureau (Cole has apparently withheld

deposit of these materials so that he can write his memoirs). The
George Graff papers reveal details of his involvement with the
New Rochelle project during the 1939-1940 academic year and
contain a complete file of the Bureau newsletter, Intercultural
Education News. The Bureau for Intercultural Education records
are a collection of research materials gathered together by
Shirley Kolack and Olive Hall, two former Boston University students
who attempted to write a history of the Bureau in 1958-1959.
Noteworthy among the contents of this collection are interview
forms filled out by leaders of the Bureau and the transcription of
taped reminiscences of Stewart Cole. Finally, the Bruno Lasker
papers (BL Mss.) at Columbia University are a rich and revealing
source of information for his one year period of association with
the Bureau (1940-1941).

One can find valuable documentation on the history of the
Bureau in the records of agencies or organizations with which the
Bureau was closely associated. The minutes of the Progressive
Education Association(Teachers College Archives, Columbia
University)were helpful for the 1936 to 1938 period. The records of
the General Education Board (GEB Mss.) at the Rockefeller Archives
Center, North Tarrytown, New York,were extremely illuminating for
this period, as well as for the 1938 to 1941 period. The records of
the American Jewish Committee (AJC Mss.) were an indispensable
source of information about the history of the Bureau. Found within

the AJC records were Executive Committee minutes, reports and correspondence of the Bureau for the period 1939 to 1954. Documentation for AJC involvement with the Bureau for the pre-1939 period is sparse, however; likewise materials for the study of the internal history of AJC during this crucial period are also limited. The Morris D. Waldman papers (MDW Mss.) in the Archives of the American Jewish Committee contain some fragmentary, though important, documentation. For the later history of the Bureau (ca. 1946 to 1954), the microfilm records of the Anti-Defamation League of B'nai B'rith (Library of the Anti-Defamation League, New York City) may prove useful. The records of the National Conference of Christians and Jews (NCCJ Mss.) in the Lazarus Library of the National Conference of Christians and Jews, New York City, help to illuminate the 1929 to 1934 period when DuBois first began to conduct curriculum experiments in different school systems. The NCCJ records are, of course, useful for reconstructing the internal history of this pathbreaking organization, although they appear to have been excessively pruned before microfilming. One can find further documentation for the early days of NCCJ in the records of the National Council of Churches of Christ in America (Presbyterian Historical Society, Philadelphia). The New York Foundation (NYF Mss.) kindly made available to me its files of correspondence with NCCJ, the Progressive Education Association, and the Bureau for Intercultural Education. These files were especially useful for the 1934 to 1935 period. I was delighted to discover a wealth of

materials on the Americans All--Immigrants All radio series in

the records of the Radio Education Project of the United States

Office of Education (REP Mss.), National Archives Building, Washington,

D.C. Together with the DuBois papers, they provided abundant

documentation for the radio series.

The Service Bureau for Intercultural Education was but one

expression of a larger movement of social reform. I have attempted

in chapter II to sketch the most visible contours of this movement.

Sources for the further study of this movement are many and varied.

The International Institutes of the YWCA were powerful catalysts

for the intercultural education movement. Extensive documentation

on the activities of social workers and nationality group leaders

associated with the institute movement may be found in the records

of the American Council for Nationalities Service (ACNS Mss.), the

Records of the International Institute of Boston (Boston Mss.) and

the Records of the International Institute of St. Louis (all housed

at the Immigration History Research Center, University of Minnesota).

Louis Adamic was the most eloquent voice of the cultural integra-

tionists as well as, perhaps, the foremost ethnic spokesman during

the inter-war years. The Louis Adamic papers at Princeton University

remain, for the most part, an untapped resource. Prof. Henry A.

Christian, of Rutgers University, who has been working on a

definitive biography of the Slovenian-born writer, has kindly made available to me pertinent documentation from this collection.

Additional information about Louis Adamic may be found in the

records of the Carnegie Corporation (Archives of the Carnegie

Corporation, New York City). The Carnegie Corporation was a

key agency in defining, and in proposing solutions to, the immigrant

and second generation problems. A history of the Corporation might

prove to be an important and enlightening study. Leonard Covello

was a major exponent of the cultural integrationist perspective,

who was intimately acquainted with the educational problems of

second generation youth. The Leonard Covello papers (Balch

Institute, Philadelphia) offer a rich and voluminous record of his

career--helpful also for the history of the Service Bureau and for

the history of intercultural experiments at Benjamin Franklin High

School. Finally, the records of the New York City Board of Education,

recently acquired by Teachers College Archives, Columbia University,

contain important documentation on intergroup education programs in

the New York City public schools.

The period during which research for this study was undertaken

proved to be a propitious time for reaching and interviewing the

surviving veterans of the intercultural education movement, most

of whom were more than willing to share with me their memories and

their strong convictions. During the last four years, interviews were

conducted with Everett R. Clinchy (December 10, 1973), Leonard

Covello (June 30, 1975), Rachel Davis DuBois (February 26, 1974),

Theresa M. Durlach (June 24, 1974), Miriam R. Ephraim

(August 18, 1975), George Graff (August 22, 1974), Read Lewis

(December 13, 1974), Joseph Roucek (June 24, 1976), Frank N. Trager

(August 5, 1975), and Sidney Wallach (August 8, 1975). Tapes were

made of the Ephraim, Graff, Roucek, Trager and Wallach interviews

and deposited at the Immigration History Research Center, University

of Minnesota. I have also benefited from correspondence with

Dr. Stewart Cole and the late Frederick L. Redefer.

On May 25, 1977, the Institute of Philosophy and Politics

of Education at Teachers College, Columbia University--as part

of its "New York City Project" on the history of education during

the Depression Decade--sponsored an oral history symposium

on the intercultural education movement. Participants in the

symposium were: Maurice Bleifeld (teacher at Benjamin Franklin

High School), Rachel Davis DuBois, Francis Bosworth (Director

of the Bureau's "Living Newspaper Project"), Rita Morgan

(community organizer for Benjamin Franklin High School), and

John Slawson (Vice-president of the American Jewish Committee).

The three-hour session was taped and a transcription will be made

and deposited in the archives of Teachers College.

SELECT BIBLIOGRAPHY

A. BOOKS

Abbott, Grace. The Immigrant and the Community. New York, 1917.

Adamic, Louis. Dynamite: The Story of Class Violence in America. New York, 1931.

————. Laughing in the Jungle. New York, 1932.

————. My America. New York, 1938.

————. Native's Return. New York,1934.

————. Two-Way Passage. New York, 1941.

Addams, Jane. Twenty Years at Hull House. New York, 1910.

Adler, Alfred. The Science of Living. New York, 1929.

Adorno, T. W.; Frenkel-Brunswik, Elsei; Levinson, Daniel J.;
    Sanford, R. Nevitt. The Authoritarian Personality.
    New York, 1950.

Alland, Alexander. American Counterpoint. New York, 1943.

Allen, James S. The Negro Question in the United States.
    New York, 1936.

American Council on Education, Committee on Intergroup Education
    in Cooperating Schools. Literature for Human Understanding.
    Washington, D.C., 1948.

American Jewish Committee, Department of Scientific Research. A
    Brief Survey of the Major Agencies in the Field of Intercultural
    Education. New York, 1950.

295

Baker, Newton D.; Hayes, Carlton J. H.; Straus, Roger W. The
    American Way: A Study of Human Relations among Protestants,
    Catholics and Jews. New York, 1936.

Becker, John. The Negro in American Life. New York, 1934.

Benedict, Ruth. Patterns of Culture. Cambridge, 1934.

Boas, Franz. Anthropology and Modern Life. New York, 1928.

_____. The Mind of Primitive Man. New York, 1938.

Bogardus, Emory S. Essentials of Americanization. Los Angeles, 1923.

Bowers, C. A. The Progressive Educator and the Depression: the
    Radical Years. New York, 1969.

Brameld, Theodore. Minority Problems in the Public School: A Study
    of Administrative Policies and Practices in Seven School
    Systems. New York, 1946.

Brown, Francis J., and Roucek, Joseph Slavey, eds. Our Racial and
    National Minorities: Their History, Contributions and
    Present Problems. New York, 1937.

_____. One America: The History, Contributions and Present
    Problems of our Racial and National Minorities. 2nd ed.
    New York, 1945.

Brown, Lawrence Guy. Immigration, Cultural Conflicts and Social
    Adjustments. New York, 1933.

Brown, Spencer. They see for Themselves: A Documentary Approach
    to Intercultural Education in the High Schools. New York,
    1945.

Bryson, Lyman; Finkelstein, Louis; and MacIver, R. M. Approaches
    to Group Understanding. Sixth Symposium of the Conference
    on Science, Philosophy and Religion. New York, 1947.

Callahan, Raymond E. Education and the Cult of Efficiency.
    Chicago, 1962.

Carlson, John Roy [Arthur Derounian.] Under Cover: My Four Years
    in the Nazi Underworld of America. New York, 1943.

Cavert, Samuel McCrea. Church Cooperation and Unity in America, A Historical Review: 1900-1970. New York, 1970.

Chato, Clarence I. and Halligan, Alice. The Story of the Springfield Plan. New York, 1945.

Child, Irwin L. Italian or American? The Second Generation in Conflict. New Haven, 1943.

Christian, Louis A. Louis Adamic: A Checklist. Kent, 1971.

Clinchy, Everett R. All in the Name of God. New York, 1934.

_____. Intergroup Relations Centers. New York, 1949.

Cohen, George. The Jews in the Making of America. Boston, 1924.

Cohen, Naomi W. Not Free to Desist: the American Jewish Committee. Philadelphia, 1972.

Cole, Stewart G., and Cole, Mildren Wiese. Minorities and the American Promise: The Conflict of Principle and Practice. New York, 1954.

Cook, Lloyd Allen. Community Backgrounds of Education: a Textbook in Educational Sociology. New York, 1938.

Council Against Intolerance in America. An American Answer to Intolerance. New York, 1939.

Covello, Leonard. The Heart is the Teacher. New York, 1958.

_____. The Social Background of the Italo-American School Child; A Study of the Southern Italian Family Mores and their Effect on the School Situation in Italy and America. Totowa, N. J., 1972.

Creel, George. How we Advertised America. New York, 1920.

Cremin, Lawrence A. The Transformation of the School: Progressivism in American Education, 1876-1957. New York, 1961.

Davis, Allen F. Spearheads for Reform: The Social Settlement and the Progressive Movement, 1890-1914. New York, 1967.

Dawidowicz, Lucy. The War Against the Jews. New York, 1975.

Diederich, Paul B., and Van Til, William. The Workshop: A Summary of Principles and Practices of the Workshop Movement. New York, 1945.

Diggins, John B. Mussolini and Fascism: the View from America. Princeton, 1972.

Dollard, John. Caste and Class in a Southern Town. New York, 1937.

Drachsler, Julius. Democracy and Assimilation: the Blending of Immigrant Heritages in America. New York, 1920.

DuBois, Rachel Davis. Adventures in Intercultural Education: A Manual for Secondary School Teachers. New York, 1939.

_____. Build Together Americans: Adventures in Intercultural Education. New York, 1945.

_____. The Contribution of Racial Elements to American Life. Philadelphia, 1930.

_____. Education in Worldmindedness: A Series of Assembly Programs Given by Students at Woodbury High School, Woodbury, New Jersey, 1927-1928. Philadelphia, 1928.

_____. Get Together Americans: Friendly Approaches to Racial and Cultural Conflicts through the Neighborhood-Home Festival. New York, 1943.

_____. National Unity through Intercultural Understanding. Washington, D.C., 1942.

_____. Neighbors in Action: A Manual for Local Leaders in Intergroup Relations. New York, 1950.

_____. Pioneers of the New World: Series III of Assembly Programs Given by Students of Woodbury, New Jersey, High School. Philadelphia, 1930.

_____. A School and Community Project in Developing Sympathetic Attitudes toward other Races and Nations. New York, 1934.

_____, and Li, Mew-Soong. The Art of Group Conversation, New York, 1963.

_____, and Nelson, Rosie. Methods of Achieving Racial Justice: Discussion Outline for Church, School and Adult Education Groups. New York, 1936.

_____, and Schweppe, Emma, eds. The Germans in American Life. New York, 1935.

_____, and Schweppe, Emma, eds. The Jews in American Life. New York, 1935.

DuBois, W. E. Burghardt. The Gift of the Black Folk. Boston, 1924.

Duncan, Ethel M. Democracy's Children. New York and Philadelphia, 1945.

Eaton, Allen H. Immigrant Gifts to American Life: Some Experiments in Appreciation of the Contributions of our Foreign-Born Citizens to American Culture. New York, 1932.

Edman, Marian, and Collins, Laurentine B. Promising Practices in Intergroup Education. New York, 1947.

Feinberg, Walter. Reason and Rhetoric: The Intellectual Foundations of Liberal Educational Reform. New York, 1975.

Fineberg, Solomon Andhil. Overcoming Anti-Semitism. New York, 1943.

Fosdick, Raymond B. Adventure in Giving: The Story of the General Education Board. New York, 1962.

Gerson, Louis L. The Hyphenate in Recent American Politics and Diplomacy. Lawrence, Kansas, 1964.

Graham, Patricia Albjerg. Progressive Education: From Arcady to Academe: A History of the Progressive Education Association, 1919-1955. New York, 1967.

Halper, Albert. Good-bye, Union Square: A Writer's Memoir of the Thirties. Chicago, 1970.

Handlin, Oscar, ed. Children of the Uprooted. New York, 1966.

_____. The Uprooted: The Epic Story of Great Migrations that Made the American People. New York, 1951.

Hartmann, Edward George. The Movement to Americanize the Immigrant. New York, 1948.

Hayes, Carlton J. H. Nationalism: A Religion. New York, 1960.

Herberg, Will. Protestant - Catholic - Jew: An Essay in American Religious Sociology. Garden City, 1955.

Higham, John. Send these to Me: Jews and other Immigrants in Urban America. New York, 1975.

_____. Strangers in the Land: Patterns of American Nativism, 1860-1925. New York, 1963.

Itzkoff, Seymour W. Cultural Pluralism and American Education. Scranton, 1969.

Jaworski, Irene D. Becoming American: The Problems of Immigrants and their Children. New York, 1950.

Jones, Maldwyn Allen. American Immigration. Chicago, 1960.

Kaplan, Mordecai M. Judaism as a Civilization: Toward a Reconstruction of American Jewish Life. New York, 1934.

Karelsen, Frank E., Jr. Human Relations: A Challenge to our Public Schools. New York, 1947.

Katz, Michael B. Class, Bureacracy, and Schools: The Illusion of Educational Change in America. New York, 1971.

_____. The Irony of Early School Reform: Educational Innovation in Mid-nineteenth Century, Massachusetts. Boston, 1968.

Kilpatrick, William Heard, ed. The Educational Frontier. New York, 1933.

Konopka, Gisella. Eduard C. Lindeman and Social Work Philosophy. Minneapolis, 1958.

Krug, Edward A. The Shaping of the American High School. New York, 1964.

Kutak, Robert I. The Story of a Bohemian-American Village: A Study of Social Persistence and Change. Louisville, 1933.

Lasker, Bruno. Democracy Through Discussion. New York, 1949.

_____. Race Attitudes in Children. New York 1929.

Lazaron, Morris S. Common Ground: A Plea for Intelligent Americanism. New York, 1938.

Leuchtenburg, William E. The Perils of Prosperity, 1914-1932. Chicago, 1958.

Lewin, Kurt. Resolving Social Conflicts: Selected Papers on Group Dynamics. New York, 1948.

Linkh, Richard M. American Catholicism and European Immigrants. New York, 1975.

Locke, Alain, ed. The New Negro. New York, 1925.

_____, and Stern, Bernhard J., eds. When Peoples Meet: A Study in Race and Culture Contacts. New York, 1942.

McWilliams, Carey. Louis Adamic and Shadow-America. Los Angeles, 1935.

Mangione, Jerre. The Dream and the Deal: The Federal Writers' Project, 1935-1943. Boston, 1972.

Marty, Martin E. Righteous Empire: the Protestant Experience in America. New York, 1970.

Mead, Margaret. Coming of Age in Samoa. New York, 1928.

Miller, Herbert A. The Schools and the Immigrant. Cleveland, 1916.

Murphy, Albert J. Education in World-mindedness. New York, 1931.

National Council for the Social Studies. Democratic Human Relations. Sixteenth Yearbook of the National Council for the Social Studies. Hilda Taba and William VanTil, eds. Philadelphia, 1945.

_____. Diversity within National Unity. A Symposium of the twenty-fourth annual meeting of the NCSS, Nov. 25, 1944. Washington, D.C., 1945.

National Education Association. Department of Supervisors and Directors of Instruction. Americans All: Studies in Intercultural Education. Washington, D.C., 1942.

Newmann, George Bradford. A Study of International Attitudes of High School Students. New York, 1926.

Newman, William M. American Pluralism: A Study of Minority Groups and Social Theory. New York, 1973.

Novak, Michael. The Rise of the Unmeltable Ethnics: Politics and Culture in the Seventies. New York, 1971.

Park, Robert E. On Social Control and Collective Behavior. Chicago, 1967.

_____. Race and Culture. Chicago, 1950.

_____. Society: Collective Behavior, News and Opinion, Sociology and Modern Society. Glencoe, Ill., 1955.

_____, and Burgess Ernest E. Introduction to the Science of Sociology. Chicago, 1924.

_____, and Miller, Herbert E. Old World Traits Transplanted. New York, 1921.

Perkinson, Henry J. The Imperfect Panacea: American Faith in Education, 1865-1965. New York, 1968.

Pitt, James E. Adventures in Brotherhood. New York, 1955.

Powdermaker, Hortense. Probing our Prejudices: A Unit for High School Students. New York, 1944.

Prescott, Daniel. Education and International Relations. Cambridge, Mass., 1930.

Reseck, Carl, ed. War and the Intellectuals: Essays by Randolph S. Bourne, 1915-1919. New York, 1964.

Robertson, Wanda. An Evaluation of the Culture Unit Method for Social Education. New York, 1950.

Rohrbough, Katherine Ferris. Fun and Festival among America's Peoples. New York, 1943.

Rugg, Harold. America and her Immigrants. New York, 1926.

Sayre, Jeanette. An Analysis of the Radio Broadcasting Activities of Federal Agencies. Studies in the Control of Radio, No. 3 [June, 1941]. Published by the Radio Broadcasting Research Project at the Littauer Center, Harvard University.

Schachner, Nathan. The Price of Liberty: A History of the American Jewish Committee. New York, 1948.

Shombaugh, Mary Effie. Folk Festivals for Schools and Playgrounds. New York, 1932.

Sickels, Alice L. Around the World in St. Paul. Minneapolis, 1945.

Sims, Mary S. The Natural History of A Social Institution: The Young Women's Christian Association. New York, 1936.

Smith, William Carlson. Americans in the Making: A Natural History of the Assimilation of Immigrants. New York, 1939.

_____. Americans in Process: A Study of our Citizens of Oriental Ancestry. Ann Arbor, 1937.

Spicer, Dorothy G. Folk Festivals and the Foreign Community. New York, 1923.

Squire, James R. A New Look at Progressive Education. Yearbook of the Association for Supervision and Curriculum Development. Washington, 1972.

Steinberg, Milton. The Making of the Modern Jew. New York, 1948.

_____. A Partisan Guide to the Jewish Problem. New York, 1945.

Stocking, George W., Jr. Race, Culture and Evolution: Essays in the History of Anthropology. New York, 1968.

Stoker, Spencer. The Schools and International Understanding. Chapel Hill, 1933.

Stonequist, Everett V. The Marginal Man. New York, 1937.

Stott, William. Documentary Expression in Thirties America. New York, 1974.

Strong, Donald S. Organized Anti-Semitism in America: The Rise of Group Prejudice During the Decade 1930-1940. Washington, D.C., 1941.

Strong, Edward K. The Second-Generation Japanese Problem. New York, 1934.

Szasz, Margaret. Education and the American Indian: The Road to Self-Determination, 1928-1973. Albuquerque, 1974.

Talbot, Winthrop. Americanization. New York, 1917.

Tennenbaum, Samuel. William Heard Kilpatrick. New York, 1951.

Tesconi, Charles, and Morris, Van Cleve. The Anti-Man Culture: Bureau-technocracy and the Schools. Urbana, Ill. 1972.

Thompson, Frank F. Schooling of the Immigrant. New York, 1920.

Trasher, Frederick. The Gang; A Study of 1,313 Gangs in Chicago. Chicago, 1963.

Tipton, James H. Community in Crisis: The Elimination of Segregation from the Public School System. New York, 1953.

Tyack, David B. The One Best System: A History of American Urban Education. Cambridge, Mass., 1974.

Urofsky, Melvin. American Zionism from Herzl to the Holocaust. Garden City, 1975.

Vickery, William E., and Cole, Stewart G. Intercultural Education in American Schools. New York, 1943.

Waldman, Morris D. Nor by Power. New York, 1953.

Ware, Caroline F. Grenwich Village, 1920-1930: A Comment on American Civilization in the Post-War Years. New York, 1935.

Warner, W. Lloyd, and Lunt, Paul S. The Social Life of a Modern Community. New Haven, 1941.

Watson, Goodwin. Action for Unity. New York, 1947.

Wise, James Waterman. The Jew in American Life. New York, 1946.

Woofter, T.J. Races and Ethnic Groups in American Life. New York, 1933.

Wolters, Raymond. Negroes and the Great Depression: The Problem of Economic Recovery. Westport, Conn., 1970.

Wyman, David S. Paper Walls: America and the Refugee Crisis, 1938-1941. Amherst, 1968.

Young, Donald R. Research Memorandum on Minority Peoples in the Depression. Bulletin No. 31. Social Sciences Research Council. New York, 1937.

Young, James O. Black Writers of the Thirties. Baton Rouge, 1973.

Young, Pauline V. The Pilgrims of Russian-Town. Chicago, 1932.

Young Women's Christian Association. Second Generation Youth: Report of the Commission on First Generation Americans. New York, 1930.

_____. What it Means to be a Second-Generation Girl: Talks Given at the Second-Generation Youth Dinner of the National Board of the YWCA, April 30, 1975. New York, 1935.

B. THESES, DISSERTATIONS AND UNPUBLISHED STUDIES

Chalip, Alice Grace. "A Descriptive Study of the Group Conversation Method of Rachel Davis DuBois." Unpublished masters thesis, California State University, Hayward, 1974.

DuBois, Rachel Davis. "Adventures in Intercultural Education." Unpublished Ph.D. dissertation, School of Education, New York University, 1940.

McBride, Paul Wilbert. "The Cultural Cold War: Immigrants and the Quest for Cultural Monism, 1890-1917." Unpublished Ph.D. dissertation, Department of History, University of Georgia, 1972.

Passi, Michael. "Mandarins and Immigrants: The Irony of Ethnic Studies in America since Turner." Unpublished Ph.D. dissertation, Department of History, University of Minnesota, 1971.

Peebles, Robert Whitney. "Leonard Covello: A Study of an Immigrant's Contribution to New York City." Unpublished Ph. D. dissertation, School of Education, New York University, 1967.

Pitkin, Victor E. "A Resource Unit for the Training of Secondary Teachers in Problems and Issues involving Minority Groups with Special Reference to Negro-White Relationships." Unpublished Ph. D. dissertation, School of Education, New York University, 1950.

Powell, James Henry. "The Concept of Cultural Pluralism in American Social Thought, 1915-1965." Unpublished Ph.D. dissertation, University of Notre Dame, 1971.

Preston, Roy Leslie. "Intercultural Education in Minnesota." Unpublished master's thesis, Department of Education, University of Minnesota, 1950.

Seamans, Herbert Lee. "Pioneer Programs in Intergroup Education: A History of the Commission on Educational Organizations of the National Conference of Christians and Jews, 1939-1957." Unpublished manuscript, 4 vols., 1959 (Copy on file at the Lazarus Library of NCCJ, New York City).

Wacker, Roland Frederick. "Race and Ethnicity in American Social Science: 1900-1950." Unpublished Ph. D. dissertation, Department of History, University of Michigan, 1975.

Weinberg, Daniel Erwin. "The Foreign Language Information Service and the Foreign Born, 1918-1939: A Case Study of Cultural Assimilation Viewed as a Problem in Social Technology." Unpublished Ph. D. dissertation, Department of History, University of Minnesota, 1973.

C. ARTICLES

Adamic, Louis. "Thirty Million New Americans." Harper's Monthly Magazine, CLXIX (November, 1934), 684-94.

Allport, Floyd H. "Culture Conflict vs. the Individual as Factors in Delinquency." Social Forces, IX (June, 1931), 493-97.

Alpern, Hymen. "The Role of the High Schools in Improving Intercultural Relations." Journal of Educational Sociology, XVI (February, 1943), 363-67.

Bodnar, John. "Materialism and Morality: Slavic-American
    Immigrants and Education, 1890-1940." Journal of Ethnic
    Studies, III (Winter, 1976), 1-20.

Bradley, Phillips. "Political Aspects of Cultural Pluralism."
    Journal of Educational Sociology, XII (April, 1939), 492-98.

Bremer, Edith Terry. "Development of Private Social Work with the
    Foreign Born." Annals of the American Academy of
    Political and Social Science, CCLXII (March, 1949), 139-47.

Brown, Francis J. "Sociology and Intercultural Understanding."
    Journal of Educational Sociology, XII (February, 1939),
    328-31.

Buroker, Robert L. "From Voluntary Association to Welfare State:
    The Illinois Immigrants' Protective League, 1908-1926."
    Journal of American History, LVII (December, 1971), 643-60.

Christian, Henry A. "'What else have you in Mind?' Louis Adamic
    and H. L. Mencken." Menckeniana, No. 47 (Fall, 1973),
    1-12.

Citron, Abraham; Reynolds, Collins; and Tayler, Sarah. "Ten
    Years of Intercultural Education in Educational Magazines."
    Harvard Educational Review, XV (March, 1945), 129-33.

Clark, Marion G. "Three Generations." Progressive Education, X
    (May, 1933), 273-76.

Cohen, David K. "Immigrants and the Schools." Review of Educational
    Research, XL (February, 1970), 13-28.

Cordasco, Francesco. "The Children of Immigrants in the Schools."
    Education and the Many Faces of the Disadvantaged:
    Cultural and Historical Perspectives. Edited by
    William M. Brickman and Stanley Lehrer. New York, 1972.

Cotton, Thomas L. "Group Approach." Proceedings of the National
    Conference of Social Work (1925), 360-65.

Covello, Leonard. "A High School and its Immigrant Community--a
    Challenge and an Opportunity." Journal of Educational
    Sociology, IX (February, 1936), 331-46.

_____. "Neighborhood Growth through the School." Progressive Education, XV (February, 1938), 126-39.

Daniel Walter G. "Negro Welfare and Mabel Carney at Teachers College, Columbia University." The Journal of Negro Education, II (October, 1942), 560-62.

DuBois, Rachel Davis. "Building Tolerant Attitudes in High School Students." The Crisis, XL (October, 1931), 334, 336.

_____. "Can we Help to Create an American Renaissance?" The English Journal, XXVII (November, 1938), 733-40.

_____. "Intercultural Education and Democracy's Defense." Friends Intelligencer, February 1, 1941.

_____. "Intercultural Education at Benjamin Franklin High School." High Points in the Work of the High Schools of New York City, XIX (December, 1937), 23-29.

_____. "Intercultural Education in the Philadelphia Schools." Philadelphia Teacher and Workshop, VII (January, 1941), 5.

_____. "Measuring and Building Attitudes." Friends Intelligencer, June 14, 1930, 467-68.

_____. "The Need for Sharing Cultural Values." Friends Intelligencer, February 11, 1939, 84-85.

_____. "The New Frontier." Opportunity, XII (February, 1934), 40-41.

_____. "Our Enemy--the Stereotype." Progressive Education, XII (March, 1939), 418-24.

_____. "A Philosophy of Intercultural Relations." World Order, IV (July, 1938), 138-42.

_____. "Shall we Emotionalize our Students?" Friends Intelligencer, December 3, 1932, 973-74.

_____. "Sharing Cultural Loyalties through Festival Making." Childhood Education, XVIII (April, 1942), 348-352.

Ephraim, Miriam R. "Service for Education in Human Relations." Selected Writings of Miriam R. Ephraim. New York: National Jewish Welfare Board, 1966.

308

Feinberg, Walter. "Progressive Education and Social Planning." *Teachers College Record*, LXXIII (May, 1972), 485-506.

Frontiers of Democracy (Special issue entitled "Minorities and American Education"), VI (April 15, 1940).

Glicksberg, Charles I. "Intercultural Education: Utopia or Reality?" *Common Ground*, VI (Summer, 1946), 61-67.

Glueck, Eleanor T. "Culture Conflict and Delinquency." *Journal of Mental Hygiene*, XXI (January, 1937), 46-66.

————. "Newer Ways of Crime Control." *Harvard Educational Review*, IX (March, 1939), 184-203.

Grossman, Mordecai. "The Schools Fight Prejudice: An Appraisal of the Intercultural Education Movement." *Commentary*, I (April, 1946), 35-42.

Hansen, Marcus Lee. "The Third Generation in America." *Commentary*, XIV (November, 1952), 492-500.

Hersey, Evelyn. "The Emotional Conflicts of the Second Generation: A Discussion of American-born Children of Immigrant Parents." *Interpreter Release Clip Sheet*, XI (July 10, 1934), 83-89.

History of Education Quarterly (Special issue devoted to the revisionist critique of John Dewey), XV (Spring, 1975).

Hoppock, Anne. "Schools for the Foreign Born in a New Jersey County." *Progressive Education*, X (April, 1933), 189-93.

Hurlbutt, Mary E. "The World Crisis and New Americans." *The Women's Press*, (February, 1939), 58-60.

Journal of Educational Sociology (Special issue entitled "United We'll Stand" sponsored by the National Conference of Christians and Jews), XVI (February, 1943).

Keliher, Alice V. "What Shall we Do about Hatred?" *Progressive Education*, XVI (November, 1939), 485-87.

Kennedy, Ruby Jo Reeves. "Single or Triple Melting Pot? Intermarriage Trends in New Haven, 1870-1940." *The American Journal of Sociology*, XLIX (January, 1944), 331-39.

309

Kilpatrick, William Heard. "Education and Intolerance." The
    Social Frontier, V (May, 1939).

Kolack, Shirley, and Kolack, Sol. "The Life and Death of a
    Voluntary Organization." Adult Leadership, XV
    (March, 1967), 313-14, 333.

Lapolla, Mazzini S. "The Italian American High School Girl."
    High Points in the Work of the High Schools of New York
    City, XVI (May, 1934), 20-24.

Levy, John. "Conflicts of Culture and Children's Maladjustments."
    Mental Hygiene, XVII (January, 1933), 41-50.

Lewis, Read. "Immigrants and their Children." Interpreter Releases,
    XII (April 30, 1935), 171-81.

Liebman, Charles S. "Reconstructionism in American Jewish Life."
    American Jewish Yearbook: 1970. New York and Philadelphia:
    The American Jewish Committee and the Jewish Publication
    Society of America, 1970, pp. 3-100.

Marcus, Grace. "The Emotional Conflicts of the Second Generation."
    Interpreter Release Clip Sheet, XI (July 10, 1934), 90-92.

Marshall, James. "How the Schools can Help to Solve the Second
    Generation Problem." Interpreter Releases, XII
    (May 13, 1935), 194-96.

Melkonian, Bertha. "America's Cultural Heritage: What it might
    Mean to the Social Studies Programs of the Public Schools
    (An Account of an Experiment Directed by Mrs. Rachel Davis-
    DuBois of the Institute for Education in Human Relations,
    at Roosevelt Junior High School, San Francisco)."
    San Francisco Teachers Bulletin, XX (February, 1937), 7-11.

Meras, Edmund A. "World-mindedness." Journal of Higher Education,
    III (May, 1932), 246-52.

Mohl, Raymond A., and Betten, Neil. "Ethnic Adjustment in the
    Industrial City: The International Institute of Gary, 1919-1940."
    International Migration Review, VI (Winter, 1972), 361-76.

_____. "Paternalism and Pluralism: Immigrants and Social
    Welfare in Gary, Indiana, 1906-1940." American Studies, XV
    (Spring, 1974), 5-30.

Noggle, Burt. "The Twenties: A New Historiographical Frontier." Journal of American History, LIII (September, 1966), 299-314.

Oralo, Pedro T., and associates. "An Indian School Serves its Community." Progressive Education, XV (February, 1938), 153-55.

Pangburn, Weaver W. "Cleveland Leads the Way." Fraternity, II (February, 1930), 3-4.

Park, Robert E. "Human Migration and the Marginal Man." American Journal of Sociology, XXXIII (May, 1928), 881-93.

Rugg, Harold. "Education and International Understanding." Progressive Education, VIII (April, 1931), 294-302.

Ryan, Carson V. "Science with the Eastern Cherokee Indians." Progressive Education, XV (February, 1938), 143-46.

Schibsby, Marian. "When the Immigrant Goes to School." The Interpreter, V (December, 1926), 4-12.

Seamans, Herbert L. "Schools and the Jews." Frontiers of Democracy, VI (April 15, 1940), 211.

Sitkoff, Harvard. "Racial Militancy and Interracial Violence in the Second World War." Journal of American History, LVIII (December, 1971), 661-81.

Stein, Howard F., and Hill, Robert F. "The Limits of Ethnicity." The American Scholar, Spring, 1977, 181-89.

Stonequist, Everett V. "The Problem of the Marginal Man." American Journal of Sociology, XLI (July, 1935), 1-12.

Studebaker, John W. "Scaling Cultural Frontiers." Journal of Educational Sociology, XII (April, 1939), 487-91.

Tyack, David B. "New Perspectives on the History of American Education." The State of American History. Edited by Herbert J. Bass. Chicago, 1970.

Vecoli, Rudolph J. "Contadini in Chicago: A Critique of The Uprooted." Journal of American History, LI (December, 1964), 404-17.

_____. "Ethnicity: A Neglected Dimension in American History." *The State of American History*. Edited by Herbert J. Bass. Chicago, 1970.

Villchur, Mark. "Cherishing Cultural Heritages." *Journal of Adult Education*, III (June, 1931), 321-26.

Wilcox, Preston R. "The Community-centered School." *The School House and the City*. Edited by Alvin Toffler. New York, 1968.

Wirth, Louis. "Culture Conflict and Misconduct." *Social Forces*, IX (June, 1931), 484-92.

Woody, Thomas. "Nationalistic Education and Beyond." *Educational Review*, LXXVI (September, 1928), 99-110.

Young, Pauline V. "Social Problems in the Education of the Immigrant Child." *American Sociological Review*, I (June, 1936), 419-29.

INDEX

Abbott, Grace, 25
Adamic, Louis, 22-3, 66-73,
  103-5, 113, 129, 139,
  152, 229, 268-9, 281
Addams, Jane, 15, 24, 80
Adler, Alfred, 39
American Council for
  Judaism, 202
American Jewish Committee,
  111, 114-5, 130, 153-4,
  158, 173, 175-8, 185-7,
  200-17, 220
Americanization movement,
  9-10, 50, 56
Americanization, scientific
  50-6, 280-1
anti-Semitism: strategies
  for dealing with, 212-17
Ashworth, Robert, 203

Baker, Newton, D., 195-6,
  206
Bayne, Edward Ashley, 221-2
Beatty, Willard W., 129, 131
Benedict, Ruth, 133, 137-9,
  144
Black-Americans, 93, 102, 163
B'nai B'rith, 189
Boas, Franz, 40
Borgeson, F.C., 129, 133,
  135-6, 148
Bourne, Randolph, 25

Boutwell, William D., 133,
  150, 160, 164
Bremer, Edith Terry, 30,
  59-60, 152, 159-60
Brown, Francis, 270
Bureau for Intercultural
  Education, see Service Bureau
  for Intercultural Education

Carnegie Foundation, 73, 152,
  268-9
Carney, Mabel, 112, 133
Carver, Dr. George Washington,
  81-2
Casa Italiana (Columbia
  University), 103
Cassidy, Florence, 60-1, 65-6,
  113, 281
Chase, Genevieve, 239-50, 263
Child, Irwin, 48
Civil Works Administration,
  111-2
Clinchy, Everett R., 96, 133,
  152, 190-2, 200, 205-7, 230-3
Cole, Stewart, 224-34, 239, 251,
  260, 264, 274
Common Ground magazine, 273
Communist Party, 125
Cotton, Tom, 65
Counts, George, 129
Covello, Leonard, 67, 103, 118-21,
  234, 277, 281

cultural integrationism, 56-75, 281-4

Davis, Ruth, 92, 162, 267
Derounian, Arthur, 222-3
Dewey, John, 140-1
Dodson, Dan, 272
DuBois, Rachel Davis:
association with the Progressive Education Association, 126-48; as consultant to the Federal Radio Project of the United States Office of Education, 149-70; differences with leadership of the Service Bureau, 218-67; early career of, 78-92; and establishment of the Service Bureau for Intercultural Education, 109-23; group conversation technique of, 277-8; as high school teacher, 84-8; intercultural education program of, 92-5; and international education, 97-102; and Quakerism, 77-9, 106-7; and the second generation, 102-6; and the separate approach to intercultural education, 121-3, 136-9, 159-70; views on Judaism, 184-5, 205, 207-12; and Workshop for Cultural Democracy, 277
DuBois, W.E.B., 82, 84, 231, 277, 281
Durlach, Theresa Mayer, 114, 133, 211, 233, 260, 264

Eaton, Allen H., 63
Eckerson, Ione, 115, 120-1
Eisenstein, Rabbi Ira, 185, 277, 281
environmentalism, 33-7
Ephraim, Miriam, 115, 184-5

Feinberg, Walter, 275-6
festivals of nations, 19, 62-7
Folk Festival Council, 65, 125
Foreign Language Information Service, 12-3, 31-2, 52-4, 72-3, 104, 177, 268-9
Foxlee, Ludmilla, 55
Frazier, E. Franklin, 41, 238
Freud, Sigmund, 38, 265

General Education Board, 134-6, 147, 235-50, 260
German-Americans, 29, 155, 161, 166, 269-70
Gerson, Louis, 7, 155
Giles, H. Harry, 271, 274-5
Graff, George, 240, 267
group conversation technique, 277-8

Handlin, Oscar, 5-7
Harper, Heber, 101
Harrison, Margaret, 137
Hartman, Edward, 10
Hartshorne, Hugh, 224-5, 233, 238, 249, 261-3, 265
Hayes, Carlton, 195-6
Herberg, Will, 199
Herring, John, 189
Hersey, Evelyn, 102
Higham, John, 3-4, 10-3
Horkheimer, Dr. Max, 214
Hull House, 25

Institute for International Education, 99
intercultural education: coining of the term, 132; definition, 20
international education movement, 97-102
International Institutes, 30, 32, 36, 55, 59-62, 64, 102, 159, 269
Irish-Americans, 166-7
Italian-Americans, 48, 155, 167, 170, 264, 266, 269-70

Japanese-Americans, 155
Jewish community, 19-20, 86, 163, 166-7, 171-217, 284
Jones, Maldwyn Allen, 4, 7

Kallen, Horace, 206
Kaplan, Mordecai M., 67, 179-84, 277
Keliher, Alice V., 133
Kilpatrick, William H., 88, 230, 233, 261, 264, 281
Klineberg, Otto, 239-50, 261, 263, 265
Kulp II, Daniel, 88-9

Lapson, Dvora, 184
Lasker, Bruno, 199, 250-9, 266, 273-4

Lazaron, Rabbi Morris S., 202
Lewin, Kurt, 213
Lewis, Read, 31, 72-3, 121, 151, 268-9
Lindeman, Eduard C., 233-4, 267, 277
Locke, Alain, 139, 148, 163

McBride, Paul, 14-15
McCarthy, Senator Joseph, 278-9
McClymer, John F., 15
McDonald, James G., 157-8
McDowell, Mary, 25
Marcus, Grace, 56
marginality, theory of, 45-7, 57-8
Marshall, John, 135, 231, 236-8
Minsky, Louis, 203
Mitchell, Ruth Crawford, 36

National Association for the Advancement of Colored People, 83-4, 91, 110, 163
National Conference of Christians and Jews, 96, 110, 131, 188-207
National Education Association, 155
Native-Americans (American Indians), 142
Nelson, Rose, 225, 267
New York City Board of Education, 219-20, 235-6
New York Foundation, 92, 130-1

Park, Robert Ezra, 6, 13, 41-50, 262-3
Passi, Michael, 13-4
Petrie, John C., 197
Polish-Americans, 141
Progressive Education Association, 126-48, 150, 209, 235; and Committee on Intercultural Education, 132-3; and Commission on Intercultural Education, 133-48; philosophy of intercultural education, 139-48
progressive education movement, 100, 106, 126-48
Puerto Rican Nationalist Party, 278

Quakers, see Society of Friends

Randolph, A. Philip, 278
Reconstructionist Movement, 179-87, 216, 281
Redefer, Frederick L., 131, 134, 139, 144-5, 226
Riggs, T. Lawrason, 197-8
Roosevelt, Franklin D., 269
Rugg, Harold, 34-5
Russell Sage Foundation, 63
Ryan, W. Carson, 132, 136-7

Schibsby, Marian, 54-5
Schweppe, Emma, 132
second generation (children of immigrants), 22-3, 102-8; and anthropology, 40-1; and cultural integration, 56-75; and environmentalism, 33-7; pre-World War I comments on, 24-6; and psychology, 38-9; reasons for growing interest in, 27-33; and scientific Americanization, 50-6; and sociology, 41-50
Seldes, Gilbert, 156, 160, 162
Service Bureau for Education in Human Relations, see Service Bureau for Intercultural Education
Service Bureau for Intercultural Education: American Jewish Committee support of, 114-5, 176-9, 205-12; early programs in the New York City metropolitan area, 115-21; establishment of, 110-5; evaluation of, 235-50; ideological divisions within, 227-67; later programs of, 274-6; period of incorporation into the Progressive Education Association, 124-48; reorganization of, 218-27, 230-34; research role in federal radio programming, 149-70
settlement houses, 14-5, 24-5, 30
Sickels, Alice, 66, 281
Sitkoff, Harvard, 276-7
Slawson, John, 215
Smith, William C., 41, 47-8
Society of Friends (Quakers), 77-84, 87, 107
Southern Christian Leadership Conference, 279
Spicer, Dorothy, 60, 64, 281

Steinberg, Rabbi Milton, 67,
  181-2, 184-5, 277, 281
Stonequist, Everett, 41, 47
Strauss, Roger W., 190, 201-2
Studebaker, John, 152, 167,
  226

Taylor, Philip, 4-5
Teachers College (Columbia
  University), 111, 129
Thrasher, Frederick, 41, 133
Toigo, Avenire, 210
Trager, Frank N., 220-1, 230,
  233-4

United States Office of Education, 149-70

Wallach, Sidney, 153, 177, 202-
  3, 208-9, 212, 220
Weinberg, Daniel, 12-3, 18
Weinstein, Rabbi Jacob, 114-5
Wirth, Louis, 41
Wise, Rabbi Stephen S., 175
Women's International League for
  Peace and Freedom, 80-1, 88
Wood, L. Hollingsworth, 223,
  232, 234, 267
Works Progress Administration
  (WPA), 92
World War I, 27-9

Young, Donald, 238, 261, 264
Young Men's Christian Association, 51
Young, Pauline, 41, 48
Young Women's Christian Association, 19, 30, 55, 59, 60-2, 64,
  113, 269

Zorbaugh, Harvey, 41, 239